THE BOOK OF F#

THE BOOK
OF F#

Breaking Free with Managed
Functional Programming

by Dave Fancher

**no starch
press**

San Francisco

Printed in the USA

ISBN-10: 1-59327-552-8
ISBN-13: 978-1-59327-552-5

Publisher: William Pollock
Production Editor: Alison Law
Cover Illustration: Chris Gould
Interior Design: Octopod Studios
Developmental Editors: Seph Kramer and William Pollock
Technical Reviewers: Kevin Miller and Tomas Petricek
Copyeditor: Rachel Monaghan
Compositors: Laurel Chun and Susan Glinert Stevens
Proofreader: James Fraleigh

For information on distribution, translations, or bulk sales, please contact No Starch Press, Inc. directly:

No Starch Press, Inc.
245 8th Street, San Francisco, CA 94103
phone: 415.863.9900; fax: 415.863.9950; info@nostarch.com; www.nostarch.com

Library of Congress Cataloging-in-Publication Data

Fancher, Dave.
  The book of F# : breaking free with managed functional programming / by Dave Fancher.
      pages cm
  Includes index.
  ISBN 978-1-59327-552-5 -- ISBN 1-59327-552-8
  1. F# (Computer program language) I. Title. II. Title: Book of F-sharp.
  QA76.73.F163F36 2014
  005.1'17--dc23
                                2014000831

About the Author

Dave Fancher has been developing software with the .NET Framework for more than a decade. He is a familiar face in the Indiana development community as both a speaker and participant in user groups around the state. In July 2013, Dave was recognized as a Microsoft MVP (Most Valuable Professional) for Visual F#. When not writing code or writing about code at *davefancher.com*, he can often be found watching a movie or gaming on his Xbox One.

About the Technical Reviewer

Over the last 14 years, Kevin Miller has worked on exciting projects with truly great people while unsuccessfully pleading with compilers to break their steadfast rules. He enjoys studying the inherent beauty of logic, and when inspired by the muses, actually codes something deserving a modicum of pride from time to time. His interests lie in security, distributed systems, and data, but he has a short attention . . . squirrel!

BRIEF CONTENTS

CONTENTS IN DETAIL

3
FUNDAMENTALS   25

11
ASYNCHRONOUS AND PARALLEL PROGRAMMING 229

12
COMPUTATION EXPRESSIONS 257

INDEX 271

FOREWORD

I met Dave at the Microsoft MVP Summit in Redmond in 2013. We witnessed something unexpected: F# caught fire. The language hadn't changed drastically, but the attitudes of the developers at the Summit had. During the past year, MVPs had been learning about functional programming, and there was a new excitement around the language. Over the week, I learned of several C# MVPs who were jumping ship to F#. Dave and I talked about the transformation. We also talked about ethics in the context of object-oriented (OO) and functional programming (FP). Here is my story about that . . .

During college in the early 90s, I was immersed in operations management where the focus was quality, continuous improvement, just-in-time strategy, and waste elimination. W. Edwards Deming was a hero to my professors, and we studied Deming's huge impact on Japanese manufacturing from the 1950s onward. Finding the root cause of defects and fixing them at the source was "the good." Shipping defective product or tacking inspection at the end of the line was "the bad." These ideas resonated with me deeply.

Continuous improvement seemed more than just a way to make widgets; it felt like a way to live life. It echoed Socrates's concept of virtue; it evoked the story of Siddhartha, who sought truth over comfort. These are ideas about "what should be," about merit, about substance over rhetoric, about correctness.

After graduation I rolled into a software development career. Depending on the company, it was either clown cars and cowboys, or rigid waterfall. Both were exciting, but no one in either environment was talking about quality or continuous improvement. When I would bring it up, I would get sad smiles from grizzled developers. Their eyes said, "Son, don't you realize this is war?" The operating systems were crashy, the dev tools were buggy, and everything was closed source and proprietary. Thucydides said war is "a rough master that brings most men's characters to a level with their fortune." Likewise, when the development environment is bad, most developers will write bad code.

In 2001, a group of conscientious software developers got together in Snowbird, Utah and signed the Agile Manifesto. About a year later I discovered it. From my perspective, it seemed like a retelling of Deming, operations management, and Lean manufacturing. It was the first time in my career that I'd heard developers discussing quality and continuous improvement. There was hope!

After five years of test-driven development, pair programming, the SOLID principles (single responsibility, open/closed, Liskov substitution, interface segregation, and dependency inversion), and Scrum, my hope had mostly worn away. I continued to fight my tools, and it remained difficult to build quality software. Without discipline it was a train wreck. With discipline, process, and diligence, it was a hard slog.

Through pure good luck I encountered Erlang in 2007, and in 2009 I began working with F#. Functional programming consumed me. I learned about immutability, recursion, pattern matching, higher-order functions, referential transparency, code as data, and separation of behavior from data. As I learned and practiced I began to see the huge cost of OO. So much of what made my day-to-day coding life miserable was solvable with Erlang and F#. As I told people about FP, I again received those sad smiles that asked, "Don't you know we are at war?" I took it differently this time. I decided, "OK, sure. Let's call it war. I'll be on the side that's looking at the root cause of defects. I'll be on the side that wants to fix the problem at the source."

The next stage for Agile must be to fully unravel itself from OO.

Object-oriented programming had boldly promised "to model the world." Well, the world is a scary place where bad things happen for no apparent reason, and in this narrow sense I concede that OO does model the world. OO as we have it mingles data and behavior; the result is low cohesion and tight coupling. In OO, there is shared mutable state, which makes concurrency impossibly difficult. In OO, logic is nondeterministic. In OO, the result of a function doesn't simply depend on the arguments we pass in. The result may vary depending on arguments passed on previous calls to the function. How about mutations from other functions? How about data passed to the constructor? How about properties and fields? How about access from other threads? With every method call, we worry about the whole environment. Joe Armstrong describes the problem with OO languages like this: "They've got all this implicit environment that they carry around with them. You wanted a banana, but what you got was a gorilla holding the banana and the entire jungle." OO is a dangerous place.

Alan Kay once said, "I invented the term *object-oriented* and I can tell you I did not have C++ in mind." What Alan Kay described was message passing, isolation between objects, and polymorphism. That describes the functional programming language Erlang better than it describes Java! So what the devil happened? Were C++, Java, and C# billion-dollar mondegreens (misheard lyrics)? Just imagine Alan Kay as Jimi Hendrix with a whole industry in an OO haze, mouthing, "'Scuse me while I kiss this guy." Who sold us this mess?

I'll wind down with a lie that OO people who are learning FP tell one another: "Learning FP will make you a better OO programmer." It rings true, and in the short run it may even *be* true, but as you internalize immutability, recursion, pattern matching, higher-order functions, code as data, separation of behavior from data, and referential transparency, you will begin to despise OO. Personally, I went from being a Microsoft C# MVP to feeling guilt every time I created a new class file. Once you understand the defects that can be avoided, it stops being a technical choice and becomes an ethical one.

The good news is F# is a great language, and this is a fantastic book. They both create an easy pathway from the OO world to a cleaner, safer functional world. I'm delighted you're about to walk this path.

Bryan Hunter
CTO, Firefly Logic

PREFACE

Ever since I started touting the benefits of F#, people have asked me why I chose to learn F# over other functional languages like Scala, Erlang, or Haskell. This line of questioning presupposes that I intentionally set out to learn a functional language. In reality, adopting F# was an organic progression from C#.

My F# story begins late in the summer of 2010. I was burning out and my career was stagnating. My employer at the time was fairly risk-averse and had proprietary frameworks for nearly every facet of the application. After an extended amount of time in this environment, I lost sight of what I loved about developing software and did the worst thing anyone in this industry can do: I stopped learning.

It was around this time that the company hired a new architect who brought with him not only a wealth of technical knowledge but also something I'd lost: passion for the craft. His excitement reminded me of what I'd forgotten and gave me the kick I needed to get back in the game.

With renewed interest, I started looking at some of the technologies I missed while I was in that rut. Of everything I looked at, the one that really caught my attention was LINQ, a domain-specific language built upon functional principles to provide a unified mechanism for data access across disparate formats. It has been said that LINQ is a gateway drug for functional programming, and in my case, this was definitely true. I'd never really done any "true" functional programming before LINQ, so it was an exciting new world for me. Like many developers learning LINQ, I was introduced to it through the query syntax, but as my comfort level increased, I gradually started exploring how it worked.

Not long into my studies, I learned that query expressions were added only after some usability studies revealed that developers were confused by the lambda expressions and method chaining syntax. What struck me about this was how natural the method syntax felt. I even found myself favoring it over the query syntax in most cases. (Confession: To this day I can't seem to remember the method syntax for an outer join.) As I continued to work with LINQ, I began to realize that the method syntax felt natural because it matched the way I think. I didn't have terms for them at the time, but the functional concepts of delegation, higher-order functions, and composability really matched up with my mental model of how the world works.

It didn't take long for me to start carrying over the functional concepts I learned from LINQ into other areas of our application. In doing so, I found that the quality of my work was improving and my code was getting more predictable. Despite this newfound power, I found myself getting increasingly frustrated with C#, but I couldn't pinpoint exactly what was bothering me.

I was mowing the lawn on a hot, summer afternoon when I had my epiphany. On a whim, I'd included *Hanselminutes* #311 in that day's yardwork podcast selection. The guests, Richard Minerich and Phillip Trelford, were discussing F#, a functional language built upon the .NET platform. I was already intrigued, but then Phillip made a quip that perfectly summarized one of my gripes about C#'s repetitive nature: Writing C# feels like filling out government forms in triplicate. As the conversation continued, Richard and Phillip touched on several other points, like improved predictability of code and streamlined type creation, that really struck a chord with me. By the end of the podcast, I was hooked and determined to take advantage of this powerful language called F#.

Since that day—despite its reputation as a niche language—F# has become one of the primary tools in my developer toolbox. It has played an important role in each of my recent projects, as my go-to language for business logic, unit testing, and prototyping. I even used F# to successfully orchestrate queue-based communication between services in a distributed application. As you read this book, it is my hope that you'll recognize how F# can make you more productive and improve the quality of your code, regardless of the type of project you're working on.

ACKNOWLEDGMENTS

Although my name is on the cover, *The Book of F#* wouldn't have been possible without the efforts of numerous people.

First, I need to thank the team at No Starch Press. Without them, writing a book would still be an item on my bucket list. In particular, I need to thank Bill Pollock and Alison Law. Bill's encouragement, especially early in the process, gave this first-time author the confidence to take on this project. Alison's experience was invaluable as she guided me through the waters of the publishing world and helped me prioritize the work.

To my good friend and official technical reviewer, Kevin Miller: thank you, thank you, thank you. Kevin went well beyond what I ever expected by taking as many as five passes over each chapter and regularly diving into the F# language spec in his attempts to find errors within the text and the code samples. Beyond his technical review duties, Kevin often acted as a sounding board for my sometimes crazy ideas. His dedication, suggestions, and attention to detail helped shape this book, and for that I'm truly grateful.

Another big thank you to Tomas Petricek. His community involvement and willingness to share his deep knowledge of F# was invaluable to me when I began learning the language. Tomas's technical review of Chapters 11 and 12 really helped smooth out some of the rough edges, and this book has benefited greatly from his input.

Next, thank you to my friends and coworkers, who put up with months of my talking about F# and the writing process. (Sorry, you haven't heard the last of it, either!) In particular, I need to thank Brian Kline. Brian read every word of this book as someone wanting to learn F#. No matter how many times I read through a chapter, he always managed to find a few typographical errors or point out areas where different wording would improve the message.

I'd never have had the opportunity to write this book if F# didn't exist. For that, I thank the F# team for creating such an incredible language. Along those lines, I owe a debt of gratitude to the F# community for being so welcoming and engaging. Without the many community resources available to help people get started with F#, I don't know that I'd have ever adopted it as part of my toolkit.

Finally, thank you to the people who were affected the most by this project: my family. I need to thank my parents not only for giving me life (as my mother likes to remind me), but also for letting me regularly take over a room in their house and escape into the creative process during weekend visits. Of course, I don't know if I could have completed this project without the love and support of my wife, Esther, and my daughter, Nadia. Thank you for understanding the late nights and reclusive weekends that were necessary to make this dream a reality. I love you all.

INTRODUCTION

From the beginning, one of the promises of the .NET Framework has been *language interoperability*; that is, developers targeting the platform could write code in one language and interact with code written in another language through the *Common Language Infrastructure (CLI)*. Early examples often included a library written in C# utilizing a library written in Visual Basic, or vice versa. Ideally, this would allow developers to solve different problems using the best language for the job. In practice, things didn't really work out that way, as developers tended to adopt either C# or Visual Basic and build entire solutions with that language. This is hardly surprising given that, with few exceptions, the differences between the languages have historically been purely syntactic (and the languages have only grown closer as the platform has matured).

Now, after more than a decade, F# has emerged as the third major language in the .NET ecosystem. But what does F# offer that the traditional .NET languages do not, and why should you care?

F# brings functional programming to .NET development. While both C# and Visual Basic have some functional aspects, they are, first and foremost, object-oriented languages; they're concerned primarily with behavior and managing an ever-changing system state. In contrast, F# is a functional-first language, concerned with the application of functions to data. This difference has a dramatic impact not only on how you write code, but also on how you think about it.

As you read through this book, you'll learn how F#'s functional nature enforces a variety of constraints that may seem limiting at first, but once you embrace them you'll likely find that your code is smaller, more correct, and more predictable. Furthermore, you'll discover how F#'s many unique constructs simplify common development tasks, thus allowing you to focus on the problem you're trying to solve rather than the plumbing required by the compiler. These aspects make F# a perfect complement to C# and Visual Basic, often paving the way toward realizing .NET's goal of mixed-language solutions.

Whom Is This Book For?

I have been developing software professionally with C# on the .NET platform since its earliest public releases back in 2002 and 2003. Thus, I wrote this book for people like me: experienced .NET developers looking to break into functional programming while retaining the safety net of the tools and libraries they're already using.

While this book is written with an emphasis on .NET development, experienced developers approaching F# from other backgrounds should still find plenty of value within these pages, as the principles covered aren't typically platform specific.

How Is This Book Organized?

The Book of F# is divided into 12 chapters intended to introduce you to each of the major language features. I recommend that you read this book from beginning to end rather than skipping around, as each chapter builds upon the concepts introduced by its predecessors.

Chapter 1: "Meet F#"   Provides your first glimpse of F# and describes its place within the .NET ecosystem. In this chapter, you'll learn what you need to begin coding in F#, how projects are structured, and some of the nuances that can catch newcomers to the language off guard.

Chapter 2: "F# Interactive"   Covers the F# Interactive environment, an indispensable *read-evaluate-print loop (REPL)* tool that ships with F#. Here you'll see how F# Interactive can help you explore a problem domain and even let you use F# as a scripting language backed by the full power of the .NET Framework.

Chapter 3: "Fundamentals" Teaches you about the fundamentals of F#. Topics covered in this chapter include default immutability, bindings, core data types, type inference, imperative flow control, and generics. Even though many of the concepts addressed in this chapter will be familiar to experienced developers, I encourage you to read through it because F# often allows you to use them in unexpected ways.

Chapter 4: "Staying Objective" Provides an in-depth look at F#'s object-oriented capabilities. In this chapter, you'll see how to develop rich object models every bit as robust as those developed in more established object-oriented languages like C# or Visual Basic.

Chapter 5: "Let's Get Functional" Takes you on a journey into managed functional programming by introducing you to concepts like functions as data, currying, partial application, and delegation. Additionally, you'll learn about several of the F# data structures typically associated with functional programming.

Chapter 6: "Going to Collections" Explores how the various .NET collection types, like arrays and sequences, are represented in F#. You'll also be introduced to several new collection types, including F#'s lists, sets, and maps.

Chapter 7: "Patterns, Patterns, Everywhere" Introduces one of F#'s most powerful constructs: the match expression. Here you'll uncover the various ways you can decompose complex types and branch your code, all within a single expression.

Chapter 8: "Measuring Up" Shows you how to add another degree of safety to your code by enforcing units of measure (such as inches, feet, meters, and so on) on your numeric types.

Chapter 9: "Can I Quote You on That?" Explains quoted expressions—F#'s version of LINQ's expression trees. Here you'll see how to compose, decompose, and apply quoted expressions.

Chapter 10: "Show Me the Data" Explores some F#-specific ways to access data, including query expressions and one of F#'s most exciting features: type providers.

Chapter 11: "Asynchronous and Parallel Programming" Provides a brief introduction to asynchronous and parallel programming with F#. Topics include consuming the Task Parallel Library from F#, asynchronous workflows, and agent-based programming using `MailboxProcessor<'T>`.

Chapter 12: "Computation Expressions" Discusses how to create computation expressions (often called *monads* in other functional languages) to control how data flows from expression to expression.

Additional Resources

As an open source language managed by the F# Software Foundation, F# is backed by a welcoming community of developers around the world, covering a wide range of disciplines. Although I've tried to provide comprehensive explanations and examples throughout the book, if you would like to explore a topic in more detail, you may find these resources helpful.

The Book of F# **companion page** *(http://nostarch.com/f_sharp)*   This is your source for content updates and the code examples used within this book.

The F# Software Foundation *(http://fsharp.org/)*   This should be your first stop. Here you'll find links to all of the language documentation, including the language reference, the language specification, component design guidelines, and more.

F# for Fun and Profit *(http://fsharpforfunandprofit.com/)*   Here you'll find a plethora of examples covering virtually every aspect of the language.

Try F# *(http://www.tryfsharp.org/)*   This browser-based tool lets you experiment with the language and learn it through guided tutorials.

1

MEET F#

Originally developed at Microsoft Research, Cambridge, F# is a functional-first, multi-paradigm language. In plain terms, that means that while F#'s syntax and constructs emphasize writing code that applies functions to data, it's also a full-featured, object-oriented language with a few imperative constructs tossed in for good measure.

F# dates back to 2002, but the first major release didn't appear until Microsoft made version 1.0 available in 2005. F# is descended from the ML language and was heavily inspired by OCaml in particular. Early in its development, the F# team strived to maintain syntactic compatibility with ML, but over time the language has diverged a bit. Gradually, F# has found its place as a first-class citizen of Visual Studio, with project templates available out-of-the-box in every version starting with Visual Studio 2010. F#'s latest release accompanies Visual Studio 2013 and has been designated as version 3.1.

Despite its inclusion in Visual Studio, F# has developed an undeserved reputation as a niche language useful only in academia or highly specialized financial software. As a result, it has failed to secure widespread adoption, particularly in enterprise software, but that seems to be changing as developers are starting to understand the virtues of functional languages. The fact that F# is an open source language licensed under the Apache 2.0 license and there are compilers available on every major platform is also helping the language gain traction. Microsoft continues to contribute heavily to F#, but the language itself is managed by the independent F# Software Foundation.

The goal of this chapter is to give you an idea of how F# programs are organized at both the Visual Studio project and code levels. As you learn the language, you'll find that F# truly is a general-purpose language capable of meeting the demands of most modern software development tasks.

Unless otherwise noted, the examples in this book were developed with F# 3.1 in Visual Studio 2013 (Professional and Ultimate editions). If, for any reason, you're not using Visual Studio, don't fret; the majority of the examples within this book are applicable no matter which platform you're using.

NOTE   *Although I don't specifically cover them, if you intend to follow along with a development environment other than Visual Studio, the F# Software Foundation has plenty of resources to help you get started on its website at* http://fsharp.org/. *You can also try F# in your browser at* http://www.tryfsharp.org/.

F# in Visual Studio

Because this book is primarily intended for experienced .NET developers, I'll assume you already know how to create projects in Visual Studio. I'll go right into introducing the different F# project templates that are available to you and follow that with a brief discussion about file organization within an F# project.

Project Templates

Each of the Visual F# project templates is listed under the Visual F# category in the New Project dialog, but the category's location within the list will vary according to your IDE settings. If the Visual F# category isn't listed immediately under Installed Templates, check under the Other Languages node. If you still don't see it, make sure the F# components are installed. Figure 1-1 shows each template as it would appear with the IDE configured for F# development and targeting .NET 4.0.

As you can see, there are five templates available. The template names are pretty intuitive, but here's a rundown:

Console Application   Creates a new command-line application.

Library   Creates a new library you can reference from other applications or libraries.

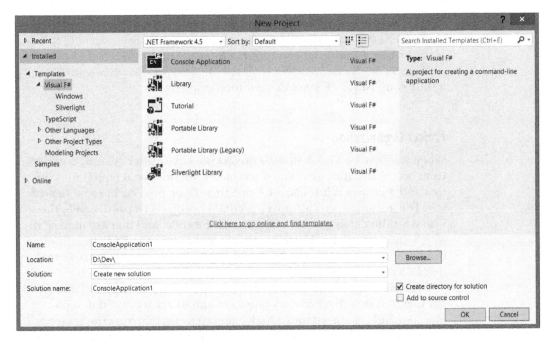

Figure 1-1: F# project templates in Visual Studio 2013

Tutorial   Is a quick way to peek into what F# has to offer, but it's not very useful for starting new projects.

Portable Library   Creates a portable class library that can be used by both .NET 4.5 and Windows Store applications.

Portable Library (Legacy)   Creates a portable class library that can be used by both .NET 4.0 and Silverlight applications.

Silverlight Library   Creates a new library you can reference in a Silverlight application.

Once you've created a project with any of these templates, you should see the familiar Visual Studio interface with the text editor, Solution Explorer, and any other windows you may normally have open. Depending on whether you've previously experimented with F#, you may also see the F# Interactive window.

Among the templates that are conspicuously missing are those for Windows Forms applications, WPF applications, and ASP.NET applications. A key reason for the omission is that many of the designer tools haven't been updated to support generating or understanding F# code. Despite the lack of built-in templates, you can still construct applications with F# using these technologies, but typically you have to do more manual work.

NOTE *The F# Community Templates repository on GitHub hosts a number of additional templates. At the time of this writing, the repository contains only a handful of templates for Visual Studio, but over time it's likely that templates for other editors, such as Xamarin Studio, will be added to the mix. You can find the repository at* https://github.com/fsharp/FSharpCommunityTemplates/.

Project Organization

When you first see Visual Studio's project workspace after creating a project from one of the aforementioned templates, you may be tempted to think that an F# project is just like a C# or Visual Basic project. In some regards, it is. For instance, you can start executable projects by pressing F5, the Visual Studio debugger can step through F# code, and files are managed with Solution Explorer. However, project organization in F# is very different from that of the traditional .NET languages. In fact, you'll probably find that F#'s code structure is almost as foreign as the language itself.

Traditional .NET projects generally follow the convention of one type per file; that is, individual data types are almost always stored in separate files and organized into a folder hierarchy that mirrors the project's namespaces. Aside from avoiding circular assembly references, there are very few steadfast rules on how or when something can appear within a project. Barring any accessibility modifiers (public, private, and so on), types and members are free to reference each other and their members regardless of where they are defined in the project.

Some rules are meant to be broken, but in this case F# shredded the project organization rulebook and then burned the remains. It is incredibly prescriptive about how projects are organized, and for good reason: F# code is evaluated from top to bottom. This means that not only is the order of declarations within an individual code file significant, but the order of the files within your project is significant as well!

It's common for new F# programmers to add a new file to the project, fill in some definitions, and then get compiler errors stating that the new definitions are missing. This is usually because the programmer forgot to move the newly created file above the files that will use the definitions. Fortunately, changing file order within an F# project is relatively painless because there are context menu items and hotkeys to move files up and down, as shown in Figure 1-2.

The other major implication of F#'s top-down evaluation order is that folders are not allowed. Folders wouldn't necessarily break the evaluation order, but they certainly do complicate it, so there's no option within the IDE to add them.

You might be wondering what advantage such an evaluation structure could possibly offer. The primary benefit is that the compiler can make more assumptions about your code and, as a result, give you type inference capabilities unrivaled by any other .NET language. Furthermore, this evaluation structure avoids inadvertent recursive definitions (when two or more types depend on each other). This makes you think a bit more about how and where your types are used, and it forces you to be explicit about recursive definitions where they're appropriate.

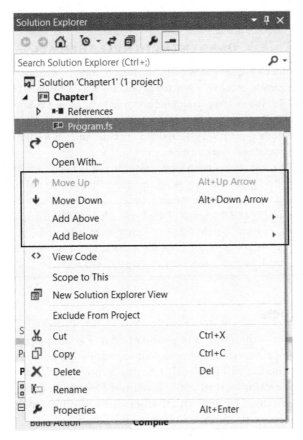

Figure 1-2: Move and Add options in Solution Explorer's context menu

Significance of Whitespace

Newcomers to F# are usually quick to notice the absence of braces or BEGIN and END delimiters. Rather than relying on syntactic tokens to denote code blocks, the designers of F# decided to make whitespace significant.

Code that is inside a block must be indented farther than the line that opens the block. For example, when you define a function, the lines belonging to the function's body must begin to the right of the first character of the function declaration. It doesn't really matter how far the lines are indented, only that they are indented and that the indentation level is consistent for each line in a block.

With most programming languages, this is the point where the age-old debate of tabs versus spaces would flare up, but this is not the case in F#. The F# compiler rules with an iron fist on this matter and expressly forbids tabs because the number of spaces that a given tab character represents is unknown. When you begin writing F#, you'll probably want to configure the options for Visual Studio's text editor to insert spaces in place of tabs.

ONE SYNTAX TO RULE THEM ALL

To say that F# requires consistent indentation or that it expressly forbids tabs isn't completely accurate. F# actually has two syntax formats: verbose and lightweight. The verbose format requires you to be more explicit with your code but isn't as sensitive to indentation. Under verbose syntax you denote the end of a code block not by decreasing the indentation level, but by using additional keywords like end and done.

In F#'s infancy, verbose format was the norm, but as the language has matured, the lightweight syntax has gained favor and is now the default. Of course, there are other differences between verbose and lightweight syntax, but they are beyond the scope of this book. None of the examples in this book use verbose syntax, but should you yearn to write more code, you can revert to verbose syntax by opening a code file with the #light off directive.

Grouping Constructs

There are two primary ways to group code in F#: namespaces and modules. In single-file projects, declaring a namespace or module is optional, as the contents of the file will implicitly become a module with the same name as the file—for example, if your file is named *Program.fs*, the module will automatically be named Program. In all other cases, though, each file must begin with a namespace or module declaration.

Namespaces

F# namespaces are the same as in C# and Visual Basic in that they allow you to group related code by a name to reduce the likelihood of a naming conflict. Namespaces can include modules and type definitions but cannot directly include any values or functions.

You declare namespaces with the namespace keyword followed by an identifier. For example, a namespace for the code in this book might look like this:

```
namespace TheBookOfFSharp
```

You can also declare more granular namespaces by nesting them. Nested namespaces are declared with fully qualified names, with each level separated by a dot (.). For instance, we could group all the code for this chapter in a nested namespace like this:

```
namespace TheBookOfFSharp.Chapter1
```

Just as in the other .NET languages, you can split namespaces across files and assemblies. You can also declare multiple namespaces within a single file, but you cannot nest them inline; each namespace declaration must be a top-level block.

In the event that you want to place code in .NET's global namespace, you can declare the namespace with the global keyword as follows:

```
namespace global
```

Whenever you declare a namespace, other code already loaded into that namespace is immediately made available to your code. For all other cases, though, you must either fully qualify the type or module names or import them using the open keyword, as you would with a using directive in C# or an Imports statement in Visual Basic. The following snippet shows both approaches:

```
// Fully qualified name
let now = System.DateTime.Now

// Imported namespace
open System
let today = DateTime.Now.Date
```

Modules

Modules are similar to namespaces in that they allow you to logically group code. Unlike namespaces, however, they can directly contain values and functions. In practice, modules are more closely related to classes containing only static members in other .NET languages; in fact, that's how they're represented in the compiled assembly.

Modules fall into one of two categories: top-level and local. *Top-level* modules contain all the code in a single implementation file. By contrast, *local* modules are used when multiple modules or types not belonging to a module are defined in the same file.

You declare modules with the module keyword followed by an identifier, like this:

```
module TheBookOfFSharp
```

Unlike namespaces, module definitions cannot span multiple files, but you can define multiple modules within a single file. You can also nest modules directly within a parent module like this:

```
module OuterModule
  module NestedModule =
    do ()
```

When you want to use both a namespace and a top-level module, F# provides a convenient syntactic shortcut that combines them into a single declaration. To take advantage of this, simply include the fully qualified name before the module name, as shown here:

```
module TheBookOfFSharp.Chapter1.QualifiedModule
```

In the preceding snippet, we declare a module named `QualifiedModule` within the `TheBookOfFSharp.Chapter1` namespace.

As a final note, you can import module members through the `open` keyword as though they belong to a namespace. For instance, to import any types defined in `QualifiedModule`, we could write:

```
open TheBookOfFSharp.Chapter1.QualifiedModule
```

To simplify this process for commonly used modules, you can decorate the module with the `AutoOpen` attribute like this:

```
[<AutoOpen>]
module TheBookOfFSharp.Chapter1.QualifiedModule
```

By applying this attribute to a module, whenever you explicitly open the namespace containing the module, the module will also be opened.

Expressions Are Everywhere

One of F#'s distinguishing characteristics is that it is an *expression-based* language; that is, nearly everything that's evaluated returns a result. As you learn F#, you'll quickly discover that writing applications and libraries is an exercise in combining expressions to produce results. This is a stark contrast to languages like C#, where typically only methods (and operators) return a result. In F#, seemingly familiar constructs like if...else gain new life because, like all expressions, the if...else expression returns a result. Consider the following snippet, which uses C#'s if...else statement to print a string indicating whether a number is even or odd:

```
// C#
var testNumber = 10;
string evenOrOdd;

if (testNumber % 2 == 0)
    evenOrOdd = "even";
else
    evenOrOdd = "odd";

Console.WriteLine(evenOrOdd);
```

Now, compare that with this functionally equivalent code in F#, which uses the if...else expression instead:

```
// F#
let testNumber = 10
let evenOrOdd = if testNumber % 2 = 0 then "even" else "odd"
Console.WriteLine evenOrOdd
```

The first thing you probably noticed is that the F# version is more concise. What might not be immediately apparent, though, is that the F# version eliminates the mutable state that's present in the C# version (evenOrOdd is uninitialized before it is assigned a value). This isn't necessarily an issue in this simple example because the mutable state is isolated, but in larger applications, mutable state contributes to a fragile and often unpredictable code base.

You might argue (correctly) that we could write the C# code using C#'s conditional operator instead of the if...else statement to achieve the same effect as the F# code. But the main point of this example is that even seemingly familiar constructs return values in F#.

Application Entry Point

In an F# application, the initializations defined in the last file of the project are used as the application's entry point by default. For more control over how your application starts, you can define a let bound function as the application's entry point by decorating it with the EntryPoint attribute. This allows you to use an arbitrary function for what would be the Main method or procedure in a C# or Visual Basic application, respectively. Accordingly, the decorated function must accept a string array and return an integer to be valid. Such a function would typically follow this pattern:

```
[<EntryPoint>]
let main argv =
  // initialization code
  0
```

Implicit Return Values

Because F# is a language steeped in expressions, the F# compiler can make more assumptions about your code. Because all expressions return a value and all functions are expressions, it is implied that all functions will return a value. Therefore, the compiler can assume that the last expression evaluated within a function is the function's return value; you don't need to explicitly state it as such with a keyword like return.

As an example, consider the main function from the previous section. In that function, 0 is implicitly returned because it's the final expression evaluated in the function. Similarly, consider this function, which simply adds two integers:

```
let add x y = x + y
```

Here, the add function accepts two parameters, x and y, and contains only a single expression: an addition operation. Because the addition operation is the last expression evaluated when add is invoked, add implicitly returns the result of that operation.

Your First F# Program

Now that you've learned how to structure an F# project, it's time to see some "real" F# code that goes beyond basic syntax. Although the instant gratification of a traditional "Hello world"–type application is a nice confidence booster when you're starting out with a new language, I've decided to forego that approach in favor of an example that both is useful and provides a nice sampling of many of F#'s capabilities: a Reverse Polish Notation (RPN) calculator.

RPN is a postfix notation for mathematical expressions; that is, it's a manner of expressing computations where each operator immediately follows its operands. For example, to express computing the sum of 1 and 2, we'd normally write 1 + 2; when using RPN, however, we'd write 1 2 +.

You typically implement RPN calculators by iterating over a sequence of numbers and operators. Each item is inspected and numbers are pushed onto a stack, whereas operators pop the appropriate number of operands from the stack, evaluate, and push the result back onto the stack. At the end of the process, the sole item remaining in the stack should be the expression's result. Figure 1-3 roughly illustrates how this process looks when applied to the expression 4 2 5 * +.

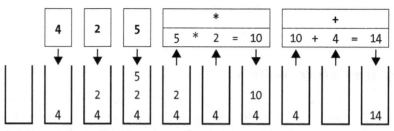

Figure 1-3: Application of Reverse Polish Notation

Working from left to right, you can see how items are added to and removed from the stack, ultimately producing 14 as the result. As you're about to see, though, implementing a basic RPN calculator in F# takes only a few lines of code and doesn't even require managing a mutable stack!

If you'd like to follow along with this example in Visual Studio, create a new project using the F# Application template. When you're ready, replace the text editor's contents with the following code (note that F# is case sensitive):

```
module TheBookOfFSharp.RpnCalculator

open System

let evalRpnExpr (s : string) =
  let solve items current =
    match (current, items) with
      | "+", y::x::t -> (x + y)::t
      | "-", y::x::t -> (x - y)::t
      | "*", y::x::t -> (x * y)::t
      | "/", y::x::t -> (x / y)::t
      | _ -> (float current)::items
  (s.Split(' ') |> Seq.fold solve []).Head

[<EntryPoint>]
let main argv =
  [ "4 2 5 * + 1 3 2 * + /"
    "5 4 6 + /"
    "10 4 3 + 2 * -"
    "2 3 +"
    "90 34 12 33 55 66 + * - + -"
    "90 3 -" ]
  |> List.map (fun expr -> expr, evalRpnExpr expr)
  |> List.iter (fun (expr, result) -> printfn "(%s) = %A" expr result)
  Console.ReadLine() |> ignore
  0
```

When you've finished entering the RPN calculator code, press F5 and observe the output. You should see the results depicted in Figure 1-4.

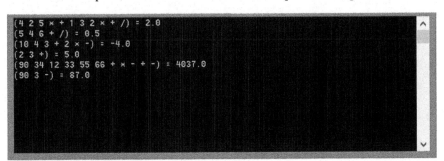

Figure 1-4: Reverse Polish Notation calculator results

Don't be discouraged if the RPN calculator code doesn't make much sense right now; that's the point! For now it's enough to recognize that the entire RPN calculation is contained within the evalRpnExpr function. I like starting with this example because it not only shows some idiomatic F# code, but it also demonstrates a number of important concepts, such as default immutability, functions as data, pattern matching, recursion, library functions, partial application, F# lists, and pipelining. These concepts work together to create highly expressive and predictable code. Throughout this book, you'll explore each of these concepts and many more in detail. As you progress through the book, I encourage you to revisit this example periodically to see just how much functionality is contained within such a small program.

Summary

Despite a reputation as a niche language, F# is an expressive, functional-first, multiparadigm language rooted in ML and useful for most modern software development activities. As you'll see in the coming chapters, writing F# effectively is about learning how to combine the types, functions, and values you'll define in namespaces and modules into expressions. That said, traditional .NET developers will have to adjust to some of the language's nuances like top-down evaluation, whitespace significance, and implicit returns. Once you get over the initial learning curve, however, you'll see how F#'s simple yet expressive syntax will enable you to solve complex problems while producing code that is more stable and predictable.

2

F# INTERACTIVE

If the prospect of doing true functional programming against the .NET Framework isn't compelling enough, the productivity gains available through F# Interactive (FSI) should be. FSI is a *read-evaluate-print loop (REPL)* utility you can use to explore problem domains and test code as you write. It also doubles as a script host that allows you to leverage the elegance of F# and the power of the .NET Framework to automate common tasks. How can a compiled language like F# be used interactively? Because behind the scenes FSI compiles its input to dynamically generate assemblies.

Running F# Interactive

There are two ways to work in FSI: via the F# Interactive window in Visual Studio or the *fsi.exe* console application. The choice is usually one of convenience. I typically prefer to work in the F# Interactive window because it easily integrates into my Visual Studio development workflow. I generally use the window for exploratory tasks and reserve the console for script execution.

To open the F# Interactive window in Visual Studio, press CTRL-ALT-F; you should see a prompt like that shown in Figure 2-1. By default, *fsi.exe* is available only through the Visual Studio command prompt shortcuts and not through the basic Windows command prompt. If you want to make *fsi.exe* available from another prompt, you'll need to add its location to your path environment variable. By default, F# is installed to *%PROGRAMFILES(x86)%\Microsoft SDKs\F#\3.0\Framework\v4.0* (*%PROGRAMFILES%* on 32-bit systems).

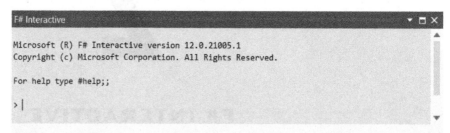

```
Microsoft (R) F# Interactive version 12.0.21005.1
Copyright (c) Microsoft Corporation. All Rights Reserved.

For help type #help;;

> |
```

Figure 2-1: The F# Interactive window in Visual Studio 2013

In addition to just opening the Interactive window, you can send code to the window with ALT-ENTER, in which case the results from executing that code will also be shown. This makes it very easy to test new concepts: If you're not sure how well something will work, you can typically try it immediately by writing a bit of code, sending it to FSI, and inspecting the result.

Sending code from the text editor isn't the only way to evaluate expressions in FSI; you can also run code directly from its prompt. This flexibility is great for productivity because you can work on a block of code in the text editor, send it to FSI, and then experiment with it interactively in the FSI window itself.

There is an important difference between entering code directly in the Interactive window versus sending code from the text editor. When you send code from the editor, it's compiled and executed automatically, whereas code entered directly won't execute until you terminate it with a double semicolon pattern (;;). For example, to perform simple addition you could either enter 1 + 1 into the text editor and send it to FSI, or enter 1 + 1;; directly at the FSI prompt. Both approaches yield the same result, but because double semicolons must be used to denote the end of the code input, FSI lets you enter and execute multiple lines of code directly at the prompt.

NOTE *Even though multiple-line entry at the prompt is possible, it's often more trouble than it's worth because if you make a silly typing mistake you must start over. I tend to use single-line statements at the prompt as much as possible. (Fortunately, recovering from such mistakes is usually just a matter of correcting the mistake and trying again.)*

F# Interactive Output

One thing that makes FSI so useful is that it reports back everything that it does. Whenever you execute code in FSI, it displays val followed by the identifier name, data type, and value for each binding it creates. For example, when you define and invoke a function, FSI will create two bindings: one for the function itself and one for the result, as shown here.

```
> let add a b = a + b
let sum = add 1 2;;

val add : a:int -> b:int -> int
val sum : int = 3
```

The it Identifier

You don't always have to explicitly define bindings in FSI; in most interactive sessions you can simply evaluate an expression. For example, you can call the add function without defining the sum identifier like this.

```
> add 1 2;;
val it : int = 3
```

When you don't explicitly name something (as when performing a simple calculation or checking the output of a function), FSI automatically binds the result to the it identifier. You can refer to it in subsequent evaluations but be aware that, as in *Highlander*, there can be only one; whenever FSI implicitly binds something, the value is replaced. You can see this behavior by evaluating multiple expressions without explicitly binding the results to an identifier, as shown here.

```
> it;;
val it : int = 3

> add 3 4;;
val it : int = 7

> it;;
val it : int = 7
```

The bottom line when it comes to the it identifier is love it, use it, but don't rely on it.

Playing in the Sandbox

Even when running within Visual Studio, FSI is a sandbox that's isolated from and completely unaware of any code you haven't explicitly told it about. This isolation provides a layer of protection between "work" and "play," but it also means that in order for it to be useful you'll need ways to interact with the outside world. For this we turn to directives.

FSI provides several directives that you can invoke in an interactive session or a script. Among these are directives for refreshing your memory about which directives are available, loading code from other F# source files, referencing assemblies, and even providing some performance statistics.

#help

If you forget any of the directives, you can invoke the #help directive at the FSI prompt for a listing of available directives and a brief description of each.

#quit

If you need to get out of FSI from the command prompt, use the #quit directive to end the session. Although you can use #quit within the FSI window in Visual Studio, I suggest using the Reset Interactive Session context menu item shown in Figure 2-2 because it clears previous output and begins a new session automatically.

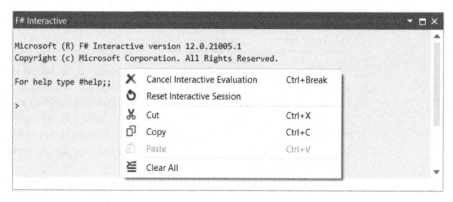

Figure 2-2: Reset Interactive Session context menu item

#load

One way to load existing code into an FSI session is with the #load directive as shown next. The #load directive accepts one or more string parameters containing the absolute or relative paths to external source files. FSI should load, compile, and execute the listed files (in order) and make their contents available in the current session.

```
> #load @"D:\Dev\FSharp\Samples\Chapter2\MySourceFile.fs";;
[Loading D:\Dev\FSharp\Samples\Chapter2\MySourceFile.fs]
-- snip --
```

Although you can include multiple source files in a single #load directive, it's often easier to include each with a separate directive. The reason is that if you're actively working on one of the files and you break something, the compiler highlights the entire directive as a problem. By using multiple directives, you can more quickly isolate the troublesome file.

#r

The #r directive is to assemblies what the #load directive is to source files. You can use #r to reference any .NET assembly (with the usual restrictions around target framework and platform). If the assembly you need is already located in one of the folders included in the assembly search path, identify it by name or you'll need to include the full path. For example, if you need to load System.Configuration, you can use:

```
> #r "System.Configuration";;
--> Referenced 'C:\Program Files (x86)\Reference Assemblies\Microsoft\
Framework\.NETFramework\v4.5\System.Configuration.dll'
```

FSI responds with the full path of each assembly it loads in this manner.

#I

When you need to reference multiple assemblies from a folder that is not already included in the search path, you can add the folder to the assembly search path in FSI with the #I directive.

```
> #I @"D:\Dev\FSharp\Samples\Chapter2\Bin\Debug";;
--> Added 'D:\Dev\FSharp\Samples\Chapter2\Bin\Debug' to library include path
```

Once the folder is added to the search path, you should be able to reference assemblies in it by name instead of by their full path.

#time

The #time directive provides extra visibility into what your code is doing by printing some statistics along with its output. You can enable timing information by using the #time directive with the on string argument.

```
> #time "on";;
--> Timing now on
```

With timing enabled, the statistics will be computed each time code is executed in FSI. These statistics include real time, CPU time, and the number of garbage collection operations over all three generations. For example, to help optimize a slow function you could invoke it with timing enabled and see something like this:

```
> DoSomethingSlow();;
Real: 00:00:01.095, CPU: 00:00:01.107, GC gen0: 25, gen1: 23, gen2: 23
val it : unit = ()
```

When you're done with the statistics and no longer want to see them in the FSI output, disable them with the #time directive and the off string argument.

```
> #time "off";;
--> Timing now off
```

Scripting

As F# is a .NET language, most of your F# code will be placed in *.fs* files and compiled into assemblies to be used by larger applications. When coupled with FSI, though, F# can serve as a scripting language so you can leverage its power to automate common tasks with full support from the .NET Framework.

For example, say you want to concatenate several PDF files into one document. You could write a console application for this, but it's trivial to write it as a script using the open source PDFsharp library to manipulate the individual PDFs. That script would take about 30 lines of code, including blank lines. By providing terse syntax and exposing the power of the .NET Framework, F# is ideal for such a task.

Creating scripts as *.fsx* files offers a few benefits. For one, the directives described in "Playing in the Sandbox" on page 15 are FSI features, so they aren't allowed in standard source files. Also, because *.fsx* files are associated with *fsi.exe*, you can execute them directly from a shell context menu as shown in Figure 2-3. This makes it easy to run scripts like the PDF concatenation as needed.

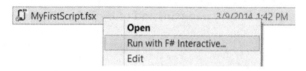

Figure 2-3: Run with F# Interactive context menu item

To add scripts to a project, select the project in Solution Explorer, press CTRL-SHIFT-A to open the **Add New Item** dialog, and select **F# Script File** as shown in Figure 2-4.

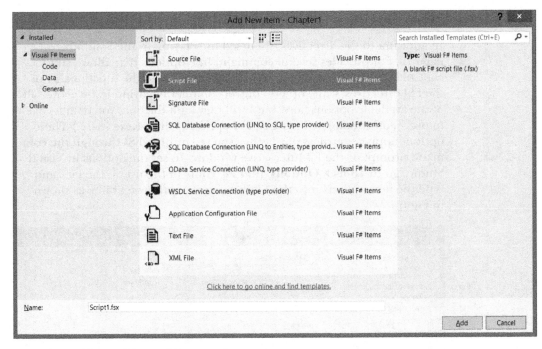

Figure 2-4: Adding an F# script file to a project

To quickly create a standalone *.fsx* file in Visual Studio 2013, press
CTRL-N to open the **New File** dialog, select **Script** from the menu on the
left, and locate the **F# Script File** option as shown in Figure 2-5.

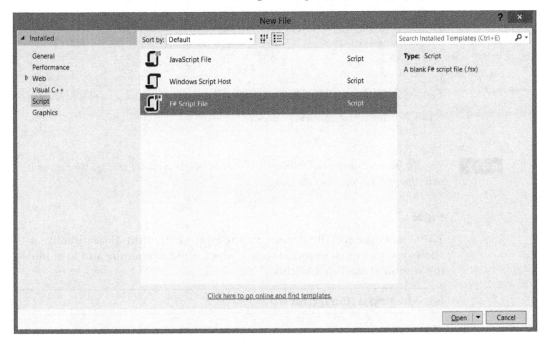

Figure 2-5: Creating a standalone F# script file

F# Interactive Options

In addition to the directives discussed in "Playing in the Sandbox" on page 15, FSI provides several command-line options that allow you to control it. Some of these options offer alternatives to the functionality of the FSI directives, while others control compiler behavior. I won't cover all of the available options here, but I will highlight the ones you're most likely to use. (For a complete listing of FSI options, run `fsi.exe -help`.) These options apply regardless of whether you're running FSI through the command prompt or the F# Interactive window. To set the options in Visual Studio, go to **Tools ▸ Options**, find **F# Tools** in the list on the left, and type the new options into the **F# Interactive options** text box as shown in Figure 2-6.

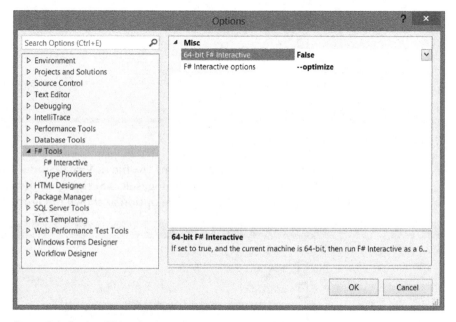

Figure 2-6: Setting F# Interactive options

NOTE   *The F# Interactive options setting in Visual Studio is a global setting. Changing it will affect all instances of the window.*

--load

The `--load` option is the command-line equivalent of the `#load` directive. It allows you to specify external source files for FSI to compile and load into the session at startup, like this:

```
fsi --load:MyFirstScript.fsx
```

The --load option doesn't process any directives in the specified file, so if any directives must be evaluated use the --use option instead.

--use

Like --load, the --use option loads external source files, but it also processes directives such as #load or #I upon loading the file.

```
fsi --use:MyFirstScript.fsx
```

--reference

Just as you can use --load or --use to import a source file, you can use the --reference option (or its short form, -r) to reference an external assembly. This has the same effect as the #r directive.

```
fsi --reference:System.Configuration
```

As with the #r directive, be sure to include the full path to the assembly if it's not in a location already included in the search path.

--lib

The --lib option serves the same role as the #I directive by adding the specified folder to the assembly search path. Its short form is -I.

```
fsi --lib:D:\Dev\FSharp\Samples\Chapter2\Bin\Debug
```

--define

As with other .NET languages, F# allows you to define conditional compilation symbols (like the predefined DEBUG and RELEASE symbols in Visual Studio) that can affect how code is compiled. To define symbols for use within an FSI session, use the --define option.

```
fsi --define:DEBUG
```

FSI and the F# compiler automatically define certain symbols for you, depending on how your code is compiled. For example, when you are running code compiled in an FSI session, whether by entering it at a prompt, sending it from the text editor, or importing another file, FSI defines the INTERACTIVE symbol. Directly compiled F# code gets the COMPILED symbol instead. These symbols become important when code must behave differently under an FSI session than in a compiled assembly due to environmental differences.

--exec

By default the FSI process doesn't terminate when it finishes evaluating a script. To force it to quit rather than return you to the FSI prompt, specify the --exec option.

```
fsi --load:MyFirstScript.fsx --exec
```

Now, when the script completes you'll automatically be returned to the command prompt.

--

If your code expects command-line arguments, you can send them to FSI with the -- option; this is essentially a delimiter that tells FSI to treat all remaining arguments as arguments to the code rather than to FSI itself.

```
fsi --load:MyFirstScript.fsx --exec -- Dave
```

When code that's dependent on command-line arguments might be executed from either an FSI session or a compiled assembly, you should use the INTERACTIVE and COMPILED symbols to ensure that the parameters are read correctly. For example, in a typical .NET application you'd use System.Environment.GetCommandLineArgs() to resolve the arguments. The same holds true for COMPILED code, but in INTERACTIVE code the execution process is actually FSI rather than your assembly. Therefore, the GetCommandLineArgs method returns all arguments passed to the FSI process rather than only the ones intended for your script! To account for this difference, interactive code should typically call fsi.CommandLineArgs instead. You can easily change this behavior with conditional compilation, like this.

```
let getCommandLineArgs() =
#if INTERACTIVE
   fsi.CommandLineArgs
#else
   System.Environment.GetCommandLineArgs()
#endif

getCommandLineArgs() |> printfn "%A"
```

Fortunately, both functions return the same result: a string array that includes the script/executable name as the first item. This greatly simplifies any argument-parsing code you have, because the end result is the same.

--quiet

Depending on what your script is doing, FSI can be pretty chatty and sometimes results can get lost in the noise. To tell FSI to be quiet, use the --quiet option.

```
fsi --quiet
```

The --quiet option suppresses virtually everything FSI would normally output, including bindings, file loads, and assembly references (but not statistics when timing is enabled). FSI will still display error messages and anything your code sends to the console.

--optimize

The --optimize option controls whether compiler optimizations will be applied to the code. It's enabled by default in Visual Studio.

--tailcalls

We'll look at tail recursion in detail in Chapter 5, but for now just know that the --tailcalls option controls whether the compiler will optimize for tail-recursive functions. This option is enabled by default in FSI.

Summary

In this chapter you've learned how F#'s REPL tool, F# Interactive, can help you explore a problem and find a path to the solution. You've also learned how you can customize the behavior of FSI through directives and command-line options. In the next chapter, we'll begin exploring the F# language itself by learning about a variety of key features that apply regardless of whether you're programming in a functional, object-oriented, or imperative style.

3

FUNDAMENTALS

In the previous chapter, you learned how F# Interactive can enhance your workflow through rapid feedback and task automation. Now we'll put that knowledge to work as we explore some basic language features. The concepts introduced in this chapter apply regardless of whether you're programming primarily in an imperative, object-oriented, or functional style.

Most of this chapter focuses on how F# handles concepts central to the .NET Framework, like the core data types, enumerations, flow control, generics, and exception handling. You'll also learn how F# can help you write more predictable code through controlling side effects, default immutability, type inference, and option types. Regardless of the subject, though, you should start seeing how F# distinguishes itself as a compelling alternative to C# and Visual Basic.

Immutability and Side Effects

If you're coming to F# from a primarily object-oriented background, the feature you may find the most challenging to adjust to is *default immutability*. This is a radical departure from traditional .NET languages that place few restrictions on what can change and when. Programs written in languages without default immutability can be unpredictable because system state (program data) can change at almost any time. We refer to these changes as *side effects*.

Some side effects, like writing to the console, are relatively benign, but what about when they affect shared resources? What if invoking a function changes a value that's used elsewhere? Will a function always yield the same result regardless of when it's called? Consider this C# example that references a public field for some multiplication:

```
//C#
using System;
using System.Linq;

class Example
{
  public static int multiplier = 1;

  private static void ❶Multiply(int value)
  {
    var result = value * multiplier;
    Console.WriteLine("{0} x {1} = {2}", value, ❷multiplier++, result);
  }

  static void Main()
  {
    var range = Enumerable.Range(1, 100);
    foreach(var i in range)
    {
      Multiply(i);
    }
  }
}

// First 10 results
// 1 x 1 = 1
// 2 x 2 = 4
// 3 x 3 = 9
// 4 x 4 = 16
// 5 x 5 = 25
// 6 x 6 = 36
// 7 x 7 = 49
// 8 x 8 = 64
// 9 x 9 = 81
// 10 x 10 = 100
```

In this example, the Multiply method ❶ has a side effect where the multiplier is incremented ❷. As long as nothing changes anywhere else in the program it's somewhat predictable, but as soon as you change the order of calls to the Multiply method, introduce another call to the Multiply method, or change the multiplier field through some other mechanism, all future results are brought into question.

To further complicate the issue, consider what happens when multiple calls to Multiply are made in parallel, in this revision of the Main method:

```
//C#
static void Main()
{
    var range = Enumerable.Range(1, 100);
    System.Threading.Tasks.Parallel.ForEach(range, i => Multiply(i));
}

// First 10 results
// 1 x 1 = 1
// 6 x 3 = 18
// 7 x 4 = 28
// 5 x 2 = 10
// 10 x 6 = 60
// 11 x 7 = 77
// 12 x 8 = 96
// 13 x 9 = 117
// 14 x 10 = 140
// 15 x 11 = 165
```

There's no guarantee as to which operation will execute first when running in parallel, so running this 10 times is likely to give you 10 different results. The unpredictability that comes from using mutable values is why *global state* (values accessible from anywhere within your application) is generally considered harmful. Properly managing global state requires discipline that can be increasingly difficult to enforce as teams and projects grow.

Functional Purity

Functional languages like F# are often described in terms of their mathematical purity. In *purely* functional languages like Haskell, programs are composed entirely of deterministic *expressions* that always return a value, and side effects are expressly forbidden except in certain specific circumstances. In contrast, F# is an *impure* functional language. As such, it takes an important step toward improving predictability by making values immutable by default.

That's not to say that F# can't use variables in the traditional sense; it just means that in order to change a value, you must explicitly allow it and should restrict the value's scope as much as possible. By keeping the scope narrow, you can code in a primarily functional style but switch to a more imperative or object-oriented style in isolated fragments as appropriate.

By managing side effects through default immutability, F# code is more naturally suited for execution in parallel and concurrent environments. In many cases, carefully controlling what can change reduces, if not eliminates, the need to lock shared resources and ensures that multiple processes don't attempt to make potentially conflicting or behavior-altering changes to the overall system state. This added safety is increasingly important as software development evolves to take advantage of the multiprocessor or multicore systems that are so ubiquitous in modern computing.

Bindings

Bindings are F#'s primary way of identifying values or executable code. There are three types of bindings—let, use, and do—and each has a specific purpose.

let Bindings

let bindings simply associate names with values. They are the most common and versatile binding type. (I briefly introduced let bindings in Chapter 2.) You create a let binding with the let keyword. For example, to bind an integer value you would use something like this:

```
let intValue = 1
```

Similarly, to bind a string you could use:

```
let strValue = "hello"
```

But let bindings aren't restricted to simple assignments. You can also use them to identify functions or other expressions:

```
let add a b = a + b
let sum = add 1 2
```

Literals

Although the let bindings we've seen so far are immutable, they can't be considered constant values in the traditional .NET sense. Bindings are more like readonly variables in C# (ReadOnly in Visual Basic) than they are constants, in that their values are resolved at run time rather than replaced inline at compile time. You can define a true .NET constant value, called a *literal* in F#, by decorating a binding with the Literal attribute. (F# follows the same convention as other .NET languages by making the Attribute suffix optional, so in this example both Literal and LiteralAttribute are acceptable.)

```
[<Literal>]
let FahrenheitBoilingPoint = 212
```

This causes the compiler to treat the definition the same as a const in C# (Const in Visual Basic), meaning that the value will be compiled inline wherever it is used. As such, bindings decorated as Literal must be a full constructed value type, string, or null.

Mutable Bindings

If you try to change the value of a default binding with the assignment operator (<-), the compiler will tell you that you can't.

```
let name = "Dave"

name <- "Nadia"
// Error - immutable binding
```

To make a binding mutable, simply include the `mutable` keyword in its definition. Once a mutable binding is defined, you can change its value at will.

```
let mutable name = "Dave"

name <- "Nadia"
// OK - mutable binding
```

There is, of course, a caveat: Mutable bindings don't play nicely with *closures* (inline functions that can access bindings visible within the scope where they're defined).

```
// Horrible, invalid code
let addSomeNumbers nums =
  let ❶mutable sum = 0
  let add = ❷(fun num -> sum <- sum + num)
  Array.iter (fun num -> add num) [| 1..10 |]
```

In this example, the mutable binding, sum ❶, is captured by the add closure ❷. If you try to compile this code, the compiler politely informs you of the error and instructs you to either eliminate the mutation or use another mutable construct, a *reference cell*, instead.

Reference Cells

Reference cells are like mutable bindings in that their values can be changed at run time, but they work much differently. A reasonable way to think of reference cells is that they are to pointers what mutable bindings are to traditional variables. That said, reference cells aren't really pointers either because they're concrete types that encapsulate a mutable value rather than pointing to a particular resource or memory address.

You create a new reference cell like a typical `let` binding except that you include the `ref` operator before the bound value.

```
let cell = ref 0
```

Accessing and changing a reference cell's value requires a different syntax than a standard binding because we need to affect the encapsulated value rather than the reference cell itself.

```
❶ cell := 100
   printf "%i" ❷!cell
```

As you can see at ❶, the := operator is used to change the reference cell's value, and at ❷ the ! operator is used to return the cell's value.

use Bindings

F# provides a binding mechanism for types that implement the IDisposable interface in a way that's similar to C#'s using statement. In F#, when you want the compiler to insert a call to an IDisposable object's Dispose method, you can create a use binding with the use keyword.

Like the using statement, which delimits the block where the IDisposable object is in scope, objects created through use bindings are disposed of when their enclosing block terminates; that is, if a use binding is created at the top level of a function, the object will be disposed of immediately after the function returns. Similarly, if a use binding is created within a nested construct, like a loop, the object will be disposed of when the iteration completes.

The following example shows this principle in action:

```
open System

let ❶createDisposable name =
  printfn "creating: %s" name
  ❷{ new IDisposable with
    member x.Dispose() =
      printfn "disposing: %s" name
  }

let ❸testDisposable() =
  use root = createDisposable "outer"
  for i in [1..2] do
    use nested = createDisposable (sprintf "inner %i" i)
    printfn "completing iteration %i" i
  printfn "leaving function"
```

In this example, the createDisposable function ❶ writes a message to the console telling you that a disposable object is being created. It then returns an object that prints a message when it's disposed of ❷. The testDisposable function ❸ repeatedly invokes the createDisposable function both inside and outside of a simple for loop and writes out messages telling you when each block is terminating.

Invoking the testDisposable function produces the following output that shows when each object is created and disposed of in relation to its containing block.

```
creating: outer
creating: inner 1
completing iteration 1
```

```
disposing: inner 1
creating: inner 2
completing iteration 2
disposing: inner 2
leaving function
disposing: outer
```

A simple and more practical example of a use binding is writing some text to a file, like this:

```
open System.IO
❶ let writeToFile filename buffer =
    ❷use fs = ❸new FileStream(filename, FileMode.CreateNew, FileAccess.Write)
    fs.Write(buffer, 0, buffer.Length)
```

Notice at ❶ that a let binding is used for the writeToFile function (functions are data in F#) and that at ❷ a use binding is used in conjunction with the new keyword ❸ to create the FileStream. (The new keyword is optional in F#, but by convention it's included whenever an IDisposable object is created to indicate that the object should be disposed of. If you create a use binding without the new keyword, the compiler will issue a warning.)

use bindings can't be used directly within a module, primarily because modules are essentially static classes that never go out of scope. If you try to define a use binding directly within a module, you'll receive a compiler warning along with a note that the binding will be treated as a let binding instead, like this:

```
warning FS0524: 'use' bindings are not permitted in modules and are
treated as 'let' bindings
```

using Function

For more control over an IDisposable, turn to the using function. Although not a binding in its own right, using offers functionality that's a bit more like C#'s using statement: Give it an IDisposable and a function that accepts the instance, and using automatically calls Dispose when it completes, as shown here:

```
open System.Drawing
using (Image.FromFile(@"C:\Windows\Web\Screen\img100.jpg"))
    (fun img -> printfn "%i x %i" img.Width img.Height)
```

In some ways using is more powerful than its C# counterpart because, like every expression in F#, it returns a value. Consider this revision of the previous example:

```
open System.Drawing
❶ let w, h = using (Image.FromFile(@"C:\Windows\Web\Screen\img100.jpg"))
                (fun img -> ❷(img.Width, img.Height))
❸ printfn "Dimensions: %i x %i" w h
```

Instead of writing the dimensions to the console within the function passed to the using function at ❷, we return them as a *tuple* (a simple type containing multiple data items) and bind each component value to meaningful names as shown at ❶, before writing them to the console at ❸. Even in this simple example you can begin to see how F#'s composable, expressive syntax leads to more understandable solutions by eliminating most of the *plumbing code* (code you have to write to satisfy the compiler), allowing you to focus on the problem itself.

Replicating the using Function in C#

I like F#'s using function so much that I've created a couple of static helper methods for use in my C# projects.

```
// C#
public static class IDisposableHelper
{
  public static TResult Using<TResource, TResult>
    (TResource resource, Func<TResource, TResult> action)
      where TResource : IDisposable
  {
    using(resource) return action(resource);
  }

  public static void Using<TResource>
    (TResource resource, Action<TResource> action)
      where TResource : IDisposable
  {
    using(resource) action(resource);
  }
}
```

They're not exactly pretty, but they get the job done.

Now here's the C# version of the preceding examples using my helper functions.

```
// C#
// using System.Drawing
IDisposableHelper.Using(
  Image.FromFile(@"C:\Windows\Web\Screen\img100.jpg"),
  img => Console.WriteLine("Dimensions: {0} x {1}", img.Width, img.Height)
);

var dims =
  IDisposableHelper.Using(
    Image.FromFile(@"C:\Windows\Web\Screen\img100.jpg"),
    img => Tuple.Create(img.Width, img.Height)
  );

Console.WriteLine("Dimensions: {0} x {1}", dims.Item1, dims.Item2);
```

Although the code looks and behaves like the F# version, I find the F# version much cleaner, especially with its syntactic support for tuples.

do Bindings

The final type of binding is the do binding, defined with the do keyword. Unlike the other binding types, do bindings don't attach values to a name; they're used whenever you need to execute some code outside the context of a function or value definition.

do bindings are commonly used within looping constructs, sequence expressions, class constructors, and module initialization. We'll look at each scenario in turn as we encounter them in later chapters.

Identifier Naming

We've seen quite a few identifiers already, but we haven't really looked at what makes something a valid identifier. Like any programming language, F# has naming rules.

Identifiers in F# are pretty typical of most programming languages. In general, F# identifiers must start with an underscore (_), an uppercase letter, or a lowercase letter, followed by any combination thereof. Numbers are also valid characters in identifiers so long as they are not the first character. For example, the following are valid identifiers.

```
let myIdentifier = ""
let _myIdentifier1 = ""
```

The most interesting thing about identifiers in F# is that there's an alternative *quoted identifier* format with fewer restrictions. By enclosing an identifier in double backtick characters (``), you can use virtually any string as a valid F# identifier, like so.

```
let ``This is a valid F# identifier`` = ""
```

It's usually best to use quoted identifiers sparingly, but they can be incredibly useful in certain situations. For example, they're often used for naming unit tests. By using quoted identifiers for test names, you can focus on describing the test rather than arguing over naming conventions. If you're using a test framework (like NUnit), the full quoted name in the test list clarifies what is being tested.

Core Data Types

As a .NET language, F# supports the full range of Common Language Infrastructure (CLI) types. Each of the core primitives and even some more complex types, like System.String, are exposed as *type abbreviations* (convenient aliases for existing types). Many of these even have additional syntax support to enhance *type inference* (the compiler's ability to automatically determine data types) or otherwise simplify working with them.

Boolean Values and Operators

The bool type abbreviation exposes the standard System.Boolean structure. Just as in other languages, bool can have one of two values: true and false.

The F# language includes a few operators for comparing Boolean values, as listed in Table 3-1.

Table 3-1: Boolean Operators

Operator	Description
not	Negation
||	OR
&&	AND

The OR and AND operators are short-circuited so they immediately return when the expression on the left satisfies the overall condition. In the case of the OR operator, if the expression on the left is true, there is no need to evaluate the expression on the right. Similarly, the AND operator will evaluate the expression on the right only when the expression on the left is true.

Numeric Types

F# offers the same selection of numeric types as in other .NET languages. Table 3-2 lists commonly used numeric types along with their corresponding .NET type, value range, and suffix.

Table 3-2: Common Numeric Types

Type Abbreviation	.NET Type	Range	Suffix
byte	System.Byte	0 to 255	uy
sbyte, int8	System.SByte	-128 to 127	y
int16	System.Int16	$-32,768$ to $32,767$	s
uint16	System.UInt16	0 to 65,535	us
int, int32	System.Int32	-2^{31} to $2^{31}-1$	
uint, uint32	System.UInt32	0 to $2^{32}-1$	u, ul
int64	System.Int64	-2^{63} to $2^{63}-1$	L
uint64	System.UInt64	0 to $2^{64}-1$	UL
decimal	System.Decimal	$-2^{96}-1$ to $2^{96}-1$	M
float, double	System.Double	64-bit double precision number precise to approximately 15 digits	

Type Abbreviation	.NET Type	Range	Suffix
float32, single	System.Single	32-bit single precision number precise to approximately 7 digits	F, f
bigint	System.Numerics .BigInteger	No defined upper or lower bounds	I
nativeint	System.IntPtr	32-bit platform-specific integer	n
unativeint	System.UIntPtr	32-bit unsigned platform-specific integer	un

In general, the suffixes are used more frequently in F# than in other .NET languages because they provide the compiler with all of the information it needs to correctly infer the type.

Numeric Operators

As you might expect, F# includes a number of built-in operators for working with the numeric types. Table 3-3 lists commonly used arithmetic, comparison, and bitwise operations.

Table 3-3: Numeric Operators

Operator	Description
+	Unary positive (does not change the sign of the expression) Unchecked addition
-	Unary negation (changes the sign of the expression) Unchecked subtraction
*	Unchecked multiplication
/	Unchecked division
%	Unchecked modulus
**	Unchecked exponent (valid only for floating-point types)
=	Equality
>	Greater than
<	Less than
>=	Greater than or equal
<=	Less than or equal
<>	Not equal
&&&	Bitwise AND
|||	Bitwise OR
^^^	Bitwise exclusive OR
~~	Bitwise negation
<<<	Bitwise left shift
>>>	Bitwise right shift

It's important to note that although most of the operators in Table 3-3 work with any numeric type, the bitwise operators work only against the integral types. Also, because of the way floating-point numbers are represented in memory you should avoid using the equality operators with them directly or you may see incorrect results, as shown here:

```
> let x = 0.33333
let y = 1.0 / 3.0
x = y;;

val x : float = 0.33333
val y : float = 0.3333333333
val it : bool = false
```

Instead of using the equality operator (=), you can calculate the difference between the two floating-point values and verify that the difference is within a threshold. I generally prefer to define this type of operation as a function for reusability.

```
> open System
let approximatelyEqual (x : float) (y : float) (threshold : float) =
  Math.Abs(x - y) <= Math.Abs(threshold)
approximatelyEqual 0.33333 (1.0 / 3.0) 0.001;;

val approximatelyEqual : x:float -> y:float -> threshold:float -> bool
val it : bool = true
```

Numeric Conversion Functions

When you're working with numeric data types in F#, there are no implicit type conversions. This is largely because type conversions are considered side effects, and computation problems arising from implicit type conversions are often difficult to locate.

To work with different numeric types in the same expression, you'll need to explicitly convert them using the appropriate built-in conversion functions. Each conversion function has the same name as the target type abbreviation, which makes them really easy to remember. For instance, to convert an integer value to a float you'd call the float function, as shown in this example.

```
let marchHighTemps = [ 33.0; 30.0; 33.0; 38.0; 36.0; 31.0; 35.0;
                       42.0; 53.0; 65.0; 59.0; 42.0; 31.0; 41.0;
                       49.0; 45.0; 37.0; 42.0; 40.0; 32.0; 33.0;
                       42.0; 48.0; 36.0; 34.0; 38.0; 41.0; 46.0;
                       54.0; 57.0; 59.0 ]
let totalMarchHighTemps = List.sum marchHighTemps
let average = totalMarchHighTemps / float marchHighTemps.Length
```

Characters

As a .NET language, F# carries on the tradition of using 16-bit Unicode for character data. Individual characters are represented by System.Char and exposed to F# via the char type abbreviation. You can bind most individual Unicode characters to an identifier by wrapping them in single quotes, while the remaining characters are represented with escaped character codes, as shown here.

```
> let letterA = 'a'
let copyrightSign = '\u00A9';;

val letterA : char = 'a'
val copyrightSign : char = '©'
```

In addition to the Unicode character escape code, F# has a few other escape sequences for some common characters, as listed in Table 3-4.

Table 3-4: Common Escape Sequences

Character	Sequence
Backspace	\b
Newline	\n
Carriage return	\r
Tab	\t
Backslash	\\
Quotation mark	\"
Apostrophe	\'

Strings

Strings are sequential collections of char and are represented by the string type abbreviation. There are three types of strings in F#: string literals, verbatim strings, and triple-quoted strings.

String Literals

The most common string definition is the *string literal*, which is enclosed in quotation marks as follows.

```
> let myString = "hello world!";;
val myString : string = "hello world!"
```

String literals can contain the same characters and escape sequences described in Table 3-4. Newlines within the string literal are retained unless they're preceded by a backslash (\) character. If a backslash is present, the newline character will be removed.

Verbatim Strings

Verbatim strings are much like string literals except that they are preceded by the @ character and ignore escape sequences. You can embed quotation marks within the string, but they must be written as "", like this:

```
> let verbatimString = @"Hello, my name is ""Dave""";;
val verbatimString : string = "Hello, my name is "Dave""
```

Not parsing escape sequences makes verbatim strings a good choice for representing system paths containing backslashes, provided that you don't have them stored in a configuration setting somewhere. (You're not hard-coding your paths, right?)

Triple-Quoted Strings

As the name implies, *triple-quoted strings* are enclosed in triple quotation marks like """Klaatu barada nikto!""". Triple-quoted strings are like verbatim strings in that they ignore all escape sequences, but they also ignore double quotes. This type of string is most useful when you're working with format-ted character data that naturally contains embedded quotes, like XML documents. For example:

```
> let tripleQuoted = """<person name="Dave" age="33" />""";;
val tripleQuoted : string = "<person name="Dave" age="33" />"
```

String Concatenation

When you want to combine multiple strings, you can concatenate them in a variety of ways. First, there's the traditional Concat method on the System.String class. This method is exactly what you'd expect from other .NET languages.

```
> System.String.Concat("abc", "123");;
val it : string = "abc123"
```

WARNING *Be careful when using String.Concat to not accidentally use the concat extension method defined in FSharp.Core. The concat extension method has more in common with the String.Join method than it does with String.Concat.*

You can also use the operators + and ^ to make the code a bit cleaner. For example:

```
> "abc" + "123";;
val it : string = "abc123"
```

The + operator is preferred, particularly in cross-language scenarios, because it's defined on System.String. The ^ operator is provided for ML com-patibility, and the compiler will issue a warning if you use it in your code.

Type Inference

I've been very careful not to explicitly state any data types in examples so far in order to illustrate one of F#'s most interesting features: type inference. *Type inference* means that the compiler can often deduce data types based on individual values and usage. In fact, F#'s type inference capabilities are so powerful that they often give newcomers to F# the impression that the language is dynamically typed when it's actually statically typed.

F# certainly isn't the first .NET language to include type inference. C# supports type inference through the var keyword, as does Visual Basic when Option Infer is enabled. However, while the type inference in C# and Visual Basic helps avoid some explicit type declarations, it works only in very limited situations. Furthermore, while both C# and Visual Basic can infer data types for individual values, they still generally require you to explicitly specify types in multiple places. In contrast, F#'s top-down evaluation takes type inference to levels never before seen in .NET.

F#'s type inference capabilities permeate the entire language. You've seen examples of type inference previously, ranging from simple values to function parameters and return types, but this feature even enters into F#'s object-oriented features.

At the risk of jumping too far ahead, let's examine how much F#'s type inference helps with a simple class definition, beginning with an example in C#.

```
// C#
using System;

public class Person
{
  public Person(Guid id, string name, int age)
  {
    Id = id;
    Name = name;
    Age = age;
  }

  public Guid Id { get; private set; }
  public string Name { get; private set; }
  public int Age { get; private set; }
}
```

Even in this simple example, C# requires no fewer than six explicit type declarations. If you wanted to take it a step further and define readonly backing variables rather than using auto-implemented properties with private setters, you'd take the number of type declarations up to nine!

Now let's look at an equivalent class in F#.

```
type Person (id : System.Guid, name : string, age : int) =
  member x.Id = id
  member x.Name = name
  member x.Age = age
```

Yes, those two definitions are indeed the same class! Not convinced? Figure 3-1 shows how each class looks in the compiled assemblies according to the decompiler, ILSpy.

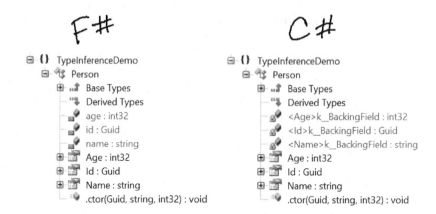

Figure 3-1: Comparison of compiled F# and C# classes

NOTE *There is a subtle difference between the two classes that isn't pictured. The C# class sets the property values via the private setters, whereas the F# class foregoes the private setters and relies exclusively on the backing variables.*

As you can see in the decompiled code, the classes are virtually identical. Ignoring the other syntactic differences between the two languages (object-oriented programming is covered in Chapter 4), you can see F#'s type inference in action throughout this example. In F# we needed to specify the data types for each member only once in the constructor, and in many cases the compiler can infer it there, too. Even each property's data type is automatically inferred from that one definition!

In cases where the compiler can't infer the type, you can add a *type annotation* to tell it what the type should be. You can use type annotations anywhere you introduce a new value. For example, you can include a type annotation in a let binding like this:

```
let i : int = 42;;
```

You can also annotate each part of a function definition. A function that adds two integers might be annotated like this:

```
let add (a : int) (b : int) : int = a + b
```

In this example, no type inference is performed because the definitions explicitly specify the type.

Nullability

If project structure differences and immutability aren't enough to make your head spin, F# has yet another trick for you: null is almost never used! You can't create null values directly with F# without resorting to a library function, and types defined in F# allow null as a valid value only if they're decorated with the AllowNullLiteral attribute. If not for the need to interoperate with .NET assemblies written in languages that lack the same restrictions, null probably wouldn't be included in the language at all.

By placing such tight restrictions around nulls, the F# language designers have greatly reduced the possibility of encountering stray null references, particularly when you're working entirely within F#. This means that you get to spend less time checking to see if every reference type instance is null before doing anything with it.

That said, null is still a valid keyword in F#, and you will find that you do need to use it from time to time, particularly as you work with assemblies written in other .NET languages. Usually, you'll pass null as a parameter to a library function or verify that the return value of a library function isn't null.

Options

Although F# strives to eradicate nulls from your software, there are times when something legitimately doesn't have a value. Without nulls this could seem like a problem, but the language has you covered.

Rather than simply allowing null to be valid for every reference type, F# takes an opt-in approach via the Option<'T> type. This type is a generic *discriminated union* with two values: Some('T) and None. In some ways options are like nullable types, but their explicit nature makes it obvious that a meaningful value might not be present. (We'll cover discriminated unions in Chapter 5. Generics are covered later in this chapter.)

Options are so important in F# that they have syntactic support in type annotations through the option keyword, as shown here:

```
> let middleName : string option = None;;
val middleName : string option = None

> let middleName = Some("William");;
val middleName : string option = Some "William"
```

Options are also how the compiler represents optional parameters for constructors or methods. You make a parameter optional by prefixing it with a question mark (?). Optional parameters are allowed only at the end of the parameter list, as shown here:

```
type Container() =
  member x.Fill ❶?stopAtPercent =
    printfn "%s" <| match (❷defaultArg stopAtPercent 0.5) with
                    | 1.0 -> "Filled it up"
                    | stopAt -> sprintf "Filled to %s" (stopAt.ToString("P2"))
let bottle = Container()
```

In the preceding example, ❶ is the optional `stopAtPercent` parameter. The function needs to account for the cases when `stopAtPercent` is `None`. One common way to provide a default value in these cases is with the `defaultArg` function ❷. This function is kind of like C#'s null coalescing operator (`??`) except that it works with options instead of nulls. The `defaultArg` function accepts an option as its first argument and returns its value when it is `Some<_>`; otherwise, it returns the second argument.

Unit Type

Expressions must always evaluate to a value, but sometimes they're evaluated solely for a side effect, such as writing to a log or updating a database. In these cases, turn to the unit type. The unit type, represented by `()` (an empty pair of parentheses), is a concrete type with a single value that signifies that no particular value is present, so the result of any expression that returns unit can safely be ignored. (In some ways, unit is like a manifestation of the void return type in C# in that it should be returned whenever a function doesn't really return anything, but it's also used syntactically to signify parameterless functions.)

Whenever an expression returns a value other than unit, F# expects you to do something with it. The compiler doesn't care whether you bind the value to an identifier or pass it as an argument to a function; it just wants you to use it. When you don't do something with the return value, the compiler warns that the expression should have type unit because it may actually indicate a program error (the warning is displayed only in compiled code and doesn't appear in FSI). For example:

```
let add a b = a + b
// Compiler warning
add 2 3
```

If you don't want to do anything with the return value, you can pass the result to the `ignore` function, which accepts a single, unconstrained generic argument and returns unit.

```
let add a b = a + b
// No warning
add 2 3 |> ignore
```

In this example, the `add` function's result is sent to the `ignore` function via the *forward pipelining operator* (`|>`). This operator evaluates the expression on the left and sends the result as the last argument to the expression on the right. We'll look at the forward pipelining operator in detail on page 107.

Enumerations

Enumerations help you write more readable code by letting you assign descriptive labels to integral values. F# enumerations compile to the same CLI type as in other .NET languages, so all of the capabilities and restrictions that apply in C# or Visual Basic apply in F# too.

The basic syntax of an enumeration in F# is:

```
type enum-name =
    | value1 = integer-literal1
    | value2 = integer-literal2
    -- snip --
```

However, unlike in C# and Visual Basic, F# doesn't automatically generate a value for each label in an enumeration, so you need to explicitly provide one. For example, if your program represents each day of the week as an integer, you might define a DayOfWeek enumeration like this:

```
type DayOfWeek =
| Sunday = 0
| Monday = 1
| Tuesday = 2
| Wednesday = 3
| Thursday = 4
| Friday = 5
| Saturday = 6
```

Should you want to base your enumerations on an integral type other than int, simply include the appropriate suffix for the data type in the label definition. For example, you could easily change the preceding DayOfWeek sample to use sbyte as its underlying type by changing the suffix on each value:

```
type DayOfWeekByte =
| Sunday = 0y
| Monday = 1y
| Tuesday = 2y
-- snip --
```

Flags Enumerations

The enumerations we've seen so far represent only single values. However, it's common for each label to represent a value by position in a bit mask so that multiple items can be combined.

For example, consider the case of the RegexOptions enumeration from the System.Text.RegularExpressions namespace. This enumeration allows you to control how the regular expression engine processes the pattern by combining multiple values with the logical or operator, like this:

```
open System.Text.RegularExpressions
let re = new Regex("^(Didactic Code)$",
                RegexOptions.Compiled ||| RegexOptions.IgnoreCase)
```

To achieve this same result in your own enumerations, include the Flags attribute and use values that are powers of two.

```
open System

[<Flags>]
type DayOfWeek =
| None = 0
| Sunday = 1
| Monday = 2
| Tuesday = 4
| Wednesday = 8
| Thursday = 16
| Friday = 32
| Saturday = 64
```

NOTE *The Flags attribute isn't required, but it's good practice to include it to show other developers how the enumeration should be used.*

You can now represent the days in a weekend by combining the Saturday and Sunday values as we did previously.

```
let weekend = DayOfWeek.Saturday ||| DayOfWeek.Sunday
```

If you know that several values will be commonly combined, consider including those combinations in your enumeration definition. F# doesn't allow referencing the other values in the definition by name, but you can still provide the appropriate corresponding integral value. In the case of DayOfWeek you could provide Weekdays and WeekendDays with the values 62 and 65, respectively.

```
open System

[<Flags>]
type DayOfWeek =
-- snip --
| Weekdays = 62
| WeekendDays = 65
```

It's easy to determine whether a particular enumeration value has a particular flag set with the HasFlag method of System.Enum.

```
> DayOfWeek.Weekdays.HasFlag DayOfWeek.Monday;;
val it : bool = true
> DayOfWeek.Weekdays.HasFlag DayOfWeek.Thursday;;
val it : bool = true
> DayOfWeek.Weekdays.HasFlag DayOfWeek.Sunday;;
val it : bool = false
```

Reconstructing Enumeration Values

Using named labels for integral values is a great way to avoid *magic numbers* (numbers without any apparent meaning) in your code, but what if you save off the underlying value (say, to a database) and later want to reconstruct the original enumeration value from it? The built-in enum function allows you to do just that for integer (int32) values.

```
> enum<DayOfWeek> 16;;
val it : DayOfWeek = Thursday
```

When the enumeration's underlying type is something other than int32, use the EnumOfValue function from the Microsoft.FSharp.Core.LanguagePrimitives module namespace instead.

```
> open Microsoft.FSharp.Core.LanguagePrimitives
EnumOfValue<sbyte, DayOfWeek> 16y;;
val it : DayOfWeek = Thursday
```

NOTE *Enumeration types aren't constrained to the values identified by labels, so when using these functions be sure to create only enumeration values that you've accounted for in your code.*

Flow Control

Despite its emphasis on functional programming, F# fully supports several imperative constructs for looping and branching. These are particularly useful in combination with other constructs like *sequence expressions* (particularly the looping constructs), but they're certainly useful in other contexts as well.

Looping

Recursion is the preferred looping mechanism in functional programming, but F# also includes a few approaches typically found in imperative languages. These looping structures are similar to those of other languages.

NOTE *F# doesn't provide mechanisms (like break or continue) for premature termination, so take extra care when using loops.*

while Loops

The simplest iterative structure is the while...do loop. As you might expect, this construct evaluates a Boolean expression and iterates as long as that condition is true. while loops are useful when you need to iterate an unknown number of times, but because they inherently rely on a state change, they can't be used in pure functional programming. The body of the loop can be any expression that returns unit.

One scenario in which while loops are helpful is responding to user input. In the following example, the echoUserInput function uses a while loop to echo whatever the user enters at the console until it encounters the word quit.

```
let echoUserInput (getInput : unit -> string) =
  let mutable input = getInput()
  while not (input.ToUpper().Equals("QUIT")) do
    printfn "You entered: %s" input
    input <- getInput()

echoUserInput (fun () -> printfn "Type something and press enter"
                         System.Console.ReadLine())
```

for Loops

When you know how many iterations you need to perform, you can turn to one of the for loop variations: simple or enumerable. *Simple* for loops are pretty restrictive in that they can iterate only over a range of integers and always return unit. Attempting to return something other than unit will result in a compilation error.

Simple for loops are useful when you know how many times you need to iterate. Here, the numbers 0 through 100 are printed in the body of a simple for loop:

```
for i = 0 to 100 do printfn "%i" i
```

By replacing the to keyword with the downto keyword, you can make a simple for loop count down instead.

```
for i = 100 downto 0 do printfn "%A" i
```

The more powerful variation of the for loop is the *enumerable* for loop. In some ways, the enumerable for loop is similar to C#'s foreach loop in that it operates over any sequence (collection types implementing IEnumerable<'T>). For instance, the enumerable for loop makes it easy to iterate over a range of integers, like this:

```
for i in [0..10] do
  printfn "%A" i
```

In reality, though, the enumerable for loop is a fancy syntactic shortcut for applying F#'s powerful pattern-matching capabilities over a sequence. With pattern matching, you can extract values from more complex types and even perform some rudimentary filtering right in the loop definition! No LINQ required!

```
❶ type MpaaRating =
   | G
   | PG
   | PG13
   | R
   | NC17

❷ type Movie = { Title : string; Year : int; Rating : MpaaRating option }

❸ let movies = [ { Title = "The Last Witch Hunter"; Year = 2014; Rating = None }
                 { Title = "Riddick"; Year = 2013; Rating = Some(R) }
                 { Title = "Fast Five"; Year = 2011; Rating = Some(PG13) }
                 { Title = "Babylon A.D."; Year = 2008; Rating = Some(PG13) } ]

❹ for { Title = t; Year = y; Rating = Some(r) } in movies do
     printfn "%s (%i) - %A" t y r
```

At ❶ we see a discriminated union representing the rating scale, at ❷ a record type representing a movie with an optional rating, at ❸ an F# list, and finally at ❹ the for...in loop with a pattern match to find all movies that have been rated. The compiler will highlight the pattern match and warn you about not having a covering case, but that's okay because we're using it as a filter.

NOTE   *Don't worry about all this discussion of pattern matching, discriminated unions, record types, and other functional concepts yet. We'll explore each in detail in Chapters 5 and 7.*

Branching

F# offers only a single imperative construct for branching: the if...then...else expression, as shown next. This expression evaluates a Boolean expression in the if part. When that expression evaluates to true, the then branch is executed; otherwise, the else branch is executed (if one is present).

```
let isEven number =
  if number % 2 = 0 then
    printfn "%i is even" number
  else
    printfn "%i is odd" number
```

You can chain multiple if...then...else expressions together with the elif keyword (a shortcut for else if), as shown next. This has the same effect as nesting them, though the result is much more readable.

```
let isEven number =
  if number = 0 then
    printfn "zero"
  elif number % 2 = 0 then
    printfn "%i is even" number
  else
    printfn "%i is odd" number
```

Because the if...then...else expression returns a value, constructs like C#'s conditional operator (?:) aren't necessary. You should know, though, that because the expression returns a value it behaves a bit differently depending on how it's being used. When only the if branch is specified, its expression must evaluate to unit, but when both the if and else branches are specified, their expressions must both evaluate to the same type.

In each example so far, the result of the if...then...else expression has been unit, but what happens if you change the function to use sprintf instead of printfn like this?

```
let isEven number =
  if number = 0 then
    sprintf "zero"
  elif number % 2 = 0 then
    sprintf "%i is even" number
  else
    sprintf "%i is odd" number
```

Instead of printing the message to the console, the isEven function actually returns the message as a string. You can see this by invoking the function in FSI like so:

```
> isEven 0;;
val it : string = "zero"
> isEven 1;;
val it : string = "1 is odd"
> isEven 2;;
val it : string = "2 is even"
```

Generics

Don Syme, the designer and architect of F#, was heavily involved in the research and development of what eventually became generics in the .NET Framework. With a heritage like that, it's no surprise that generics in F# are incredibly robust, in some ways even more powerful than in other .NET languages.

Generics allow you to define functions, classes, methods, interfaces, and structures that can work directly with any data type. Without generics, the only way to write type-safe code that works with multiple data types is to write a separate implementation for each type. However, this approach is limiting, because any new type that relies on that code will need its own implementation. Generics abstract away this complexity by generating these implementations for you based on the type parameters you've supplied in your code.

To show how useful generics really are, consider how one of the original .NET collection types, the `ArrayList`, compares to its cousin, the generic list. The `ArrayList` class is a collection type that has been around since the earliest days of .NET and well before generics were available in the framework. In order for it to hold data of any type, it needed to treat every element as `System.Object`. As a result, code written with `ArrayList` almost always involved excessive type conversions of elements in the list. Worse, there was no way to enforce consistency between elements, so although a developer might believe that every element in the list was a string, it could very well also contain integers, floats, or instances of any other data type. This type of code was highly error prone and often had a negative impact on performance.

The generic `List<'T>` class, on the other hand, can be instantiated to work with any specific data type. It removes all ambiguity about what its elements are and typically eliminates the type conversions (subclassing notwithstanding), which leads to more reliable and efficient code.

Since their beginning, generics have played a starring role in virtually every innovation in .NET development, including LINQ and the Task Parallel Library. In some ways, they play an even greater part in F# development than in traditional .NET development because of their role in the type inference process and concepts like statically resolved type parameters (discussed in "Statically Resolved Type Parameters" on page 52).

In F#, most generic type parameters are named with a leading apostrophe. For example, `'a`, `'A`, and `'TInput` are all valid type parameter names. By convention, F# uses sequential lowercase identifiers for inferred type parameters, whereas user-defined type parameters begin with an uppercase character.

Automatic Generalization

F#'s type inference feature favors generic types whenever possible through a process called *automatic generalization*. Here it is in action:

```
> let toTriple a b c = (a, b, c);;
val toTriple : a:'a -> b:'b -> c:'c -> 'a * 'b * 'c
```

In this example the `toTriple` function converts its three parameters into a three-item tuple (sometimes called a triple). We'll explore the arrows and tuples in detail in Chapter 5; for now just recognize that the compiler automatically generalized each of the three parameters to the types `'a`, `'b`, and `'c`, respectively.

Whether the compiler can automatically generalize a parameter depends largely on how and where it's used. Automatic generalization is attempted only with immutable values on complete function definitions with explicit parameters.

Explicit Generalization

If the compiler can't automatically generalize a parameter, or you want more control over it, you can explicitly generalize a parameter with a type annotation. This is especially useful when you want to constrain the types allowed. You could rewrite the previous toTriple example with explicit type parameters as follows:

```
> let toTriple (a : 'A) (b : 'B) (c : 'C) = (a, b, c);;
val toTriple : a:'A -> b:'B -> c:'C -> 'A * 'B * 'C
```

When type parameters are unconstrained, you're fairly limited in what you can do with them. Generally, you can use them only with other unconstrained generic types or functions, and good luck invoking any methods beyond those defined on System.Object. To do something that depends on some aspect of the type, such as calling an interface method, you'll need to add a *constraint*.

If you're familiar with generic constraints in C# or Visual Basic, you may have been frustrated by the lack of things you can actually constrain. In those languages you can constrain type parameters only to reference types, value types, types with a default constructor, types that derive from a particular class, and types that derive from a particular interface. F# supports each of these but also adds a few other constraints.

> **NOTE** *Most constraint types apply to standard type parameters, but a few apply only to an F#-specific form of type parameters called* statically resolved type parameters. *In the following examples, you'll see these constraints defined in inline functions with a type parameter that uses a caret (^) instead of an apostrophe. Statically resolved type parameters are described later in this section.*

You apply constraints by following the generic type annotation with when and the constraint. You can specify multiple constraints by combining them with and.

Subtype constraints   A subtype constraint limits the acceptable types to the constraint type itself or any type that derives from that type. When the constraint type is an interface, the provided type needs to implement that interface.

```
let myFunc (stream : 'T when 'T :> System.IO.Stream) = ()
```

Nullness constraints   A nullness constraint limits the acceptable types to those where null is a valid value.

```
let inline myFunc (a : ^T when ^T : null) = ()
```

Member constraints   A member constraint ensures that the supplied type includes a member with a specific signature. You can constrain the types based on either instance or static members.

```
// instance member
let inline myFunc
  (a : ^T when ^T : (member ReadLine : unit -> string)) = ()

// static member
let inline myFunc
  (a : ^T when ^T : (static member Parse : string -> ^T)) = ()
```

Default constructor constraints   A default constructor constraint ensures that the supplied type has a default constructor.

```
let myFunc (stream : 'T when 'T : (new : unit -> 'T)) = ()
```

Value type constraints   A value type constraint restricts the supplied type to any .NET value types except System.Nullable<_>.

```
let myFunc (stream : 'T when 'T : struct) = ()
```

Reference type constraints   A reference type constraint ensures that the supplied type is a .NET reference type.

```
let myFunc (stream : 'T when 'T : not struct) = ()
```

Enumeration constraints   An enumeration constraint limits the supplied types to enumerations with a specific underlying type.

```
let myFunc (stream : 'T when 'T : enum<int32>) = ()
```

Delegate constraints   A delegate constraint restricts the provided types to delegate types with a particular set of arguments and return type. Delegate constraints are intended primarily for use with traditional .NET event handlers.

```
open System
let myFunc (stream : 'T when 'T : delegate<obj * EventArgs, unit>) = ()
```

Unmanaged constraints   Unmanaged constraints restrict the provided type to unmanaged types like some of the numeric primitives and enumeration types.

```
let myFunc (stream : 'T when 'T : unmanaged) = ()
```

Equality constraints   An equality constraint restricts the provided type to types that support equality. This constraint is considered weak because it's satisfied by nearly every CLI type.

```
let myFunc (stream : 'T when 'T : equality) = ()
```

Comparison constraints   Comparison constraints are satisfied only by types that implement System.IComparable, arrays, nativeint, and unativeint unless the type has the NoEquality attribute.

```
let myFunc (stream : 'T when 'T : comparison) = ()
```

Flexible Types

Although not strictly generic constructs, *flexible types* are a syntactic shortcut for subtype constraints. They're particularly useful with the function arguments of a higher-order function where automatic type conversion normally doesn't automatically occur.

You can specify a flexible type by prefixing a type name with a # character within a type annotation.

```
let myFunc (stream : #System.IO.Stream) = ()
```

Wildcard Pattern

When you want to use a generic type as a parameter but want the compiler to infer the type, you can use the *Wildcard pattern* in place of a named type parameter. The Wildcard pattern is represented with an underscore.

```
let printList (l : List<_>) = l |> List.iter (fun i -> printfn "%O" i)
```

The preceding function will print each element in an F# list with its ToString function regardless of what type is contained in the list.

Statically Resolved Type Parameters

F# has two classifications of generics. The first (which we've focused on almost exclusively so far) is standard generics, the same generics as in other .NET languages. The second, called *statically resolved type parameters*, is specific to F# and identified by a caret (^) instead of an apostrophe. Statically resolved type parameters force the compiler to resolve the types at compile time rather than run time. The implication is that the compiler generates a version of the generic type for each resolved type rather than a single version.

Statically resolved type parameters are primarily intended for use with inline functions and are especially well suited for custom operators, as shown here.

```
let inline (!**) x = x ** 2.0
```

When this operator is compiled, it uses static resolution with a constraint to ensure that any types that use it include the Pow function in their definition based on the use of the ** operator.

```
val inline ( !** ) :
  x: ^a -> ^a when ^a : (static member Pow :  ^a * float -> ^a)
```

When Things Go Wrong

Despite your best efforts and the extra safety that F# provides, things can and will go wrong. Proper error handling is a critical piece of any program. F# builds upon the standard .NET exception mechanisms with additional syntactic support that allows you to *throw* (or *raise* in F# parlance) and handle exceptions with ease. (For convenience, the standard exception type, System.Exception, is abbreviated as exn.)

Handling Exceptions

Error conditions are always a possibility, so it's important to know how to handle them properly when they arise. F# provides two constructs for error handling: try...with and try...finally. These constructs are strictly independent of each other; that is, there is no try...with...finally construct in F#. If you need both a with and a finally block, you'll generally nest a try... with block within a try...finally block, although the nesting order doesn't really matter.

try...with Expressions

In a try...with construct, the expressions contained within the try block are evaluated and if any raise an exception, F# pattern matching is used to locate an appropriate handler in the with block.

Input/output-related operations, like reading from a file, are great examples of where you'd use the exception-handling constructs because you're at the mercy of external factors like network availability issues or file permissions. In this example, we attempt to read a text file and write its contents to the console but do so in a try block.

```
open System.IO

try
  use file = File.OpenText "somefile.txt"
  file.ReadToEnd() |> printfn "%s"
with
| ❶:? FileNotFoundException -> printfn "File not found"
| ❷_ -> printfn "Error loading file"
```

If an exception is raised, execution passes to the with block, where the system attempts to find a handler first using ❶, a *Type-Test pattern* (a pattern that matches a specific data type). In this case, the *Wildcard pattern* ❷ (a general-purpose pattern that matches everything) is used as a general exception handler. If a suitable match isn't found, the exception bubbles up the call stack until a handler is found or the application fails.

Without delving too much into the specifics of pattern matching, we can look at a few ways to unlock the potential of the with block. As it stands now, the handler for FileNotFoundException isn't very helpful because it doesn't give any information about which file wasn't found. You can capture the exception for use in the handler by including an identifier with the as keyword in the pattern.

```
try
-- snip --
with
| :? FileNotFoundException as ❶ex ->
❷printfn "% was not found" ex.FileName
| _ -> printfn "Error loading file"
```

Now that the ex identifier is defined ❶, you can include the filename in the printed message ❷.

You can even combine cases when two or more exception types should use the same handler.

```
try
-- snip --
with
| :? FileNotFoundException as ex ->
  printfn "%s was not found" ex.FileName
| :? PathTooLongException
| :? ArgumentNullException
| :? ArgumentException ->
  printfn "Invalid filename"
| _ -> printfn "Error loading file"
```

Sometimes you may want to partially handle an exception at one level but still allow it to traverse up the call stack to another handler. You could raise the exception normally with the raise function, but in doing so you'd lose the call stack information embedded in the exception and later handlers would recognize your handler as the source of the error. To preserve the stack trace, *reraise* the exception with a function that's valid only within a with block: reraise.

```
try
-- snip --
with
| :? FileNotFoundException as ex ->
  printfn "%s was not found" ex.FileName
| _ ->
  printfn "Error loading file"
  reraise()
```

Unlike in C# and Visual Basic, F#'s try...with construct is an expression, so it returns a value. All of the examples so far have returned unit. This opens up more possibilities as to how you can use the construct, but it also means that each exception case must have the same return type as the try block.

A common practice is to have the try...with return an option type where the try block returns Some<_> and each exception case returns None. You can follow this pattern to return the contents of a text file.

```
open System
open System.Diagnostics
open System.IO

let fileContents =
  try
    use file = File.OpenText "somefile.txt"
❶ Some <| file.ReadToEnd()
  with
  | :? FileNotFoundException as ex ->
    printfn "%s was not found" ex.FileName
❷ None
  | _ ->
    printfn "Error loading file"
    reraise()
```

In this example, you can see at ❶ where an option is created with the contents of the text file and returned. Returning None from the FileNotFoundException handler is shown at ❷.

try...finally Expressions

The try...finally construct is used to execute code that must run regardless of whether the code in the try block raises an exception.

Usually, try...finally is used to clean up any resources that might have been left open by the try block, as shown here:

```
try
  use file = File.OpenText "somefile.txt"
  Some <| file.ReadToEnd()
finally
  printfn "cleaning up"
```

Raising Exceptions

An exception-handling mechanism isn't much use if you're stuck handling exceptions from library functions but can't raise your own. You can raise an exception of any type with the raise function.

```
let filename = "x"
if not (File.Exists filename) then
  raise <| FileNotFoundException("filename was null or empty")
```

In addition to raise, F# includes a sprinkling of additional functions for raising some of the more commonly used exceptions. The failwith and failwithf functions are convenient for general exceptions. Both raise a Microsoft.FSharp.Core.FailureException, but the failwithf function allows you to use the F# format strings (discussed in "String Formatting" on page 58), as shown here.

```
// failwith
if not (File.Exists filename) then
  failwith "File not found"

// failwithf
if not (String.IsNullOrEmpty filename) then
  failwithf "%s could not be found" filename
```

Another common exception type that's easily raised through a built-in function is System.ArgumentException. To conveniently raise it, use the invalidArg function.

```
if not (String.IsNullOrEmpty filename) then
  invalidArg "filename" (sprintf "%s is not a valid file name" filename)
```

Custom Exceptions

It's usually best to use predefined exception types like ArgumentException, FormatException, or even NullReferenceException, but if you must define your own exception types, you can define a new class that extends System.Exception. For example:

```
type MyException(message, category) =
  inherit exn(message)
  member x.Category = category
  override x.ToString() = sprintf "[%s] %s" category message
```

You can raise your custom exception with the raise function and handle it in a try...with or try...finally block as with any other exception type. Here you can see the custom MyException exception raised and caught.

```
try
  raise <| MyException("blah", "debug")
with
  | :? MyException as ex -> printfn "My Exception: %s" <| ex.ToString()
  | _ as ex -> printfn "General Exception: %s" <| ex.ToString()
```

There's also a lightweight alternative to creating exception classes. In F# you can define a custom exception type and its associated data with the exception keyword. Exceptions created this way are still standard .NET exceptions that derive from System.Exception, but the syntax borrows from a few functional concepts (syntactic tuples and discriminated unions, in particular) to accomplish its magic.

```
exception RetryAttemptFailed of string * int
exception RetryCountExceeded of string
```

You raise these exceptions as you would any exception. However, handling them is streamlined because you can use the same pattern-matching syntax as discriminated unions (more on pattern matching in Chapter 7) to not only determine which handler to use but also to bind the associated data to useful identifiers.

A generalized retry function might raise different exception types that indicate whether it should keep trying or give up depending on how many times it has tried to execute some action.

```
let ❶retry maxTries action =
  let ❷rec retryInternal attempt =
    try
      if not (action()) then
        raise <| if attempt > maxTries then
                   ❸RetryCountExceeded("Maximum attempts exceeded.")
                 else
                   ❹RetryAttemptFailed(sprintf "Attempt %i failed." attempt, attempt)
    with
    | ❺RetryAttemptFailed(msg, count) as ex -> Console.WriteLine(msg)
                                               retryInternal (count + 1)
    | ❻RetryCountExceeded(msg) -> Console.WriteLine(msg)
                                  reraise()
  ❼retryInternal 1

retry 5 (fun() -> false)
```

In this example, the retry function ❶ accepts two parameters. The first indicates the maximum number of attempts and the second is a Boolean-returning function to invoke. All of the work is performed within retryInternal ❷, a nested *recursive function* that calls itself and that invokes the supplied function. If the supplied function returns false, it raises either a RetryCountExceeded exception ❸ or a RetryAttemptFailed exception ❹. When RetryAttemptFailed is raised, the handler ❺ writes the exception message to the console before calling the retryInternal function again with an incremented counter. If a RetryCountExceeded exception is raised, the handler ❻ writes the exception message to the console and then reraises the exception for another handler to process. Of course, this process has to start somewhere, so we make the initial call to retryInternal ❼ with 1 to indicate the first attempt.

This syntactic simplicity does come at a cost. Despite RetryAttemptFailed and RetryCountExceeded being standard exceptions, you'll really want to keep them isolated to your F# assemblies because consuming them in other languages can be cumbersome. The associated data is defined as a syntactic tuple, so the individual values don't get descriptive names in the compiled code; instead, the values are assigned "useful" generated names like Data0 and Data1. To confuse matters even more, the compiler has no way of knowing which, if any, of the associated data items should be treated as the exception's Message property, so the default message (from the base exception class) is used.

String Formatting

You probably guessed that the tried and tested `Console.Write`, `Console.WriteLine`, and `String.Format` methods are perfectly acceptable in F#. When you need absolute control over formatting, you'll have to use them. As capable as they are, though, they don't take advantage of all that F# has to offer.

F# has its own string formatting capabilities that you can use with the `printf`, `printfn`, and `sprintf` functions, among others. Why did the language designers choose to build another formatting mechanism when .NET's built-in mechanism is already so capable? Because F#'s native formatting capabilities tie into the compiler better than the traditional ones. For one, the tokens used within the F# format strings are generally easier to remember than the format strings in the core methods, but that's not the primary advantage. What really distinguishes the F# formatting system is that it ties in to the F# type inference system! The compiler will verify that each token has a matching value and that each supplied value is the correct type for the corresponding token!

To simply format a string, you could use the `sprintf` function. For example, here's how to quickly format a basic integer value.

```
> sprintf "%d" 123;;
val it : string = "123"
```

Of course, integers aren't the only data type you can format in this manner. Table 3-5 shows a list of common format string tokens.

Table 3-5: Common Format Tokens

Token	Description
%A	Prints any value with F#'s default layout settings
%b	Formats a Boolean value as true or false
%c	Formats a character
%d, %i	Formats any integer
%e, %E	Formats a floating-point number with scientific notation
%f	Formats a floating-point number
%g, %G	Shortcut for %e or %f; the more concise one will be selected automatically.
%M	Formats a decimal value
%o	Octal
%O	Prints any value by calling its ToString method
%s	Formats a string
%x	Lowercase hexadecimal
%X	Uppercase hexadecimal

To ensure that the formatted text is at least a certain number of characters wide, you can include an optional width value after the %. (The default formatter won't truncate your data unless the format token explicitly allows it.) For example:

```
> printfn "%5s" "ABC";;
ABC

> printfn "%5s" "ABCDEFGHI";;
ABCDEFGHI
```

You can combine several modifiers with the tokens for a little extra flexibility in formatting, as listed in Table 3-6.

Table 3-6: Numeric Format String Modifiers

Modifier	Effect	Example	Result
0	When used in conjunction with a width, pads any extra space with zeros	"%010d"	"0000000123"
-	Left-justifies the text within the available space	"%-10d"	"123 "
+	Prepends a positive sign if the number is positive	"%+d"	"+123"
(space)	Prepends a space if the number is positive	"% d"	" 123"

You can also combine several modifiers within a single token. For example, you could use the token %+010d to print a number front-padded with zeros and the plus (+) sign.

Type Abbreviations

Type abbreviations allow you to define a new name for an existing type just like the core data types are exposed to F#. It's possible to do something similar in C# with the using directive, but F#'s type abbreviations allow you to use the name throughout your library (after its definition, of course) instead of only within a single file.

You define type abbreviations with the type keyword, an identifier, and the type. If you wanted to refer to System.IO.FileStream as fs, you'd use the following:

```
type fs = System.IO.FileStream
```

Comments

When you want to describe what a particular piece of code is doing, use comments. There are three ways to comment your code in F#: end-of-line comments, block comments, and XML documentation.

End-of-Line Comments

End-of-line (or *single-line*) *comments* begin with two slash characters (//). As their name implies, they include everything until the end of the line. These comments frequently appear on a line of their own but can also appear at the end of a line.

```
// This is an end-of-line comment
let x = 42 // Answer to the Ultimate Question of Life, The Universe, and Everything
```

Block Comments

Block comments are delimited with (* and *) and are typically used for comments that need to span multiple lines.

```
(* This is a block comment *)

(*
  So is this
*)
```

You can also use block comments in the middle of a line of otherwise uncommented code.

```
let x (* : int *) = 42
```

Be careful with what you include in block comments because the compiler treats their content as strings, verbatim strings, and triple-quoted strings. If you happen to include a quotation mark (or three consecutive quotation marks), the compiler will insist that you're beginning a string and will produce a syntax error if it doesn't find the corresponding closing token.

```
(* "This is ok" *)
(* """This is not *)
```

XML Documentation

Like the other .NET languages, F# allows *XML documentation comments* with triple slashes (///). These comments are technically just a special case of end-of-line comments where the compiler retains the contents to build an XML document that can eventually serve as documentation.

A complete discussion of XML documentation comments is beyond the scope of this book, but keep in mind that comments are useful for documenting your API. At a minimum I recommend using them on all of your application's public and internal types and members.

Your XML documentation comments will usually include a few elements like summary, param, and returns. summary elements briefly describe the documented code, param elements identify and describe individual function or constructor parameters, and returns elements describe a function's return value.

You might document a function that calculates some circle measurements based on its radius like this:

```
/// <summary>
/// Given a radius, calculate the diameter, area, and circumference
/// of a circle
/// </summary>
/// <param name="radius">The circle's radius</param>
/// <returns>
/// A triple containing the diameter, area, and circumference
/// </returns>
let measureCircle radius =
    let diameter = radius * 2.0
    let area = Math.PI * (radius ** 2.0)
    let circumference = 2.0 * Math.PI * radius
    (diameter, area, circumference)
```

Even if you don't intend to distribute the resulting XML file, XML documentation comments can help you by surfacing information about the documented types and members through IntelliSense. In Figure 3-2 you can see the summary from the preceding example included in the tool tip displayed when you hover the mouse over the measureCircle function in Visual Studio.

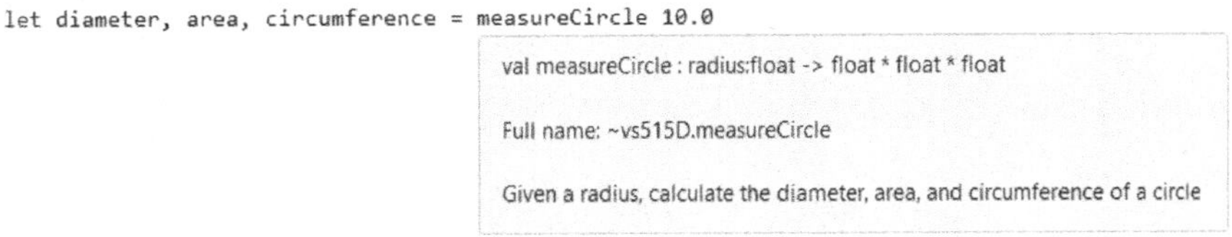

```
let diameter, area, circumference = measureCircle 10.0
```

val measureCircle : radius:float -> float * float * float

Full name: ~vs515D.measureCircle

Given a radius, calculate the diameter, area, and circumference of a circle

Figure 3-2: XML documentation in IntelliSense

There's a shortcut for XML documentation comments. When you're writing only a summary, you can simply use the triple slashes and omit the tags. Here's the summary in the previous example written using the shortcut:

```
/// Given a radius, calculate the diameter, area, and circumference
/// of a circle
let measureCircle radius =
-- snip --
```

As you can see, when your comment is too long for a single line, you can write it on multiple lines as long as each line begins with triple slashes.

Summary

In this chapter, we've explored some of the fundamental concepts of the F# language. You've seen the problems that can arise from mutable data and how F#'s default immutability, type inference capabilities, and explicit opt-in approach for valueless data can help you write more robust, fault-tolerant code. You've also learned how F# supports the core CLI types and other base capabilities of the .NET Framework like enumerations, generics, exception handling, and string formatting.

What really makes F# stand out as a viable language for your projects, though, is how it expands upon so many concepts even at this fundamental level. Constructs like use bindings that dispose of objects without requiring additional nesting levels, exception handlers that return values, and string-formatting functions that tie into the compiler can have an immediate, positive impact on your productivity.

In the next chapter, we'll build upon these concepts with a look into F#'s object-oriented capabilities. We'll see how the concepts introduced here can help you quickly develop complex libraries while keeping you focused on the problem rather than the compiler.

4

STAYING OBJECTIVE

For years, *object-oriented (OO)* development has been the de facto standard for developing business software, particularly within the enterprise, so you're probably familiar with many of its core principles. It should come as no surprise that as a .NET language, F# supports the full cast of constructs—including classes, structs, and interfaces—available in the other .NET languages. Despite its reputation as a niche language useful only for academic exercises or highly specialized software, F#'s general-purpose, multiparadigm nature makes it suitable for most development situations. With C# and Visual Basic already well established, though, why choose F# as an OO language?

A large part of the decision rests on F#'s terse syntax, but features like type inference, object expressions, and the ability to combine object-oriented and functional styles make a strong argument, too. Let's face it, though: Even if you're developing in a primarily functional manner, when you're developing software on the .NET Framework you're going to have to work with objects at some point; that's just the nature of the platform.

In this chapter, you'll learn how to create OO constructs in F# with less code, yet still build robust frameworks that can hold their own against similar frameworks built with more dedicated OO languages.

Classes

Conceptually, classes in F# are identical to classes in other OO languages in that they encapsulate related data and behavior as fields, properties, methods, and events (collectively called *members*) to model real-world objects or concepts. Like classes in C# and Visual Basic, F# classes are reference types that support single inheritance and multiple interface implementation, and can control access to their members. As with all user-defined data types in F#, you declare classes with the type keyword. (Rather than requiring different keywords for every data type you can create, the compiler infers the construct based on its structure.)

To illustrate, let's take another look at the class definition introduced in the type inference discussion in Chapter 3.

```
type Person (id : Guid, name : string, age : int) =
  member x.Id = id
  member x.Name = name
  member x.Age = age
```

There's a lot of definition packed into this example. In just four lines, there's a class with a *primary constructor* with three arguments and three implicit, read-only properties! While quite a departure from the other .NET languages, this terseness is just one of the ways that F# distinguishes itself.

Constructors

Constructors are the means by which new class instances are created and initialized. They're really specialized functions that return fully initialized class instances. Classes in F# do not require a constructor, as shown here:

```
type ConstructorlessClass = class end
```

The empty class in this example is valid F# but, unlike in C#, if you don't define a constructor, the compiler won't automatically generate a *default constructor* (a constructor with no parameters). Since a memberless class that you can't instantiate is pretty useless, your classes will typically have at least one constructor and one member.

NOTE *One reason you might choose to omit the constructor is that each of the type's members is static; that is, it applies to the type rather than an individual instance. We'll examine static members in detail a bit later in this chapter.*

As with other OO languages, you create new class instances by invoking a constructor. In the case of our `Person` class there's only one constructor, so the choice is clear.

```
let me = Person(Guid.NewGuid(), "Dave", 33)
```

Using the `new` keyword to create a new class instance is optional. By convention, you use the `new` keyword only when creating an instance of a class that implements the `IDisposable` interface.

F# constructors come in two flavors: primary constructors and additional constructors.

Primary Constructors

F# classes can have a *primary constructor* whose arguments are embedded within the type definition itself. The primary constructor's body contains a series of `let` and `do` bindings that represent the class's field definitions and initialization code.

```
type Person ❶(name : string, dob : System.DateTime) =
❷let age = (System.DateTime.Now - dob).TotalDays / 365.25
❸do printfn "Creating person: %s (Age: %f)" name age
    member x.Name = name
    member x.DateOfBirth = dob
    member x.Age = age
```

In this example, the primary constructor includes the parameter list with type annotations ❶, a single field definition for the calculated age ❷, and a do binding ❸ that prints the person's name and age when the object is constructed. All of the primary constructor's parameters are automatically available as fields throughout your class, so there's no need to explicitly map them.

The compiler can frequently infer the types for each constructor parameter, so there's often no need to include explicit type annotations. In the preceding example, a type annotation (or one on an intermediate binding with a type annotation) would still be needed for the `dob` parameter so the compiler can resolve the correct subtract operator overload. However, that's more the exception than the rule, as shown in the next example, where the compiler can infer the types for both the `name` and `age` parameters as `string` and `int`, respectively.

```
type Person (name, age) =
    do printfn "Creating person: %s (Age: %i)" name age
    member x.Name = name
    member x.Age = age

let me = Person ("Dave", 33)
```

By default, the primary constructor is public, but you can change that by including an access modifier before the parameter list. You might consider changing the primary constructor's accessibility if you were implementing the *Singleton pattern*, which specifies that only a single instance of the type can exist, as shown here:

```
type Greeter private () =
  static let _instance = lazy (Greeter())
  static member Instance with get() = _instance.Force()
  member x.SayHello() = printfn "hello"

Greeter.Instance.SayHello()
```

MORE ABOUT ACCESSIBILITY IN F#

Access modifiers limit the scope of bindings, types, and members throughout your program. F# differs from C# and Visual Basic in that it directly supports only the public, private, and internal modifiers. You can't define protected class members in F# due in part to how they complicate the functional nature of the language. F# does still honor protected members defined in other languages, so they won't be publicly accessible and you can still override them in derived classes without breaking the abstraction.

Additional Constructors

Constructors that you define beyond the primary constructor are called *additional constructors*. Additional constructors are defined with the new keyword followed by a parameter list and constructor body, as shown next. While additional constructors must always invoke the primary constructor, they may do so indirectly through another constructor, thereby allowing you to chain constructor calls.

```
type Person (name, age) =
  do printfn "Creating person: %s (Age: %i)" name age
  new (name) = Person(name, 0)
  new () = Person("")
  member x.Name = name
  member x.Age = age
```

Additional constructors can contain their own let bindings and other expressions, but unlike those in the primary constructor, any such elements will be local to the constructor where they're defined rather than exposed as fields.

Additional constructors can invoke additional code like a primary constructor, but instead of using a do binding they use the then keyword. In this example, each additional constructor includes the then keyword in order to print a message indicating which constructor is being invoked.

```
type Person (name, age) =
  do printfn "Creating person: %s (Age: %i)" name age
  new (name) = Person(name, 0)
               then printfn "Creating person with default age"
  new () = Person("")
           then printfn "Creating person with default name and age"
  member x.Name = name
  member x.Age = age
```

Classes without a primary constructor behave a bit differently at initialization. When you use them, you must explicitly define fields with the val keyword, and any additional constructors must initialize any fields not decorated with the DefaultValue attribute, as shown here:

```
type Person =
  val _name : string
  val _age : int
  new (name, age) = { _name = name; _age = age }
  new (name) = Person(name, 0)
  new () = Person("")
  member x.Name = x._name
  member x.Age = x._age
```

Self-Identifiers

Sometimes you'll want to reference a class member within a constructor. By default, class members aren't accessible because they require a recursive reference to the type, but you can enable *self-referencing* with the as keyword and a *self-identifier* like this:

```
type Person (name, age) as this =
  do printfn "Creating person: %s (Age: %i)" this.Name this.Age
  member x.Name = name
  member x.Age = age
```

You can choose any name for your self-identifiers as long as you follow the normal rules for identifiers. You could even use a quoted identifier like the following ones if you really want to irritate your future self or anyone else who's maintaining your code.

```
type Person (name, age) as ``This is a bad identifier`` =
  do
    printfn "Creating person: %s (Age: %i)"
      ``This is a bad identifier``.Name
      ``This is a bad identifier``.Age
```

```
member x.Name = name
member x.Age = age
```

It's generally best to stick with short names. Common conventions are to use either x or this. But whatever you choose, be consistent!

WARNING *The compiler will generate a warning if you define a self-identifier but don't use it in your constructor. The reason is that using the as keyword makes the class definition recursive, which results in additional run time validation that can negatively impact initializing types in your class hierarchy. Use self-identifiers in primary constructors only when you actually need them.*

Fields

Fields define the data elements associated with an object. In the previous section, we took a brief look at both ways to create fields. In this section, we'll examine field creation in more detail.

let Bindings

The first way to create fields is with let bindings in the primary constructor. These fields, which must be initialized in the primary constructor, are *always* private to the class. Although they must be initialized when they're created, you can make the value mutable as in any let binding, as shown here:

```
type Person () =
  let mutable name : string = ""
  member x.Name
    with get() = name
    and set(v) = name <- v
```

Here, a mutable let binding is used to define the backing store for the Name property.

Explicit Fields

When you want a little more control over a field or your class doesn't have a primary constructor, create an explicit field with the val keyword. Explicit fields don't need to be initialized immediately, but in classes with a primary constructor you'll need to decorate them with the DefaultValue attribute to ensure that the value is initialized to its appropriate "zero" value, like this:

```
type Person () =
  [<DefaultValue>] val mutable n : string
  member x.Name
    with get() = x.n
    and set(v) = x.n <- v
```

In this example, n is an explicit field. Because n is of type string, it's initialized to null, as you can see here:

```
> let p = Person()
p.Name;;

val p : Person
val it : string = null
```

Explicit fields are public by default, but you can make them private by including the private access modifier in the definition like this:

```
type Person () =
  [<DefaultValue>] val mutable private n : string
  -- snip --
```

Properties

Like fields, *properties* represent data associated with an object. Unlike fields, though, properties offer more control over how that data is accessed or modified by exposing the actions through some combination of get and/or set functions (collectively called *accessors*).

You can define properties either implicitly or explicitly. One guideline is to favor implicit properties when you're exposing a simple value; when you need custom logic when getting or setting a property value, use explicit properties instead.

Explicit Properties

Explicit properties are those where you define and control the backing store (typically with a let binding) and implement the get and set function bodies yourself. You define an explicit property with the member keyword followed by a self-identifier, the property name, a type annotation (if the compiler can't infer it), and the function bodies, as shown here:

```
type Person() =
  let mutable name = ""
  member x.Name
    with get() = name
    and set(value) = name <- value
```

In this example, the name field is the private backing store for the read/write Name property. Once you've created an instance of this Person class, you can assign a value to the Name property with the assignment operator, like so:

```
let me = Person()
me.Name <- "Dave"
```

Instead of using the and keyword, you can use an alternative syntax where the get and set accessors are defined as separate properties.

```
type Person() =
  let mutable name = ""
  member x.Name with get() = name
  member x.Name with set(value) = name <- value
```

Whichever syntax you choose, properties are public by default, but you can control their accessibility by inserting the access modifier (public, private, or internal) after the with (or and) keyword, like this:

```
type Person() =
  let mutable name = ""
  member x.Name
    with public get() = name
    and internal set(value) = name <- value
```

If you wanted the Name property to be read-only, you could revise the class to include the value as an argument to the primary constructor and remove the and set... line in this way:

```
type Person(name) =
  member x.Name with get() = name
```

Of course, this is F#, so although defining a read-only property is already easy, there's an even easier way with the explicit syntax.

```
type Person(name) =
  member x.Name = name
```

When you're creating a read-only property, the compiler automatically generates the get accessor function for you.

Implicit Properties

Implicit, or automatic, properties were added to F# in version 3.0 (if you're using 2.0, you'll need to use explicit properties). They're very much like auto-implemented properties in C# in that they allow the compiler to generate the proper backing store and corresponding get/set accessor bodies. Implicit properties are a lot like their explicit counterparts, but there are a few differences.

First, implicit properties are considered part of the type's initialization, so they must appear before other member definitions, typically along with the primary constructor. Next, they are defined via the member val keyword pair and must be initialized to a default value, as shown next. (They must not include a self-identifier.) And finally, their accessibility can be changed only at the property level, not the accessor level.

```
type Person() =
  member val Name = "" with get, set
```

If your implicit property is read-only, you can omit the with expression like this:

```
type Person(name) =
  member val Name = name
```

Indexed Properties

F# classes can also have *indexed properties*, which are useful for defining an array-like interface for working with sequential data. Indexed properties are defined like ordinary properties except that the get accessor includes an argument.

When you are creating indexed properties, naming one Item makes it a *default indexed property* and enables convenient syntactic support through the dot operator and a pair of brackets enclosing the index value (.[...]). For example, consider a class that accepts a string and exposes each word through a default indexer like this:

```
type Sentence(initial : string) =
  let mutable words = initial.Split ' '
  let mutable text = initial
  member x.Item
    with get i = words.[i]
    and set i v =
      words.[i] <- v
      text <- System.String.Join(" ", words)
```

Notice that the Item property is defined like a normal property with the get, and even a set, accessor. Because this indexer is just a wrapper around the words array (String.Split returns an array), it accepts an integer value and returns the corresponding word.

F# arrays are zero-based, so you can get the second word from a sentence like this:

```
> let s = Sentence "Don't forget to drink your Ovaltine"
s.[1];;

val s1 : Sentence
val it : string = "forget"
```

To change the second word, you'd reference the index in the same way and use the assignment operator (<-) like so:

```
> s.[1] <- "remember";;
val it : unit = ()
```

```
> s.[1];;
val it : string = "remember"
```

Furthermore, default indexed properties can be multidimensional. For instance, you can define one to return a specific character from a word by including two parameters.

```
type Sentence(initial : string) =
  -- snip --
  member x.Item with get(w, i) = words.[w].[i]
```

Now you can easily get the first character of the second word like this:

```
> s.[1, 0];;
val it : char = 'f'
```

But what if you want to define another indexed property to get a character out of the original string? You've already defined a default indexed property that accepts an integer, so you can't do it that way. In C#, you'd have to create this as a method, but in F# any property can be an indexed property. For example:

```
type Sentence(initial : string) =
  -- snip --
  member x.Chars with get(i) = text.[i]
```

The only caveat is that you can't use the dot/bracket syntax that you'd use with a default indexed property; you have to access the property as if it's a method (as described in "Instance Methods" on page 73) by including the index value in parentheses after the property name in this way:

```
> s.Chars(0);;
val it : char = 'D'
```

Though it looks like a method call, if the Chars indexed property included a set accessor, you'd use the assignment operator just like you would with any other property to change the underlying value.

Setting at Initialization

An alternative object initialization syntax lets you set individual property values as part of the constructor call. To use the object initialization syntax, you need only include each property name and value (separated by an equal sign) immediately following the normal constructor arguments. Let's reconsider one of the previous Person class examples to illustrate.

```
type Person() =
  member val Name = "" with get, set
```

Because the Person class has only the single, parameterless constructor, you could create an instance and then assign a value to the Name property in a second operation. But it would be much more concise to do it all at once, like this:

```
let p = Person(Name = "Dave")
```

There is one catch to using this syntax: Any properties you initialize this way must be writable.

Methods

Methods are functions that are associated with a class and that represent the type's behavior.

Instance Methods

There are two ways to define instance methods. The first form uses the member keyword to define a public method in much the same way as a property, as demonstrated by the GetArea method that follows.

```
open System

type Circle(diameter : float) =
  member x.Diameter = diameter
  member x.GetArea() =
    let r = diameter / 2.0
    System.Math.PI * (r ** 2.0)
```

Here, the Circle class is initialized with a diameter value and contains a parameterless, public method named GetArea that calculates the area of the circle. Because GetArea is an instance method, you'll need to create an instance of the Circle class to invoke it as follows:

```
> let c = Circle 5.0
c.GetArea();;

val c : Circle
val it : float = 19.63495408
```

Method Accessibility

As with properties, you can control access to methods with accessibility modifiers. For example, to make a method private you would simply include the private keyword in the method's signature, as in the GetRadius method here:

```
type Circle(diameter : float) =
  member private x.GetRadius() = diameter / 2.0
  member x.Diameter = diameter
  member x.GetArea() = System.Math.PI * (x.GetRadius() ** 2.0)
```

Alternatively, you can use a let binding to define a private function, as shown here:

```
type Circle(diameter : float) =
  let getRadius() = diameter / 2.0
  member x.Diameter = diameter
  member x.GetArea() = System.Math.PI * (getRadius() ** 2.0)
```

Named Arguments

When you call a method, you'll usually provide the arguments as a comma-delimited list with each argument corresponding to the parameter at the same position. For a bit of extra flexibility, though, F# allows *named arguments* for both methods and constructors. With named arguments, each argument is explicitly associated with a particular parameter by name. In some cases, named arguments can help clarify your code, but they also allow you to specify the arguments in any order.

The following example contains a method that calculates the Euclidean distance between two points in a three-dimensional space (RGB colors, to be exact).

```
open System
open System.Drawing

type ColorDistance() =
  member x.GetEuclideanDistance(c1 : Color, c2 : Color) =
    let getPointDistance p1 p2 = (float p1 - float p2) ** 2.0
    [ getPointDistance c1.R c2.R
      getPointDistance c1.G c2.G
      getPointDistance c1.B c2.B ] |> List.sum |> Math.Sqrt
```

You can call the GetEuclideanDistance method normally by specifying two colors, or by specifying the parameter names in the argument list like this:

```
> let d = ColorDistance()
d.GetEuclideanDistance(Color.White, Color.Black);;

val d : ColorDistance
val it : float = 441.6729559

> d.GetEuclideanDistance(c2 = Color.White, c1 = Color.Snow);;
val it : float = 7.071067812
```

You can specify named arguments in any order. You can also use named arguments with unnamed arguments, but if you do, the unnamed arguments must appear first in the argument list. Finally, because named arguments are permissible only for methods defined with the member syntax, they can't be used with functions created through let bindings.

Overloaded Methods

An *overloaded method* shares its name with one or more other methods in the same class but has a different set of parameters. Overloaded methods often define subsets of parameters, with each overload calling a more specific form with its supplied arguments and providing default values for others.

For example, if you were building a utility to tie in to your favorite version control system, you might define a Commit method that accepts a list of files, the description, and the target branch. To make the target branch optional, you could overload the Commit function as shown here:

```
open System.IO

type Repository() =
  member ❶x.Commit(files, desc, branch) =
    printfn "Committed %i files (%s) to \"%s\"" (List.length files) desc branch
  member ❷x.Commit(files, desc) =
    x.Commit(files, desc, ❸"default")
```

In this example, the overload at ❶ is responsible for committing changes to the repository, while the overload at ❷ makes the branch parameter optional when you supply the default value shown at ❸.

Optional Parameters

Even though F# supports method overloading, you probably won't use it very often because F# also supports *optional parameters*, which are generally more convenient. If you prefix a parameter name with a question mark (?), the compiler treats it as an optional parameter.

Optional parameters are a bit different in F# than they are in C# and Visual Basic. In other languages, optional parameters are defined with a default value that's used when the corresponding argument is omitted. In F#, though, the parameters are actually compiled to option<_> and default to None. (Optional parameter values behave like any other option type value, so you'll still use defaultArg or pattern matching in your method to get a meaningful value, as appropriate.)

Let's rewrite the Repository example from the previous section to use an optional parameter instead of an overloaded method.

```
open System.IO

type Repository() =
  static member Commit(files, desc, ?branch) =
    let targetBranch = defaultArg branch "default"
    printfn "Committed %i files (%s) to \"%s\"" (List.length files) desc targetBranch
```

Although you need to manage the optional parameter within the method, you now need to maintain only the one method instead of multiple, overloaded versions. As you can see, optional parameters can reduce the likelihood of defects that come from using inconsistent defaults across overloads, and they simplify refactoring because only one method needs to change.

Slice Expressions

Indexed properties, introduced in "Indexed Properties" on page 71, are great for working with a single value in an encapsulated sequence, but you'll sometimes want to work with a range of values in that sequence. Traditionally you'd have to get each item manually through the indexer, or implement IEnumerable<'T> and get the values through some combination of LINQ's Skip and Take extension methods. *Slice expressions* resemble indexed properties, except that they use range expressions to identify which items should be included in the resulting sequence.

To use slice expressions with your class, you need to implement a GetSlice method. There's really nothing special about the GetSlice method; it's just the method that the compiler looks for when it encounters the slice expression syntax. To illustrate a slice expression, let's revisit the Sentence class from the indexed properties section.

```
type Sentence(initial : string) =
  let words = initial.Split ' '
  let text = initial
  member x.GetSlice(lower, upper) =
    match defaultArg lower 0 with
    | l when l >= words.Length -> Array.empty<string>
    | l -> match defaultArg upper (words.Length - 1) with
           | u when u >= words.Length -> words.[l..]
           | u -> words.[l..u]
```

The basic class definition is the same as before, except this time we have a GetSlice() method that accepts the lower and upper bounds. (Don't dwell on the match expressions here; a full discussion is waiting for you in Chapter 7. For now it's enough to know that they're just doing some boundary checks.)

You could call this method directly in your code, but the expression form is much more convenient. For example, to retrieve the second, third, and fourth words in a sentence, you could write:

```
> let s = Sentence "Don't forget to drink your Ovaltine"
s.[1..3];;

val s : Sentence
val it : string [] = [|"forget"; "to"; "drink"|]
```

One of the nice things about slice expressions is that the bounds parameters are optional, so you can use open-ended ranges. To specify a range without a lower bound, just omit the first value (the 1) in the slice expression, which in this case is equivalent to [0..3].

```
> s.[..3];;
val it : string [] = [|"Don't"; "forget"; "to"; "drink"|]
```

Similarly, you can leave out the second parameter and get the items up to the end of the collection.

```
> s.[3..];;
val it : string [] = [|"drink"; "your"; "Ovaltine"|]
```

Like indexed properties, slice expressions can work on two dimensions, but you need to overload the GetSlice method to accept four parameters that define both pairs of lower and upper bounds. Continuing with the Sentence example, we can add a multidimensional slice overload to get a range of characters from a range of words like this:

```
type Sentence(initial : string) =
  -- snip --
  member x.GetSlice(lower1, upper1, lower2, upper2) =
    x.GetSlice(lower1, upper1)
    |> Array.map
        (fun w -> match defaultArg lower2 0 with
                  | l when l >= w.Length -> ""
                  | l -> match defaultArg upper2 (w.Length - 1) with
                         | u when u >= w.Length -> w.[l..]
                         | u -> w.[l..u])
```

To use this overload, just separate the range pairs in the slice expression with a comma.

```
> s.[1..4, ..1];;
val it : string [] = [|"fo"; "to"; "dr"; "yo"|]
```

Events

The final member type is *events*. Events are used throughout the .NET Framework with some notable examples found in the user interface components and ADO.NET. As in other .NET languages, at their core F# events are collections of functions invoked in response to some action like a button click or an asynchronous process completion.

In many ways F# events serve the same purpose as traditional .NET events, but they're a completely different mechanism. However, for cross-language compatibility, they can tie in to the .NET event system. (We'll see how your custom events can harness this capability with the CLIEvent attribute a bit later in this section.)

Basic Event Handling

Events in F# are instances of the Event<'T> class (found in FSharp.Core.Control). One of the primary features that the Event<'T> class enables is a more explicit publish/subscribe model than you might be used to. In this model you can subscribe to published events by adding event handlers to the event via a call to the Add function.

For example, the System.Timers.Timer class publishes an Elapsed event that you can subscribe to.

```
let ticks = ref 0
let t = ❶new System.Timers.Timer(500.0)
t.Elapsed.Add ❷(fun ea -> printfn "tick"; ticks := ticks.Value + 1)
❸ t.Start()
while ticks.Value < 5 do ()
t.Dispose()
```

Here we create a new instance of the Timer class at ❶. At ❷, we subscribe to the Elapsed function using a *lambda expression* (an anonymous function) as the event handler. Once the timer is started at ❸, the event handler prints tick and increments a reference cell's value (remember, closures like the one created by the lambda expression can't use mutable let bindings) every half-second, per the timer definition. When the tick counter reaches five, the loop will terminate and the timer will be stopped and disposed of.

Observing Events

The other primary benefit of F# events is that they enable you to treat events as sequences that you can intelligently partition, filter, aggregate, or otherwise act upon as they're triggered. The Event module defines a number of functions—such as add, filter, partition, and pairwise—that accept published events.

To see this principle in action, let's turn to an example in ADO.NET. The DataTable class triggers a variety of events in response to certain actions like changed or deleted rows. If you wanted to handle the RowChanged event, you could add a single event handler (just as in the previous section) and include logic to filter out the events you don't care about, or you could use the filter function from the Event module and invoke your handler only when it's needed, as follows:

```
open System
open System.Data

let dt = new DataTable("person")
dt.Columns.AddRange
  [| new DataColumn("person_id", typedefof<int>)
     new DataColumn("first_name", typedefof<string>)
     new DataColumn("last_name", typedefof<string>) |]
dt.Constraints.Add("pk_person", dt.Columns.[0], true)

let ❶h1, h2 =
❷ dt.RowChanged
    |> ❸Event.partition
        ❹(fun ea ->
            let ln = ea.Row.["last_name"] :?> string
            ln.Equals("Pond", StringComparison.InvariantCultureIgnoreCase))

❺ h1.Add (fun _ -> printfn "Come along, Pond")
❻ h2.Add (fun _ -> printfn "Row changed")
```

We'll forego a discussion of the first half of this example; for our purposes, all that's important there is that it sets up a DataTable with three columns and a primary key. What's really important here is the partition function.

In this example, we invoke the partition function at ❸ by supplying both a delegate (in the form of a lambda expression) at ❹ and the Event object published by the DataTable's RowChanged event at ❷. The partition function then returns two new events that we bind to h1 and h2 at ❶. Finally, we subscribe to both of the new events by calling their Add method at ❺ and ❻.

Now that the table structure and event handlers are in place, we can add some rows and see how the events are triggered.

```
> dt.Rows.Add(1, "Rory", "Williams") |> ignore;;
Row changed
val it : unit = ()
> dt.Rows.Add(2, "Amelia", "Pond") |> ignore;;
Come along, Pond
val it : unit = ()
```

As you can see, when the first row is added, the last name doesn't match the criteria specified in the filter, so h2 is triggered. However, the second row does match the criteria, so h1 is triggered instead.

If the syntax for calling the partition function looks backward, that's because it is; the *forward pipelining operator* (|>) applies its left operand as the final argument to the function specified by its right operand. (The forward pipelining operator is used frequently in F#, and we'll explore it in much more detail in Chapter 5.)

Custom Events

You can define your own custom events in your types. However, doing so is a bit different than in other .NET languages because events exist only as objects in F# and they lack keyword support.

The first thing you need to do, aside from defining the type, is create a field (with a let binding) for your event object. This is the object used to coordinate publishing and triggering the event. Once the field is defined, you can expose the event's Publish property to the outside world with a property of your own. Finally, you'll need to trigger the event somewhere by calling the Trigger function.

```
type Toggle() =
  let toggleChangedEvent = Event<_>()
  let mutable isOn = false

  member x.ToggleChanged = toggleChangedEvent.Publish

  member x.Toggle() =
    isOn <- not isOn
    toggleChangedEvent.Trigger (x, isOn)
```

With the type defined, you can create a new instance and subscribe to the ToggleChanged event as with any built-in type. For example, next we use a partition to create two new event handlers, one to handle when the toggle is turned on and another to handle when it is turned off. The call to Event.map simply rephrases the event by throwing away the first parameter (the source, or sender, per .NET conventions) before calling the partition function.

```
let myToggle = Toggle()
let onHandler, offHandler =
  myToggle.ToggleChanged
  |> Event.map (fun (_, isOn) -> isOn)
  |> Event.partition (fun isOn -> isOn)

onHandler |> Event.add (fun _ -> printfn "Turned on!")
offHandler |> Event.add (fun _ -> printfn "Turned off!")
```

Now every call to the Toggle method will trigger the ToggleChanged event and cause one of the two handlers to execute.

```
> myToggle.Toggle();;
Turned on!
val it : unit = ()
> myToggle.Toggle();;
Turned off!
val it : unit = ()
```

As you've just seen, the ToggleChanged event is fully enabled within F#. If your class won't be consumed outside F# assemblies, you could stop here. However, if you need to use it in assemblies written in different languages, you'll have to do one more thing: decorate the ToggleChanged property with the CLIEvent attribute.

```
[<CLIEvent>]
member x.ToggleChanged = toggleChangedEvent.Publish
```

The CLIEvent attribute instructs the compiler to include the appropriate metadata that makes the event consumable from other .NET languages.

Structures

Structures, or *structs*, are similar to classes in that they can have fields, properties, methods, and events. Structs are defined just like classes except that the type must be decorated with the Struct attribute.

```
[<Struct>]
type Circle(diameter : float) =
  member x.getRadius() = diameter / 2.0
  member x.Diameter = diameter
  member x.GetArea() = System.Math.PI * (x.getRadius() ** 2.0)
```

However, despite their similarities, behind the scenes, classes and structs are very different animals. The primary difference between them is that structs are *value types.*

This difference is significant because it affects not only how you interact with the data but also how value types are represented in the computer's memory. With both types, the runtime allocates space in memory to store the value. Value types always result in a new allocation with the data copied into that space. With reference types, the memory is allocated once and accessed via a reference that identifies its location.

When you pass a reference type to a function, the runtime creates a new reference to that location in memory rather than a copy of the data. Therefore, reference types can more easily wreak havoc through side effects, because when you pass a reference type to a function any changes that you make to that object are immediately reflected wherever that object is referenced. In contrast, passing a value type to a function creates a copy of the value so any changes to it are isolated to that one instance.

Structs are also initialized differently than classes. Unlike classes, the compiler generates a default (parameterless) constructor for structs that initializes all fields to their appropriate zero value (zero, null, and so on). This means that you can't use let bindings to create private instance fields or methods within a struct unless they're static; instead, you must use val to define struct instance fields. Also, you can't define your own default constructor, so any additional constructors you define must accept at least one parameter. (Your fields can still be mutable as long as you don't include a primary constructor.)

Because of differences in how memory is allocated for reference and value types, structs cannot contain fields of their own type. Without this restriction, the memory requirement for a struct instance would be infinitely large because each instance would recursively require enough space for another instance of the same type.

Finally, structs can implement interfaces but cannot otherwise participate in inheritance. Regardless, structs still derive from System.Object, so you can override methods (like ToString).

Inheritance

In OO programming, *inheritance* describes an *identity* relationship between two types in the way that an apple *is* a fruit. F# classes support *single inheritance*, meaning that any given class can directly inherit from only one other in order to establish a class hierarchy. Through inheritance, public (and sometimes internal) members exposed by the base type are automatically available in the derived type. You can see this principle in action in the following snippet.

```
type BaseType() =
  member x.SayHello name = printfn "Hello, %s" name
```

```
type DerivedType() =
  inherit BaseType()
```

The DerivedType defined here doesn't define any functionality of its own, but because it derives from BaseType, the SayHello method is accessible through DerivedType.

F# inheritance requires a primary constructor. To specify a base class, include the inherit keyword followed by the base type name and its constructor arguments in the primary constructor before any bindings or member definitions. For instance, a task management system might have a WorkItem class that represents all work items in the system, as well as specialized classes such as Defect and Enhancement that derive from the WorkItem class, as shown next in bold.

```
type WorkItem(summary : string, desc : string) =
  member val Summary = summary
  member val Description = desc

type Defect(summary, desc, severity : int) =
  inherit WorkItem(summary, desc)
  member val Severity = severity

type Enhancement(summary, desc, requestedBy : string) =
  inherit WorkItem(summary, desc)
  member val RequestedBy = requestedBy
```

Every .NET class, including the primitive types, ultimately participates in inheritance. Also, when you define a class without explicitly specifying a base class, the defined class implicitly inherits from System.Object.

Casting

In Chapter 3 you learned how to convert between numeric types. Types can also be converted within their type hierarchy through the upcast and downcast operators.

Upcasting

Until now I've maintained that there are no implicit conversions in F#, but that's not entirely true. The only time that types are implicitly *upcast* (converted to a type higher in their inheritance structure) is when they're passed to a method or a let-bound function where the corresponding parameter is a flexible type. In all other cases, you must explicitly cast the type with the *static cast* operator (:>).

To see the static cast operator in action, let's continue with the WorkItem example by creating a Defect and immediately casting it to a WorkItem.

```
> let w = Defect("Incompatibility detected", "Delete", 1) :> WorkItem;;
val w : WorkItem
```

The static cast operator resolves valid casts at compile time. If the code compiles, the conversion will always succeed.

Downcasting

The opposite of an upcast is a *downcast*. Downcasts are used to convert a type to something lower in its hierarchy, that is, to convert a base type to a derived type. To perform a downcast, you use the *dynamic cast* operator (:?>)

Because the WorkItem instance we created in the previous example is still a Defect, we can use the dynamic cast operator to convert it back to a WorkItem.

```
> let d = w :?> Defect;;
val d : Defect
```

Unlike the static cast operator, the dynamic cast operator isn't resolved until run time, so you may see an InvalidCastException if the target type isn't valid for the source object. For instance, if you try to downcast w to Enhancement, the cast will fail.

```
> let e = w :?> Enhancement;;
System.InvalidCastException: Unable to cast object of type 'Defect' to type 'Enhancement'.
   at Microsoft.FSharp.Core.LanguagePrimitives.IntrinsicFunctions.UnboxGeneric[T](Object source)
   at <StartupCode$FSI_0007>.$FSI_0007.main@()
Stopped due to error
```

Overriding Members

Aside from reusing code, you might use inheritance to change the functionality offered by a base class by overriding its members.

For example, the ToString method defined on System.Object is a great (and often overlooked) debugging tool whose default implementation isn't particularly informative because it just returns the type name. To make it more useful, your classes can override the default functionality and return a string that actually describes the object.

To illustrate, consider the WorkItem class from earlier. If you were to call its ToString method, you would see something like this:

```
> let w = WorkItem("Take out the trash", "It's overflowing!")
w.ToString();;

val w : WorkItem
val it : string = "FSI_0002+WorkItem"
```

NOTE   *In the preceding example, FSI_0002+ is an artifact of invoking the code in FSI. Your type name will probably differ.*

To override the default behavior and make ToString return something more useful, define a new method with the override keyword.

```
type WorkItem(summary : string, desc : string) =
  -- snip --
  override x.ToString() = sprintf "%s" x.Summary
```

If you call ToString now, the result will be the summary text instead of the type name.

```
> let w = WorkItem("Take out the trash", "It's overflowing!")
w.ToString();;

val w : WorkItem = Take out the trash
val it : string = "Take out the trash"
```

You can override a given function only once per type, but you can override it at multiple levels in the hierarchy. For instance, here's how you could override ToString again in the Defect class to display the severity of the defect:

```
type Defect(summary, desc, severity : int) =
  inherit WorkItem(summary, desc)
  member val Severity = severity
  override x.ToString() = sprintf "%s (%i)" x.Summary x.Severity
```

When overriding a *virtual member* (an abstract member with a default implementation), you can call into the base functionality through the base keyword. The base keyword behaves like a self-identifier except that it represents the base class.

Continuing with our ToString override theme, to augment the default behavior your override could call base.ToString() like this:

```
type Defect(summary, desc, severity : int) =
  -- snip --
  override x.ToString() =
    sprintf "%s (%i)" (base.ToString()) x.Severity
```

Note that the base keyword is available only in classes that explicitly inherit from another type. To use the base keyword in a class that inherits from System.Object, you would need to explicitly inherit from it as follows:

```
type WorkItem(summary : string, desc : string) =
  inherit System.Object()
  -- snip --
  override x.ToString() =
    sprintf "[%s] %s" (base.ToString()) x.Summary
```

Abstract Classes

An *abstract class* is one that can't be directly instantiated; it's accessible only through derived classes. Abstract classes typically define a common interface and optional implementation for a group of related classes that fulfill similar needs in different ways. Abstract classes are used throughout the .NET Framework; one great example is the TextWriter class in the System.IO namespace.

The TextWriter class defines a common mechanism for writing characters to *something*. It doesn't care where or how the characters are written, but it orchestrates some of the process, with the implementation details left to individual derived classes such as StreamWriter, StringWriter, and HttpWriter.

You can define your own abstract classes by decorating the type definition with the AbstractClass attribute. For example, to create a simple tree structure you could use an abstract class as follows:

```
[<AbstractClass>]
type Node(name : string, ?content : Node list) =
  member x.Name = name
  member x.Content = content
```

Abstract Members

One reason to define an abstract class is to define *abstract members*, that is, members without an implementation. Abstract members are allowed only in abstract classes (or interfaces, described in "Interfaces" on page 91) and must be implemented in a derived class. They're handy when you want to define what a class does but not how it does it.

Abstract Properties

When you want to define the data associated with a particular type but not how that data is stored or what happens when it is accessed, you can define an *abstract property* with the abstract keyword.

For example, this abstract class contains one abstract property:

```
[<AbstractClass>]
type AbstractBaseClass() =
  abstract member SomeData : string with get, set
```

AbstractBaseClass requires only that its subtypes implement the SomeData property, but they're free to implement their own storage mechanism. For instance, one derived class may use a traditional backing store, whereas another may opt to use a .NET generic dictionary as follows:

```
type BindingBackedClass() =
  inherit AbstractBaseClass()
  let mutable someData = ""
  override x.SomeData
    with get() = someData
    and set(v) = someData <- v

type DictionaryBackedClass() =
  inherit AbstractBaseClass()
  let dict = System.Collections.Generic.Dictionary<string, string>()
```

```
[<Literal>]
let SomeDataKey = "SomeData"
override x.SomeData
  with get() =
    match dict.TryGetValue(SomeDataKey) with
    | true, v -> v
    | _, _ -> ""
  and set(v) =
    match System.String.IsNullOrEmpty(v) with
    | true when dict.ContainsKey(SomeDataKey) ->
        dict.Remove(SomeDataKey) |> ignore
    | _ -> dict.[SomeDataKey] <- v
```

As you can see, both `BindingBackedClass` and `DictionaryBackedClass` derive from `AbstractBaseClass`, but they implement the `SomeData` property in very different ways.

Abstract Methods

Even though you can define abstract properties, you're much more likely to use *abstract methods*. Like abstract properties, abstract methods allow you to define a capability that derived classes must implement without specifying any of the implementation details. For example, when calculating the area of a shape, you might define an abstract `Shape` class that includes an abstract `GetArea` method.

```
[<AbstractClass>]
type Shape() =
  abstract member GetArea : unit -> float
```

Because the method doesn't have an implementation, you must explicitly define the entire signature. In this case, the `GetArea` method accepts unit and returns a float.

Overriding a method is also similar to overriding a property, as you can see in the following `Circle` and `Rectangle` classes:

```
open System

type Circle(r : float) =
  inherit Shape()
  member val Radius = r
  override x.GetArea() =
    Math.Pow(Math.PI * r, 2.0)

type Rectangle(w : float, h : float) =
  inherit Shape()
  member val Width = w
  member val Height = h
  override x.GetArea() = w * h
```

Virtual Members

Like C# and Visual Basic, F# allows *virtual members*—that is, properties or methods that can be overridden in a derived class. But unlike other .NET languages, F# takes a more literal approach to virtual members. For instance, in C# you include the `virtual` modifier in a nonprivate instance member definition, and in Visual Basic you use the `Overridable` modifier to achieve the same effect.

Virtual members in F# are closely related to abstract members. In fact, in order to create a virtual member you first define an abstract member and then provide a default implementation with the `default` keyword. For example, in the following listing the `Node` class is the basis for a simple tree structure. It provides two virtual methods, `AddChild` and `RemoveChild`, which help control the tree structure.

```
open System
open System.Collections.Generic

type Node(name : string) =
  let children = List<Node>()
  member x.Children with get() = children.AsReadOnly()
  abstract member AddChild : Node -> unit
  abstract member RemoveChild : Node -> unit
  default x.AddChild(n) = children.Add n
  default x.RemoveChild(n) = children.Remove n |> ignore
```

With this definition, all `Node` class instances (including any derived types) will allow children. To create a specialized `Node` that doesn't allow children, you could define a `TerminalNode` class and override both virtual methods to prevent children from being added or removed.

```
type TerminalNode(name : string) =
  inherit Node(name)
  [<Literal>]
  let notSupportedMsg = "Cannot add or remove children"
  override x.AddChild(n) =
    raise (NotSupportedException(notSupportedMsg))
  override x.RemoveChild(n) =
    raise (NotSupportedException(notSupportedMsg))
```

Sealed Classes

A *sealed class* is a class that cannot serve as the base class for another class. One of the most notable sealed classes in the .NET Framework is `System.String`.

You can create your own sealed classes by decorating them with the `Sealed` attribute, as shown in the following snippet:

```
[<Sealed>]
type NotInheritable() = class end
```

If you tried to create another class that inherits from the `NotInheritable` class, the compiler would raise an error like this:

```
> type InvalidClass() =
  inherit NotInheritable();;

  inherit NotInheritable();;
--^^^^^^^^^^^^^^^^^^^^^^^^

stdin(4,3): error FS0945: Cannot inherit a sealed type
```

Static Members

Fields, properties, and methods are instance members by default. You can make each static so that it applies to the type rather than a specific instance by including the static keyword before the member definition.

> **A WORD ABOUT STATIC CLASSES**
>
> In C# a *static class* is an implicitly sealed class that cannot be instantiated and in which all members are static. Most of the time in F#, when you want static class–like functionality, you'll place it in a module. However, modules have certain limitations. For example, they don't allow you to overload functions.
>
> Although F# doesn't directly support static classes the way that C# does, you can do a little syntactic dance to achieve a similar effect. To do so, omit the primary constructor (or make it private if you need a static initializer) to ensure that no instances can be created, and then verify that every member is static (the F# compiler won't enforce this for you). For completeness, decorate the class with `SealedAttribute` so that nothing inherits from it.

Static Initializers

Static initializers, or *static constructors*, execute only once per class and ensure that certain code is executed before a class is used for the first time. You create static initializers in F# through a series of static let and do bindings, just as you would when defining a primary constructor. In fact, if your class needs a static initializer, you must include a primary constructor to contain the static bindings as shown here:

```
type ClassWithStaticCtor() =
  static let mutable staticField = 0
  static do printfn "Invoking static initializer"
          staticField <- 10
  do printfn "Static Field Value: %i" staticField
```

Static initializers can access only the static members of their containing class. If you try to access an instance member from within a static initializer, you'll get a compiler error.

Static Fields

Static fields are often useful as a single reference for something you need to use repeatedly. For example, to associate certain data with the class itself, define a static field by including the static keyword before a let binding, as shown here:

```
module Logger =
  let private log l c m = printfn "%-5s [%s] %s" l c m
  let LogInfo = log "INFO"
  let LogError = log "ERROR"

type MyService() =
  static let logCategory = "MyService"
  member x.DoSomething() =
    Logger.LogInfo logCategory "Doing something"
  member x.DoSomethingElse() =
    Logger.LogError logCategory "Doing something else"
```

When the DoSomething and DoSomethingElse methods are called, each calls a function in the Logger module to write a log message in the same category but without the duplication of data.

```
> let svc = MyService()
svc.DoSomething()
svc.DoSomethingElse();;
INFO  [MyService] Doing something
ERROR [MyService] Doing something else
```

Static Properties

Properties can also be static. Here, a read-only *static property* is used to expose the number of times a particular method has been called across all instances of your class.

```
type Processor() =
  static let mutable itemsProcessed = 0
  static member ItemsProcessed = itemsProcessed
  member x.Process() =
    itemsProcessed <- itemsProcessed + 1
    printfn "Processing..."
```

Every time the Process method is called, it increments the itemsProcessed field and prints a message. To see how many times the Process method has been called across all instances, inspect the ItemsProcessed property on the Processor class itself.

```
> while Processor.ItemsProcessed < 5 do (Processor()).Process();;
Processing...
Processing...
Processing...
Processing...
Processing...
val it : unit = ()
```

This example iterates as long as the Process method has been invoked fewer than five times. Each iteration creates a new instance of the Processor class and invokes its Process method (which illustrates how the static property is instance agnostic).

Static Methods

Like other static members, *static methods* apply to a type rather than an instance. For example, static methods are commonly used in the *Factory pattern* (a common approach to creating instances of similar classes without relying on a specific implementation). In some variations of the Factory pattern, a static method returns new instances of objects that conform to a specific interface. To illustrate this concept, consider an application where you need to handle different image formats. You may have an abstract ImageReader class that other types derive from in order to handle specific formats like JPEG, GIF, and PNG.

```
[<AbstractClass>]
type ImageReader() =
  abstract member Dimensions : int * int with get
  abstract member Resolution : int * int with get
  abstract member Content : byte array with get

type JpgImageReader(fileName : string) =
  inherit ImageReader()
  -- snip --

type GifImageReader(fileName : string) =
  inherit ImageReader()
  -- snip --

type PngImageReader(fileName : string) =
  inherit ImageReader()
  -- snip --
```

A Factory method for creating instances of these classes might look something like this:

```
open System.IO

[<Sealed>]
type ImageReaderFactory private() =
  static member CreateReader(fileName) =
    let fi = FileInfo(fileName)
```

```
match fi.Extension.ToUpper() with
| ".JPG" -> JpgImageReader(fileName) :> ImageReader
| ".GIF" -> GifImageReader(fileName) :> ImageReader
| ".PNG" -> PngImageReader(fileName) :> ImageReader
| ext -> failwith (sprintf "Unsupported extension: %s" ext)
```

The static `CreateReader` method in the preceeding snippet uses F# pattern matching to create the appropriate `ImageReader` implementation based on the provided filename. When the file extension isn't recognized, it raises an exception indicating that the format isn't supported. Because the method is static, you can call it without creating an instance of the `ImageReaderFactory` class, as shown here:

```
ImageReaderFactory.CreateReader "MyPicture.jpg"
ImageReaderFactory.CreateReader "MyPicture.gif"
ImageReaderFactory.CreateReader "MyPicture.png"
ImageReaderFactory.CreateReader "MyPicture.targa"
```

Mutually Recursive Types

When two or more types depend on each other such that one cannot be used without the other, the types are said to be *mutually recursive.*

To illustrate, think of a book and its pages. The book can contain a collection of pages, but each page might also refer back to the book. Remember, F# is evaluated top-down, so which type would you define first? The book or the page? Because the book depends on its pages and the page refers back to the book, there is mutual recursion here. This means that you must define the types together using the and keyword, as shown here:

```
type Book() =
  let pages = List<Page>()
  member x.Pages with get() = pages.AsReadOnly()
  member x.AddPage(pageNumber : int, page : Page) =
    if page.Owner = Some(x) then failwith "Page is already part of a book"
    pages.Insert(pageNumber - 1, page)
and Page(content : string) =
  let mutable owner : Book option = None
  member x.Content = content
  member x.Owner with get() = owner
  member internal x.Owner with set(v) = owner <- v
  override x.ToString() = content
```

Interfaces

In OO programming, *interfaces* specify the properties, methods, and sometimes even events that a type must support. In some ways interfaces are like abstract classes, with certain important differences. For one, unlike abstract classes, interfaces cannot contain any implementations of their members; their members must be abstract. Also, because interfaces define functionality that implementers must support, all interface members are implicitly public. Finally, interfaces aren't subject to the same inheritance restrictions as classes: A class can implement any number of interfaces (and structs can, too).

Implementing Interfaces

F# approaches interface implementation a bit differently than its .NET language counterparts. C# and Visual Basic allow both implicit and explicit implementations. With *implicit implementations*, interface members are accessible directly through the implementing class, whereas with *explicit implementations*, interface members are accessible only when the implementing type is treated as the interface.

Consider this C# example with two classes that both implement the IDisposable interface:

```
// C#

class ImplicitExample : IDisposable
{
❶public void Dispose()
  {
    Console.WriteLine("Disposing");
  }
}

class ExplicitExample : IDisposable
{
❷void IDisposable.Dispose()
  {
    Console.WriteLine("Disposing");
  }
}
```

Both classes implement IDisposable, but ImplicitExample ❶ does so implicitly and ExplicitExample ❷ does it explicitly. This difference has a dramatic effect on how you call the Dispose method in each class, as shown here:

```
// C#

var ex1 = ❶new ImplicitExample();
❷ ex1.Dispose();

var ex2 = ❸new ExplicitExample();
❹ ((IDisposable)ex2).Dispose();
```

Here we instantiate ImplicitExample at ❶ and ExplicitExample at ❸. For both classes we call the Dispose method, but because Dispose is implicitly implemented in the ImplicitExample class we can call it directly through ex1, as we do at ❷. The compiler would produce an error if we tried the same approach with ex2 because `Dispose` is explicitly implemented in `ExplicitExample`. Instead, we need to cast ex2 to `IDisposable`, as shown at ❹, in order to call its `Dispose` method.

All interface implementations in F# are explicit. Though F# honors implicit interface implementations on types defined in other languages, any implementations that you define in F# will be explicit.

Implementing an interface in F# is similar to inheriting from another class except that it uses the `interface` keyword. For example, to implement `IDisposable` in one of your types, you could do this:

```
open System

type MyDisposable() =
  interface IDisposable with
    member x.Dispose() = printfn "Disposing"
```

To manually invoke the `Dispose` method on the `MyDisposable` class, you'll need to cast an instance to `IDisposable`, as shown here with the static cast operator:

```
let d = new MyDisposable()
(d :> IDisposable).Dispose()
```

Defining Interfaces

When you define a type without any constructors and only abstract members, the F# compiler infers that the type is an interface. For example, an interface for working with image data might look something like this:

```
open System.Drawing
open System.IO

type IImageAdapter =
  abstract member PixelDimensions : SizeF with get
  abstract member VerticalResolution : int with get
  abstract member HorizontalResolution : int with get
  abstract member GetRawData : unit -> Stream
```

As you can see, the `IImageAdapter` type contains no constructors and all of its four members are abstract. To define an empty, or *marker*, interface you can end the definition with the `interface end` keyword pair:

```
type IMarker = interface end
```

It's standard practice in .NET development to begin interface names with a capital letter I. You should do so for the sake of consistency.

Like classes, interfaces can inherit from each other to define more specialized contracts. Also like classes, interface inheritance is accomplished with the inherit keyword.

Let's continue our imaging example. The IImageAdapter interface is helpful for working with any image format, but some formats include capabilities not available in others. To handle these, you could define additional interfaces that represent these capabilities. For example, when working with a format that supports transparency you might create an ITransparentImageAdapter that derives from IImageAdapter, as shown here:

```
type ITransparentImageAdapter =
  inherit IImageAdapter
  abstract member TransparentColor : Color with get, set
```

Now, any types that implement the ITransparentImageAdapter must implement all members defined by both IImageAdapter and ITransparentImageAdapter.

Custom Operators

In Chapter 3 you saw numerous predefined operators for working with the built-in data types. You can use *operator overloading* to extend many of these to your types as well. By overloading operators, you can make your custom types interact a bit more naturally.

Operators in F# come in two forms: prefix and infix. *Prefix operators* are placed before their operand, whereas *infix operators* are placed between their operands. F# operators can also be *unary* or *binary*, meaning that they operate against one or two arguments, respectively. Custom operators are defined as static methods except that the name is the operator wrapped in parentheses.

Prefix Operators

When defining a prefix operator, you must begin its name with a tilde (~) to distinguish it from infix operators with the same name. The tilde is not otherwise part of the operator. To demonstrate operator overloading, we'll define a type that represents basic RGB colors. Consider this class definition:

```
type RgbColor(r, g, b) =
  member x.Red = r
  member x.Green = g
  member x.Blue = b
  override x.ToString() = sprintf "(%i, %i, %i)" r g b
```

To calculate the negative color you could define a GetNegative function, but wouldn't it be more intuitive to prefix an instance with the negative sign (-) instead?

```
type RgbColor(r, g, b) =
  -- snip --
  /// Negate a color
  static member (~-) (r : RgbColor) =
    RgbColor(
      r.Red ^^^ 0xFF,
      r.Green ^^^ 0xFF,
      r.Blue ^^^ 0xFF
    )
```

With the custom operator defined, you can now create a color instance and find its negative with a convenient syntax like this:

```
> let yellow = RgbColor(255, 255, 0)
let blue = -yellow;;

val yellow : RgbColor = (255, 255, 0)
val blue : RgbColor = (0, 0, 255)
```

Infix Operators

Creating infix operators is almost like creating prefix operators except that you omit the tilde character from the name.

Continuing with the RgbColor example, it would be nice to add and subtract two colors using the familiar and natural + and - operators.

```
open System

type RgbColor(r, g, b) =
  -- snip --
  /// Add two colors
  static member (+) (l : RgbColor, r : RgbColor) =
    RgbColor(
      Math.Min(255, l.Red + r.Red),
      Math.Min(255, l.Green + r.Green),
      Math.Min(255, l.Blue + r.Blue)
    )
  /// Subtract two colors
  static member (-) (l : RgbColor, r : RgbColor) =
    RgbColor(
      Math.Max(0, l.Red - r.Red),
      Math.Max(0, l.Green - r.Green),
      Math.Max(0, l.Blue - r.Blue)
    )
```

Now we can add and subtract colors just as we would add and subtract numbers.

```
> let red = RgbColor(255, 0, 0)
let green = RgbColor(0, 255, 0)
let yellow = red + green;;

val red : RgbColor = (255, 0, 0)
val green : RgbColor = (0, 255, 0)
val yellow : RgbColor = (255, 255, 0)

> let magenta = RgbColor(255, 0, 255)
let blue = magenta - red;;

val magenta : RgbColor = (255, 0, 255)
val blue : RgbColor = (0, 0, 255)
```

New Operators

You're not limited to overloading only existing operators. You can define custom operators using various combinations of the characters !, %, &, *, +, -, ., /, <, =, >, ?, @, ^, |, and ~. Creating custom operators can be complicated because the combination you select determines the precedence (priority) and associativity (right to left or left to right) of the operation. Furthermore, creating custom operators can hinder the comprehensibility of your code if you choose something that's not intuitive. That said, if you still want to define a new operator, the definition looks the same as an overload.

For example, in the previous section we overloaded the + operator to add two colors, but how about blending colors? The + operator would have been a nice choice for a blending operation, but because it's already being used for adding colors we can define the += operator instead.

```
type RgbColor(r, g, b) =
  -- snip --
  /// Blend two colors
  static member (+=) (l : RgbColor, r : RgbColor) =
    RgbColor(
      (l.Red + r.Red) / 2,
      (l.Green + r.Green) / 2,
      (l.Blue + r.Blue) / 2
    )
```

Now blending two colors is as easy as adding them:

```
> let grey = yellow += blue;;

val grey : RgbColor = (127, 127, 127)
```

Global Operators

Not only does F# allow you to overload operators on types, but you can also define operators globally. This lets you create new operators even for types you don't control! For example, to define any of the custom operators on the standard System.Drawing.Color struct, you could define a new operator at the global level using a let binding as follows:

```
open System
open System.Drawing

let (+) (l : Color) (r : Color) =
    Color.FromArgb(
        255, // Alpha channel
        Math.Min(255, int <| l.R + r.R),
        Math.Min(255, int <| l.G + r.G),
        Math.Min(255, int <| l.B + r.B)
    )
```

WARNING *Be careful when defining global operators. Any operator you define that conflicts with the built-in one will take priority, meaning you can inadvertently replace core functionality.*

Object Expressions

As an alternative to formal inheritance, F# provides *object expressions*, a handy construct for creating ad hoc (anonymous) types based on an existing class or interface. Object expressions are useful when you need a one-off type but don't want to create a formal type. (Although the analogy isn't perfect, you might find it helpful to think of object expressions as lambda expressions for types, because the result of an object expression is an instance of a new type that implements the interface or inherits from a base class.)

For example, consider a simplified game scenario where a character can equip a weapon. You might see a weapon interface and character class like this:

```
type IWeapon =
  abstract Description : string with get
  abstract Power : int with get

type Character(name : string, maxHP : int) =
  member x.Name = name
  member val HP = maxHP with get, set
  member val Weapon : IWeapon option = None with get, set
  member x.Attack(o : Character) =
    let power = match x.Weapon with
                | Some(w) -> w.Power
                | None -> 1 // fists
    o.HP <- System.Math.Max(0, o.HP - power)
  override x.ToString() =
    sprintf "%s: %i/%i" name x.HP maxHP
```

You can use these definitions to create a few characters:

```
let witchKing = Character("Witch-king", 100)
let frodo = Character("Frodo", 50)
```

As currently written, if either character attacked the other he wouldn't do much damage since he has only his fists. It would be nice to give each character a weapon, but all we have right now is the IWeapon interface. We could define types for every weapon we can think of, but it's much more convenient to write a function that creates weapons for us via an object expression.

Object expressions, like the one in the following forgeWeapon function, are defined with the new keyword followed by the type name, the with keyword, and the member definitions all wrapped in braces.

```
let forgeWeapon desc power =
  { new IWeapon with
      member x.Description with get() = desc
      member x.Power with get() = power }
```

With the forgeWeapon function in place, we can create some weapons for our characters.

```
> let morgulBlade = forgeWeapon "Morgul-blade" 25
let sting = forgeWeapon "Sting" 10;;

val morgulBlade : IWeapon
val sting : IWeapon
```

As you can see, both calls to forgeWeapon result in new instances of IWeapon. They can be used as if they had been formally defined through type definitions, as you can see by assigning each to a character and invoking the Attack function:

```
witchKing.Weapon <- Some(morgulBlade)
frodo.Weapon <- Some(sting)

witchKing.Attack frodo
```

Despite their convenience, object expressions aren't suitable for every situation. One of their primary drawbacks is that they must implement every abstract member from the underlying type. If the underlying interface or base class has many abstract members, an object expression can become cumbersome very quickly, so you would probably want to consider using a different construct.

Object expressions aren't limited to a single base type. To implement multiple base types with an object expression, you use an inheritance-like syntax. For instance, if you wanted weapons created through the forgeWeapon function to also implement IDisposable, you could use the following:

```
let forgeWeapon desc power =
  { new IWeapon with
      member x.Description with get() = desc
      member x.Power with get() = power
    interface System.IDisposable with
      member x.Dispose() = printfn "Disposing" }
```

Creating a new weapon is the same as earlier:

```
let narsil = forgeWeapon "Narsil" 25
```

Objects created through object expressions that include multiple base types are always treated as the type listed immediately after the new keyword, unless they're explicitly cast to one of the other types. For example, in the case of the forgeWeapon function, the returned object will be IWeapon unless you cast it to IDisposable.

```
(narsil :?> System.IDisposable).Dispose()
```

Type Extensions

When LINQ was added to the .NET Framework, one exciting feature that it introduced to C# and Visual Basic was extension methods. *Extension methods* allow you to add new methods to an existing type without relying on inheritance or other design patterns such as the Decorator pattern. F# provides similar capabilities except that it doesn't stop with methods. In F#, you can create extension methods, properties, events, and even static members!

You extend existing types in F# through *type extensions*, or *type augmentations*. Type extensions come in two flavors: intrinsic and optional.

Intrinsic extensions must be defined in the same namespace or module, and in the same source file as the type being extended. The new extensions become part of the extended type when the code is compiled and are visible through reflection. Intrinsic extensions are useful when you want to build up a type incrementally by grouping related pieces or as an alternative to building mutually recursive type definitions.

Optional extensions must be defined in a module. Like their C# and Visual Basic counterparts, they are accessible only when their containing namespace or module is open but are not visible through reflection. Optional extensions are most useful for adding custom functionality to types you don't control or that are defined in other assemblies.

Regardless of whether you're defining intrinsic or optional extensions, the syntax is the same. You begin with a new type definition. The difference is that instead of using a primary constructor and an equal sign, you use the with keyword followed by your extension definitions. For example, here we extend the Color struct (in System.Drawing) with both a static and an instance method.

```
module ColorExtensions =
  open System
  open System.Drawing
  open System.Text.RegularExpressions

  // Regular expression to parse the ARGB components from a hex string
❶let private hexPattern =
    Regex("^#(?<color>[\dA-F]{8})$", RegexOptions.IgnoreCase ||| RegexOptions.Compiled)

  // Type extension
❷type Color with
  ❸static member FromHex(hex) =
      match hexPattern.Match hex with
      | matches when matches.Success ->
        Color.FromArgb <| Convert.ToInt32(matches.Groups.["color"].Value, 16)
      | _ -> Color.Empty
  ❹member x.ToHex() = sprintf "#%02X%02X%02X%02X" x.A x.R x.G x.B
```

This optional type extension enhances the Color struct's usability by allowing you to create new instances from known hexadecimal color strings or translate the color into a hexadecimal color string. The type extension itself is at ❷. The static extension method ❸ relies on the regular expression (a domain-specific language for parsing strings) at ❶ to match and extract the hexadecimal value to convert it into the ARGB value passed to Color's constructor. The instance extension method ❹ simply returns the ARGB value formatted as a hexadecimal string.

> **CROSS-LANGUAGE CONSIDERATIONS**
>
> Despite serving a similar purpose, extension methods in F# are implemented differently than in the rest of the .NET Framework. Therefore, optional extension methods defined in F# aren't accessible as extension methods in C# or Visual Basic unless you include the Extension attribute in both the type definition and extension methods.

Summary

Despite F#'s perception as a niche functional language on the .NET Framework, you've seen in this chapter that F# is also a full-featured OO language. Numerous examples demonstrated how F#'s concise syntax aids you in developing robust OO frameworks complete with classes, structures, and interfaces. You've even seen how to implement some common design patterns like Singleton and Factory.

Although F# supports the same common OO concepts as its more established counterpart languages, you've learned how it takes familiar concepts like operator overloading, events, and extension methods and expands them into something much more powerful through observation and type augmentation. Finally, you've seen how entirely new constructs like object expressions can improve code quality by allowing you to create ad hoc types when and where you need them.

5

LET'S GET FUNCTIONAL

I've mentioned several times that F# is a functional language, but as you've learned from previous chapters you can build rich applications in F# without using any functional techniques. Does that mean that F# isn't really a functional language? No. F# is a general-purpose, multiparadigm language that allows you to program in the style most suited to your task. It is considered a functional-first language, meaning that its constructs encourage a functional style. In other words, when developing in F# you should favor functional approaches whenever possible and switch to other styles as appropriate.

In this chapter, we'll see what functional programming really is and how functions in F# differ from those in other languages. Once we've established that foundation, we'll explore several data types commonly used with functional programming and take a brief side trip into lazy evaluation.

What Is Functional Programming?

Functional programming takes a fundamentally different approach toward developing software than object-oriented programming. While object-oriented programming is primarily concerned with managing an ever-changing system state, functional programming emphasizes immutability and the application of deterministic functions. This difference drastically changes the way you build software, because in object-oriented programming you're mostly concerned with defining classes (or structs), whereas in functional programming your focus is on defining functions with particular emphasis on their input and output.

F# is an impure functional language where data is immutable by default, though you can still define mutable data or cause other side effects in your functions. Immutability is part of the functional concept called *referential transparency*, which means that an expression can be replaced with its result without affecting the program's behavior. For example, if you can replace let sum = add 5 10 with let sum = 15 without otherwise affecting the program's behavior, then add is said to be referentially transparent. But immutability and referential transparency are only two aspects of functional programming, and they certainly don't make a language functional on their own.

Programming with Functions

If you've never done any "real" functional programming, F# will forever change the way you think about functions because its functions closely resemble mathematical functions in both structure and behavior. For example, Chapter 3 introduced the unit type, but I avoided discussing its importance in functional programming. Unlike C# and Visual Basic, F# makes no distinction between functions that return values and those that don't. In fact, every function in F# accepts exactly one input value and returns exactly one output value. The unit type enables this behavior. When a function doesn't have any specific input (no parameters), it actually accepts unit. Similarly, when a function doesn't have any specific output, it returns unit.

The fact that every F# function returns a value allows the compiler to make certain assumptions about your code. One important assumption is that the result of the last evaluated expression in a function is the function's return value. This means that although return is a keyword in F#, you don't need to explicitly identify return values.

Functions as Data

A defining (and arguably the most important) characteristic of any functional language is that it treats functions like any other data type. The .NET Framework has always supported this concept to some degree with delegation, but until relatively recently delegation was too cumbersome to be viable in all but a few limited scenarios. Only when LINQ was introduced with the goodness of lambda expressions and the built-in generic delegate types (`Action` and `Func`) did delegation reach its full potential. F# uses delegation behind the scenes, but unlike C# and Visual Basic, its syntax abstracts away the delegation with the `->` token. The `->` token, generally read as "goes to" or "returns," identifies a value as a *function value* where the data type specified on the left is the function's input type and the data type on the right is its return type. For example, the signature for a function that both accepts and returns a string is `string -> string`. Similarly, a parameterless function that returns a string is represented as `unit -> string`.

Signatures become increasingly complex when you begin working with *higher-order functions*—functions that accept or return other functions. Higher-order functions are used extensively in F# (and functional programming in general) because they allow you to isolate common parts of functions and substitute the parts that change.

In some ways, higher-order functions are to functional programming what interfaces are to object-oriented programming. For example, consider a function that applies a transformation to a string and prints the result. Its signature might look something like `(string -> string) -> string -> unit`. This simple notation goes a long way toward making your code more comprehensible than when you're dealing with the delegates directly.

You can use the function signatures in type annotations whenever you're expecting a function. As with other data types, though, the compiler can often infer the function type.

Interoperability Considerations

Despite the fact that F# functions are ultimately based on delegation, be careful when working with libraries written in other .NET languages, because the delegate types aren't interchangeable. F# functions rely on the overloaded `FSharpFunc` delegate types, whereas traditional .NET delegates are often based on the `Func` and `Action` types. If you need to pass `Func` and `Action` delegates into an F# assembly, you can use the following class to simplify the conversion.

```
open System.Runtime.CompilerServices

[<Extension>]
type public FSharpFuncUtil =
  [<Extension>]
  static member ToFSharpFunc<'a, 'b> (func : System.Func<'a, 'b>) =
    fun x -> func.Invoke(x)

  [<Extension>]
  static member ToFSharpFunc<'a> (act : System.Action<'a>) =
    fun x -> act.Invoke(x)
```

The `FSharpFuncUtil` class defines the overloaded `ToFSharpFunc` method as traditional .NET extension methods (via the `ExtensionAttribute` on both the class and methods) so you can easily call them from another language. The first overload handles converting single-parameter Func instances, while the second handles single-parameter Action instances. These extension methods don't cover every use case, but they're certainly a good starting point.

Currying

Functions in F# work a bit differently than you're probably accustomed to. For example, consider the simple add function, introduced in Chapter 2.

```
let add a b = a + b
```

You might think that add accepts two parameters, but that's not how F# functions work. Remember, in F# every function accepts exactly one input and returns exactly one output. If you create the preceding binding in FSI or hover over the name in Visual Studio, you'll see that its signature is:

```
val add : a:int -> b:int -> int
```

Here, the name add is bound to a function that accepts an integer (a) and returns a function. The returned function accepts an integer (b) and returns an integer. Understanding this automatic function chaining—called *currying*—is critical to using F# effectively because it enables several other features that affect how you design functions.

To better illustrate how currying actually works, let's rewrite add to more closely resemble the compiled code.

```
> let add a = fun b -> (+) a b;;

val add : a:int -> b:int -> int
```

The most significant thing here is that both this and the previous version have exactly the same signature. Here, though, add accepts only a single parameter (a) and returns a separate function as defined by a lambda expression. The returned function accepts the second parameter (b) and invokes the multiplication operator as another function call.

Partial Application

One of the capabilities unlocked by curried functions is partial application. *Partial application* allows you to create new functions from existing ones simply by supplying some of the arguments. For example, in the case of add, you could use partial application to create a new addTen function that always adds 10 to a number.

```
> let addTen = add 10;;

val addTen : ❶(int -> int)
```

```
> addTen 10;;
val it : int = 20
```

Notice at ❶ how addTen's definition and signature are listed. Although we didn't explicitly include any parameters in the definition, the signature is still a function that both accepts and returns an integer. The compiler evaluated the curried add function as far as it could with the provided arguments (just 10, in this case) and bound the resulting function to the name, addTen.

Currying applies arguments one at a time, from left to right, so partially applied arguments must correspond to the function's first parameters.

Once you're comfortable with currying and partial application, you may start thinking that you could simulate them in C# or Visual Basic by returning Func or Action instances. Don't. Neither language is designed to support this type of functional programming, so simulating these concepts is inelegant at best and immensely error prone at worst.

Pipelining

Another feature often associated with currying (and used extensively in F#) is pipelining. *Pipelining* allows you to create your own function chains by evaluating one expression and sending the result to another function as the final argument.

Forward Pipelining

Usually you'll send values forward to the next function using the *forward pipelining operator* (|>). If you don't want to do anything with a function's result when it returns something other than unit, you can pipe the result forward to the ignore function like this:

```
add 2 3 |> ignore
```

Pipelining isn't restricted to simple scenarios like ignoring a result. As long as the last argument of the receiving function is compatible with the source function's return type, you can create complex function chains. For example, suppose you have a list of daily temperatures in degrees Fahrenheit and want to find the average temperature, convert it to Celsius, and print the result. You could do it the old-fashioned, procedural way by defining a binding for each step, or you could use pipelining to chain the steps like this:

```
let fahrenheitToCelsius degreesF = (degreesF - 32.0) * (5.0 / 9.0)

let marchHighTemps = [ 33.0; 30.0; 33.0; 38.0; 36.0; 31.0; 35.0;
                       42.0; 53.0; 65.0; 59.0; 42.0; 31.0; 41.0;
                       49.0; 45.0; 37.0; 42.0; 40.0; 32.0; 33.0;
                       42.0; 48.0; 36.0; 34.0; 38.0; 41.0; 46.0;
                       54.0; 57.0; 59.0 .]
```

```
marchHighTemps
|> List.average
|> fahrenheitToCelsius
|> printfn "March Average (C): %f"
```

Here the marchHighTemps list is piped to the List module's average function. The average function is then evaluated and its result passed on to the fahrenheitToCelsius function. Finally, the average temperature in Celsius is passed along to printfn.

Backward Pipelining

Like its forward counterpart, the *backward pipelining operator* (<|) sends the result of an expression to another function as the final argument, but does it from right to left instead. Because it changes precedence within an expression, the backward pipelining operator is sometimes used as a replacement for parentheses.

The backward pipelining operator can change the semantics of your code. For instance, in the fahrenheitToCelsius example in the previous section, the emphasis is on the list of temperatures because that's what's listed first. To change the semantics to emphasize the output, you could place the printfn function call ahead of the backward pipelining operator.

```
printfn "March Average (F): %f" <| List.average marchHighTemps
```

Noncurried Functions

Although pipelining is typically associated with curried functions, it also works with noncurried functions (like methods) that accept only a single argument. For instance, to force a delay in execution you could pipe a value into the TimeSpan class's static FromSeconds method and then send the resulting TimeSpan object to Thread.Sleep, as shown here.

```
5.0
|> System.TimeSpan.FromSeconds
|> System.Threading.Thread.Sleep
```

Because neither the TimeSpan class nor the Thread class is defined in F#, the functions aren't curried, but you can see how we can chain these functions together with the forward pipelining operator.

Function Composition

Like pipelining, *function composition* allows you to create function chains. It comes in two forms: forward (>>) and backward (<<).

Function composition is subject to the same rules as pipelining regarding inputs and outputs. Where function composition differs is that instead of defining a one-time operation, the composition operators actually generate new functions. Continuing with our average temperature example, you could easily create a new function from the List.average and fahrenheitToCelsius functions with the forward composition operator.

```
> let averageInCelsius = List.average >> fahrenheitToCelsius;;

val averageInCelsius : (float list -> float)
```

The composition operator results in a new function that accepts a list of floats and returns a float. Now, instead of calling the two functions independently, you can simply call averageInCelsius instead.

```
printfn "March average (C): %f" <| averageInCelsius marchHighTemps
```

As with pipelining, you can compose functions from noncurried functions. For instance, you could compose the forced delay example from "Noncurried Functions" on page 108 as well.

```
> let delay = System.TimeSpan.FromSeconds >> System.Threading.Thread.Sleep;;

val delay : (float -> unit)
```

As you might expect, you can now call the delay function to temporarily pause execution.

```
> delay 5.0;;
val it : unit = ()
```

Recursive Functions

There are typically three looping constructs associated with imperative code: while loops, simple for loops, and enumerable for loops. Because each relies on a state change to determine when the exit criteria have been met, you'll need to take a different approach to looping when writing purely functional code. In functional programming, the preferred looping mechanism is *recursion*. A *recursive function* is one that calls itself either directly or indirectly through another function.

Although methods within a type are implicitly recursive, let-bound functions, such as those defined within a module, are not. To make a let-bound function recursive, you must include the rec keyword in its definition, as this factorial function illustrates.

```
let rec factorial v =
  match v with | 1L -> 1L
               | _ -> v * factorial (v - 1L)
```

The rec keyword instructs the compiler to make the function name available within the function but does not otherwise change the function's signature (`int64 -> int64`).

Tail-Call Recursion

The preceding factorial example is simple, but it suffers from a major flaw. For example, consider what happens when you call `factorial 5`. On each recursive iteration (other than when the value is 1), the function calculates the product of v and the factorial of v - 1. In other words, calculating the factorial for a given value inherently requires each subsequent factorial call to complete. At run time, it looks a bit like this:

```
5L * (factorial 4L)
5L * (4L * (factorial 3L))
5L * (4L * (3L * (factorial 2L)))
-- snip --
```

The preceding snippet shows that each call is added to the stack. It's unlikely that this would be a problem with a factorial function, since the calculation can quickly overflow the data type, but more complex recursion scenarios could result in running out of stack space. To address this problem, you can revise the function to use a *tail call* by removing the dependency on subsequent iterations, as shown here:

```
❶ let factorial v =
    let ❷rec fact c p =
      match c with | 0L -> p
                   | _ -> ❸fact <| c - 1L <| c * p
    ❹fact v 1L
```

The revised factorial function ❶ creates and then calls a nested recursive function, fact ❷, to isolate the implementation details. The fact function accepts both the current iteration value (c) and the product calculated by the previous iteration (p). At ❸ (the nonzero case), the fact function makes the recursive call. (Notice how only the arguments to the recursive call are calculated here.) Finally, to initiate recursion, the factorial function ❹ invokes the first fact iteration, passing the supplied value and 1L.

Although the recursive call is still present in the code, when the F# compiler detects that no iteration is dependent on subsequent iterations, it optimizes the compiled form by replacing the recursion with an imperative loop. This allows the system to iterate as long as necessary. You can observe this optimization by examining the stack traces for each version by inserting a breakpoint and looking at the call stack window (if you're running this as a console application) or by printing out the stack information returned from `System.Diagnostics.StackTrace`, as shown here. (Note that your namespaces will likely vary.)

Standard recursion
```
   at FSI_0024.printTrace()
   at FSI_0028.factorial(Int64 v)
   at FSI_0028.factorial(Int64 v)
   at FSI_0028.factorial(Int64 v)
   at FSI_0028.factorial(Int64 v)
   at FSI_0028.factorial(Int64 v)
   at <StartupCode$FSI_0029>.$FSI_0029.main@()
   -- snip --
```

Tail recursion
```
   at FSI_0024.printTrace()
   at FSI_0030.fact@75-8(Int64 c, Int64 p)
   at <StartupCode$FSI_0031>.$FSI_0031.main@()
   -- snip --
```

Mutually Recursive Functions

When two or more functions call each other recursively, they are said to be *mutually recursive*. Like mutually recursive types (described in Chapter 4), mutually recursive functions must be defined together with the and keyword. For example, a Fibonacci number calculation is easily expressed through mutual recursion.

```
let fibonacci n =
  let rec f = function
            | 1 -> 1
            | n -> g (n - 1)
  and g = function
          | 1 -> 0
          | n -> g (n - 1) + f (n - 1)
  f n + g n
```

The preceding fibonacci function defines two mutually recursive functions, f and g. (The function keyword inside each is a shortcut for pattern matching.) For all values other than 1, f calls g. Similarly, g recursively calls itself and f.

Because the mutual recursion is hidden inside fibonacci, consumers of this code can simply call fibonacci directly. For example, to compute the sixth number in the Fibonacci sequence you'd write:

```
> fibonacci 6;;
val it : int = 8
```

Mutual recursion can be useful, but this example is really only good for illustrating the concept. For performance reasons, a more realistic Fibonacci example would likely forego mutual recursion in favor of a technique called *memoization*, where expensive computations are performed once and the results are cached to avoid calculating the same values multiple times.

Lambda Expressions

If you've ever used LINQ or done any other functional programming, you're probably already familiar with *lambda expressions* (or *function expressions*, as they're sometimes called). Lambda expressions are used extensively in functional programming. In brief, they provide a convenient way to define simple, single-use, anonymous (unnamed) functions. Lambda expressions are typically favored over let-bound functions when the function is significant only within its context (such as when filtering a collection).

Lambda expression syntax is similar to that of a function value except that it begins with the fun keyword, omits the function identifier, and uses the arrow token (->) in place of an equal sign. For example, you could express the Fahrenheit-to-Celsius conversion function inline as a lambda expression and immediately evaluate it like this:

```
(fun degreesF -> (degreesF - 32.0) * (5.0 / 9.0)) 212.0
```

Although defining ad hoc functions like this is certainly one use for lambda expressions, they're more commonly created inline with calls to higher-order functions, or included in pipeline chains.

Closures

Closures enable functions to access values visible in the scope where a function is defined regardless of whether that value is part of the function. Although closures are typically associated with lambda expressions, nested functions created with let bindings can be closures as well, since ultimately they both compile to either an FSharpFunc or a formal method. Closures are typically used to isolate some state. For instance, consider the quintessential closure example—a function that returns a function that manipulates an internal counter value, as shown here:

```
let createCounter() =
  let count = ref 0
  (fun () -> count := !count + 1
             !count)
```

The createCounter function defines a reference cell that's captured by the returned function. Because the reference cell is in scope when the returned function is created, the function has access to it no matter when it's called. This allows you to simulate a stateful object without a formal type definition.

To observe the function modifying the reference cell's value, we just need to invoke the generated function and call it like this:

```
let increment = createCounter()
for i in [1..10] do printfn "%i" (increment())
```

Functional Types

F# includes native support for several additional data types. These types—tuples, records, and discriminated unions—are typically associated with functional programming, but they're often useful in mixed-paradigm development as well. While each of these types has a specific purpose, they're all intended to help you remain focused on the problem your software is trying to solve.

Tuples

The most basic functional type is the *tuple*. Tuples are a convenient way to group a number of values within a single immutable construct without creating a custom type. Tuples are expressed as comma-delimited lists and are sometimes enclosed in parentheses. For example, the following two definitions representing geometric points as tuples are equally valid.

```
> let point1 = 10.0, 10.0;;

val point1 : float * float = (10.0, 10.0)

> let point2 = (20.0, 20.0);;

val point2 : float * float = (20.0, 20.0)
```

The signature for a tuple type includes the type of each value separated by an asterisk (*). The asterisk is used as the tuple element delimiter for mathematical reasons: Tuples represent the Cartesian product of all values their elements contain. Therefore, to express a tuple in a type annotation, you write it as an asterisk-delimited list of types like this:

```
let point : float * float = 0.0, 0.0
```

Despite some syntactic similarities, particularly when the values are enclosed in parentheses, it's important to recognize that other than the fact that they contain multiple values, tuples aren't collections; they simply group a fixed number of values within a single construct. The tuple types don't implement IEnumerable<'T>, so they can't be enumerated or iterated over in an enumerable for loop, and individual tuple values are exposed only through properties with nonspecific names like Item1 and Item2.

Extracting Values

Tuples are often useful for returning multiple values from a function or for sending multiple values to a function without currying them. For instance, to calculate the slope of a line you could pass two points as tuples to a slope function. To make the function work, though, you'll need some way to access the individual values. (Fortunately, tupled values are always accessible in the order in which they're defined, so some of the guesswork is eliminated.)

When working with *pairs* (tuples containing two values like the geometric points we discussed previously), you can use the fst and snd functions to retrieve the first and second values, respectively, as shown here.

```
let slope p1 p2 =
  let x1 = fst p1
  let y1 = snd p1
  let x2 = fst p2
  let y2 = snd p2
  (y1 - y2) / (x1 - x2)

slope (13.0, 8.0) (1.0, 2.0)
```

Notice how we define bindings for the various coordinates with the fst and snd functions. As you can see, however, extracting each value this way can get pretty tedious and these functions work only with pairs; if you were to try either against a *triple* (a tuple with three values), you'd get a type mismatch. (The reason is that at their core, tuples compile to one of the nine generic overloads of the Tuple class.) Aside from sharing a common name, the tuple classes are independent of each other and are otherwise incompatible.

A more practical approach to extract tuple values involves introducing a *Tuple pattern*. Tuple patterns allow you to specify an identifier for each value in the tuple by separating the identifiers with commas. For example, here's the slope function revised to use Tuple patterns instead of the pair functions.

```
let slope p1 p2 =
  let x1, y1 = p1
  let x2, y2 = p2
  (y1 - y2) / (x1 - x2)
```

You can see how Tuple patterns may help, but you need to be careful with them. If your pattern doesn't match the number of values in the tuple, you'll get a type mismatch.

Fortunately, unlike the pair functions, resolving the problem is simply a matter of adding or removing identifiers. If you don't care about a particular value in your Tuple pattern, you can ignore it with the Wildcard pattern (_). For instance, if you have three-dimensional coordinates but care only about the z-coordinate, you could ignore the x- and y-values as follows:

```
> let _, _, z = (10.0, 10.0, 10.0);;

val z : int = 10
```

Tuple patterns aren't limited to let bindings. In fact, we can make a further revision to the slope function and include the patterns right in the function signature!

```
let slope (x1, y1) (x2, y2) = (y1 - y2) / (x1 - x2)
```

Equality Semantics

Despite the fact that they're formally reference types, each of the built-in tuple types implements the IStructuralEquatable interface. This ensures that all equality comparisons involve comparing the individual component values rather than checking that two tuple instances reference the same Tuple object in memory. In other words, two tuple instances are considered equal when the corresponding component values in each instance are the same, as shown here:

```
> (1, 2) = (1, 2);;
val it : bool = true
> (2, 1) = (1, 2);;
val it : bool = false
```

For the same reasons that the fst and snd functions work only with pairs, comparing tuples of different lengths will cause an error.

Syntactic Tuples

So far, all of the tuples we've looked have been concrete ones, but F# also includes *syntactic tuples*. For the most part, syntactic tuples are how F# works around noncurried functions in other languages. Because F# functions always accept a single parameter, but functions in C# and Visual Basic can accept more than one, in order to call functions from libraries written in other languages you can use a syntactic tuple and let the compiler work out the details.

For example, the `String` class's `Format` method accepts both a format string and a params array of values. If `String.Format` were a curried function, you'd expect its signature to be something like `Format : format:string -> params args : obj [] -> string`, but it's not. Instead, if you hover your cursor over the function name in Visual Studio, you'll see that its signature is actually `Format(format:string, params args : obj [])  : string`. This distinction is significant because it means that the arguments must be applied as a group rather than individually as they would with curried functions. If you were to try invoking the method as a curried F# function, you'd get an error like this:

```
> System.String.Format "hello {0}" "Dave";;

System.String.Format "hello {0}" "Dave";;
^^^^^^^^^^^^^^^^^^^^^^^^^^^^^^^^^^^^^^^^

stdin(3,1): error FS0003: This value is not a function and cannot be applied
```

The correct way to call `String.Format` in F# is with a syntactic tuple, like this:

```
> System.String.Format ("hello {0}", "Dave");;
val it : string = "hello Dave"
```

You've probably noticed that F# generally doesn't require parentheses around arguments when calling a function; it uses parentheses primarily to establish precedence. Because functions are applied from left to right, you'll mainly use parentheses in a function call to pass the result of another function as an argument. In this case, the parentheses around the arguments are necessary. Without them, the left-to-right evaluation would cause the compiler to essentially treat the expression as `((System.String.Format "hello {0}"), "Dave")`. In general, it's good practice to include parentheses around syntactic tuples in order to remove any ambiguity.

Out Parameters

F# doesn't directly support out parameters—parameters passed by reference with values assigned in the method body so they can be returned to the caller. To fully support the .NET Framework, however, F# needs a way to access out parameter values. For example, the `TryParse` methods on the various numeric data type classes attempt to convert a string to the corresponding numeric type and return a Boolean value indicating success or failure. If the conversion succeeds, the `TryParse` methods set the out parameter to the appropriate converted value. For instance, calling `System.Int32.TryParse` with `"10"` would return true and set the out parameter to `10`. Similarly, calling the same function with `"abc"` would return `false` and leave the out parameter unchanged.

In C#, calling System.Int32.TryParse would look like this:

```
// C#
❶ int v;
var r = System.Int32.TryParse("10", out v);
```

The problem with out parameters in a functional language is that they require a side effect, as shown by the uninitialized variable at ❶. To work around this problem, the F# compiler converts the return value and out parameter to a pair. Therefore, when you invoke a method with an out parameter in F#, you treat it exactly like any other tuple-returning function.

Calling the same Int32.TryParse method in F# looks like this:

```
// F#
let r, v = System.Int32.TryParse "10"
```

For a behind-the-scenes look at the generated class, we can once again turn to ILSpy to see how it's represented in C#.

```
// C#
using System;
using System.Diagnostics;
using System.Runtime.CompilerServices;
namespace <StartupCode$Samples>
{
  internal static class $Samples
  {
    [DebuggerBrowsable(DebuggerBrowsableState.Never)]
    internal static readonly Tuple<bool, int> patternInput@3;
    [DebuggerBrowsable(DebuggerBrowsableState.Never)]
    internal static readonly int v@3;
    [DebuggerBrowsable(DebuggerBrowsableState.Never)]
    internal static readonly bool r@3;
    [DebuggerBrowsable(DebuggerBrowsableState.Never), DebuggerNonUserCode, CompilerGenerated]
    internal static int init@;
  ❶ static $Samples()
    {
      int item = 0;
      $Samples.patternInput@3 = ❷new Tuple<bool, int>(❸int.TryParse("10", out item), item);
    ❹$Samples.v@3 = Samples.patternInput@3.Item2;
    ❺$Samples.r@3 = Samples.patternInput@3.Item1;
    }
  }
}
```

Here, the F# compiler wrapped the Int32.TryParse call inside a static class. The generated class's static constructor ❶ invokes TryParse at ❸ and wraps the results in a tuple at ❷. Then, the internal v@3 and r@3 fields are assigned to the out parameter value and the return value at ❹ and ❺, respectively. In turn, the v and r values defined by the let binding are compiled to read-only properties that return the v@3 and r@3 values.

Record Types

Like tuples, *record types* allow you to group values in a single immutable construct. You might think of them as bridging the functional gap between tuples and your own classes. Record types provide many of the same conveniences as tuples, like simple syntax and value equality semantics, while offering you some control over their internal structure and allowing you to add custom functionality.

Defining Record Types

Record type definitions consist of the type keyword, an identifier, and a list of labels with type annotations all enclosed in braces. For example, this listing shows a simple record type representing an RGB color.

```
> type rgbColor = { R : byte; G : byte; B : byte };;

type rgbColor =
  {R: byte;
   G: byte;
   B: byte;}
```

If you take a peek at what the compiler generates from this definition, you'll see a sealed class with read-only properties, equality semantics, and a single constructor to initialize all values.

NOTE   *When defining record types on a single line, you must separate each label and type annotation pair by semicolons. If you place each pair on a separate line, you can safely omit the semicolons.*

Creating Records

New records are created via *record expressions*. Record expressions allow you to specify a value for each label in the record type. For example, you could create a new rgbColor instance using a record expression, as shown next. (Note that, as when defining a record type, you must separate each label or assignment pair by semicolons or place it on a line of its own.)

```
> let red = { R = 255uy; G = 0uy; B = 0uy };;

val red : rgbColor = {R = 255uy;
                      G = 0uy;
                      B = 0uy;}
```

Notice that nowhere in the record expression do we include an explicit reference to the rgbColor type. This is another example of F#'s type inference engine at work. Based on the labels alone, the compiler was able to infer that we were creating an instance of rgbColor. Because the compiler relies on the labels rather than position to determine the correct type, order doesn't matter. This means that you can place the label and value pairs in any order. Here, we create an rgbColor instance with the labels in G, B, R order.

```
> let red = { G = 0uy; B = 0uy; R = 255uy };;

val red : rgbColor = {R = 255uy;
                      G = 0uy;
                      B = 0uy;}
```

Unlike with tuples, we don't need to use special value extraction functions like fst or snd with record types, because each value can be accessed by its label. For instance, a function that converts an rgbColor value to its hexadecimal string equivalent might look like this:

```
let rgbColorToHex (c : rgbColor) =
  sprintf "#%02X%02X%02X" c.R c.G c.B
```

Avoiding Naming Conflicts

The compiler can usually infer the correct type, but it's possible to define two record types with the same structure. Consider what happens when you add a color type with the same structure as rgbColor.

```
> type rgbColor = { R : byte; G : byte; B : byte }
type color = { R : byte; G : byte; B : byte };;

type rgbColor =
  {R: byte;
   G: byte;
   B: byte;}
type color =
  {R: byte;
   G: byte;
   B: byte;}

> let red = { R = 255uy; G = 0uy; B = 0uy };;

val red : ❶color = {R = 255uy;
                    G = 0uy;
                    B = 0uy;}
```

Despite having two record types with the same structure, type inference still succeeds, but notice at ❶ that the resulting type is color. Due to F#'s top-down evaluation, the compiler uses the most recently defined type that matches the labels. If your goal was to define red as color you'd be fine, but if you wanted rgbColor instead you'd have to be a bit more explicit in your record expression and include the type name, as shown here:

```
> let red = { ❶rgbColor.R = 255uy; G = 0uy; B = 0uy };;

val red : ❷rgbColor = {R = 255uy;
                       G = 0uy;
                       B = 0uy;}
```

By qualifying one of the names with the type name at ❶, you bypass type inference and the correct type is resolved ❷. (Although you can technically qualify the type on any name, the convention is to do it on either the first one or all of them.)

Copying Records

Not only can you use record expressions to create new record instances from scratch, but you can also use them to create new record instances from existing ones by copying values forward and setting new values for one or more properties. The alternate syntax, called a *copy and update record expression*, makes it easy to create yellow from red, as shown here:

```
> let red = { R = 255uy; G = 0uy; B = 0uy }
let yellow = { red with G = 255uy };;

val red : color = {R = 255uy;
                   G = 0uy;
                   B = 0uy;}
val yellow : color = {R = 255uy;
                      G = 255uy;
                      B = 0uy;}
```

To specify new values for multiple properties, separate them with semicolons.

Mutability

Like virtually everything else in F#, record types are immutable by default. However, because their syntax is so convenient, they're commonly used in place of classes. In many cases, though, these scenarios require mutability. To make record type properties mutable within F#, use the mutable keyword just as with a let binding. For instance, you could make all of rgbColor's members mutable like this:

```
> type rgbColor = { mutable R : byte
                    mutable G : byte
                    mutable B : byte };;

type rgbColor =
  {mutable R: byte;
   mutable G: byte;
   mutable B: byte;}
```

When a record type property is mutable, you can change its value with the standard assignment operator (<-) like this:

```
let myColor = { R = 255uy; G = 255uy; B = 255uy }
myColor.G <- 100uy
```

Additional Members

Because record types are really just syntactic sugar for classes, you can define additional members just as you would on a class. For example, you could augment rgbColor with a method that returns its hexadecimal string equivalent like this:

```
type rgbColor = { R : byte; G : byte; B : byte }
            member x.ToHexString() =
                sprintf "#%02X%02X%02X" x.R x.G x.B
```

Now you can call the ToHexString method on any rgbColor instance.

```
> red.ToHexString();;
val it : string = "#FF0000"
```

Additional members on record types can also be static. For example, suppose you wanted to expose a few common colors as static properties on a record type. You could do this:

```
type rgbColor = { R : byte; G : byte; B : byte }
            -- snip --
            static member Red = { R = 255uy; G = 0uy; B = 0uy }
            static member Green = { R = 0uy; G = 255uy; B = 0uy }
            static member Blue = { R = 0uy; G = 0uy; B = 255uy }
```

The static Red, Green, and Blue properties behave like any other static member and can be used anywhere you need an rgbColor instance.

```
> rgbColor.Red.ToHexString();;
val it : string = "#FF0000"
```

You can also create custom operators for your record types as static members. Let's implement the addition operator to add two rgbColor instances.

```
open System
type rgbColor = { R : byte; G : byte; B : byte }
            -- snip --
            static member (+) (l : rgbColor, r : rgbColor) =
               { R = Math.Min(255uy, l.R + r.R)
                 G = Math.Min(255uy, l.G + r.G)
                 B = Math.Min(255uy, l.B + r.B) }
```

The operator overload on rgbColor is defined and invoked like any other operator:

```
> let yellow = { R = 255uy; G = 0uy; B = 0uy } +
               { R = 0uy; G = 255uy; B = 0uy };;

val yellow : rgbColor = {R = 255uy;
                         G = 255uy;
                         B = 0uy;}
```

Discriminated Unions

Discriminated unions are user-defined data types whose values are restricted to a known set of values called *union cases*. There are no equivalent structures in the other popular .NET languages.

At first glance, you might mistake some simple discriminated unions for enumerations because their syntax is so similar, but they're entirely different constructs. For one, enumerations simply define labels for known integral values, but they aren't restricted to those values. By contrast, the only valid values for discriminated unions are their union cases. Furthermore, each union case can either stand on its own or contain associated immutable data.

The built-in Option<'T> type highlights each of these points. We're really only interested in its definition here, so let's take a look at that.

```
type Option<'T> =
| None
| Some of 'T
```

Option<'T> defines two cases, None and Some. None is an empty union case, meaning that it doesn't contain any associated data. On the other hand, Some has an associated instance of 'T as indicated by the of keyword.

To demonstrate how discriminated unions enforce a specific set of values, let's define a simple function that accepts a generic option and writes out the associated value when the option is Some, or "None" when the option is None:

```
let showValue (v : _ option) =
  printfn "%s" (match v with
                | Some x -> x.ToString()
                | None -> "None")
```

When we invoke this function, we simply need to provide one of the option cases:

```
> Some 123 |> showValue;;
123
val it : unit = ()
> Some "abc" |> showValue;;
abc
val it : unit = ()
> None |> showValue;;
None
val it : unit = ()
```

Notice how in each of the three calls to showValue, we specified only the union case names. The compiler resolved both Some and None as Option<'T>. (In the event of a naming conflict, you can qualify the case names with the discriminated union name just as you would with a record type.) However, if you were to call showValue with a value other than Some or None, the compiler will raise an error like this:

```
> showValue "xyz";;

  showValue "xyz";;
  ----------^^^^^

stdin(9,11): error FS0001: This expression was expected to have type
    Option<'a>
but here has type
    string
```

Defining Discriminated Unions

Like other types, discriminated union definitions begin with the type keyword. Union cases are delimited with bars. The bar before the first union case is optional, but omitting it when there's only one case can be confusing because it will make the definition look like a type abbreviation. In fact, if you omit the bar in a single-case discriminated union and there is no data associated with the case, the compiler will treat the definition as a type abbreviation when there is a naming conflict with another type.

The normal rules for identifiers apply when you are defining union cases, with one exception: Union case names must begin with an uppercase letter to help the compiler differentiate union cases from other identifiers in pattern matching. If a case name does not begin with an uppercase letter, the compiler will raise an error.

In practice, discriminated unions typically serve one of three purposes:

- Representing simple object hierarchies
- Representing tree structures
- Replacing type abbreviations

Simple Object Hierarchies

Discriminated unions are commonly used to represent simple object hierarchies. In fact, they excel at this task so much that they're often used as a substitute for formal classes and inheritance.

Imagine working on a system that needs some basic geometry functionality. In an object-oriented environment, such functionality would probably consist of an IShape interface and a number of concrete shape classes like Circle, Rectangle, and Triangle, with each implementing IShape. A possible implementation might look like this:

```
type IShape = interface end

type Circle(r : float) =
  interface IShape
  member x.Radius = r

type Rectangle(w : float, h : float) =
  interface IShape
  member x.Width = w
  member x.Height = h

type Triangle(l1 : float, l2 : float, l3 : float) =
  interface IShape
  member x.Leg1 = l1
  member x.Leg2 = l2
  member x.Leg3 = l3
```

Discriminated unions offer a cleaner alternative that is less prone to side effects. Here's what that same object hierarchy might look like as a discriminated union:

```
type Shape =
/// Describes a circle by its radius
| Circle of float
/// Describes a rectangle by its width and height
| Rectangle of ❶float * float
/// Describes a triangle by its three sides
| Triangle of ❷float * float * float
```

The Shape type defines three cases: Circle, Rectangle, and Triangle. Each case has at least one attached value specific to the shape it represents. Notice at ❶ and ❷ how the tuple syntax is used to associate multiple data values with a case. But despite using the tuple syntax, cases don't actually compile to tuples. Instead, each associated data item compiles to an individual property that follows the tuple naming pattern (that is, Item1, Item2, and so on). This distinction is important because there's no direct conversion from a union case to a tuple, meaning that you can't use them interchangeably. The only real exception to this rule is that when the types are wrapped in parentheses the compiler will interpret the grouping as a tuple. In other words, the compiler treats of string * int and of (string * int) differently; the former is tuple-like, while the latter actually is a tuple. Unless you really need a true tuple, though, use the default format.

As you'd expect, creating Shape instances is the same as creating Option<'T> instances. For example, here's how to create an instance of each case:

```
let c = Circle(3.0)
let r = Rectangle(10.0, 12.0)
let t = Triangle(25.0, 20.0, 7.0)
```

One of the major annoyances with the tuple syntax for multiple associated values is that it's easy to forget what each position represents. To work around the issue, include XML documentation comments—like those preceding each case in this section's Shape definition—as a reminder.

Fortunately, relief is available. One of the language enhancements in F# 3.1 is support for named union type fields. The refined syntax resembles a hybrid of the current tupled syntax and type-annotated field definitions. For example, under the new syntax, Shape could be redefined as follows.

```
type Shape =
| Circle of Radius : float
| Rectangle of Width : float * Height : float
| Triangle of Leg1 : float * Leg2 : float * Leg3 : float
```

For discriminated unions defined with the F# 3.1 syntax, creating new case instances is significantly more developer friendly—not only because the labels appear in IntelliSense, but also because you can use named arguments like this:

```
let c = Circle(Radius = 3.0)
let r = Rectangle(Width = 10.0, Height = 12.0)
let t = Triangle(Leg1 = 25.0, Leg2 = 20.0, Leg3 = 7.0)
```

Tree Structures

Discriminated unions can also be *self-referencing*, meaning that the data associated with a union case can be another case from the same union. This is handy for creating simple trees like this one, which represents a rudimentary markup structure:

```
type Markup =
| ContentElement of string * ❶Markup list
| EmptyElement of string
| Content of string
```

Most of this definition should be familiar by now, but notice that the ContentElement case has an associated string and list of Markup values.

The nested Markup list ❶ makes it trivial to construct a simple HTML document like the following. Here, ContentElement nodes represent elements (such as html, head, and body) that contain additional content, while Content nodes represent raw text contained within a ContentElement.

```
let movieList =
  ContentElement("html",
    [ ContentElement("head", [ ContentElement("title", [ Content "Guilty Pleasures" ])])
      ContentElement("body",
        [ ContentElement("article",
            [ ContentElement("h1", [ Content "Some Guilty Pleasures" ])
              ContentElement("p",
                [ Content "These are "
                  ContentElement("strong", [ Content "a few" ])
                  Content " of my guilty pleasures" ])
              ContentElement("ul",
                [ ContentElement("li", [ Content "Crank (2006)" ])
                  ContentElement("li", [ Content "Starship Troopers (1997)" ])
                  ContentElement("li", [ Content "RoboCop (1987)" ])])])])])
```

To convert the preceding tree structure to an actual HTML document, you could write a simple recursive function with a match expression to handle each union case, like this:

```
let rec toHtml markup =
  match markup with
  | ❶ContentElement (tag, children) ->
      use w = new System.IO.StringWriter()
      children
        |> Seq.map toHtml
        |> Seq.iter (fun (s : string) -> w.Write(s))
      sprintf "<%s>%s</%s>" tag (w.ToString()) tag
  | ❷EmptyElement (tag) -> sprintf "<%s />" tag
  | ❸Content (c) -> sprintf "%s" c
```

The match expression is used here roughly like a switch statement in C# or a SELECT CASE statement in Visual Basic. Each match case, denoted by a vertical pipe (|), matches against an Identifier pattern that includes the union case name and identifiers for each of its associated values. For instance, the match case at ❶ matches ContentElement items and represents the associated values with the tag and children identifiers within the case body (the part after the arrow). Likewise, the match cases at ❷ and ❸ match the EmptyElement and Content cases, respectively. (Note that because match expressions return a value, each match case's return type must be the same.)

Invoking the toHtml function with movieList results in the following HTML (formatted for readability). As you look over the resulting HTML, try tracing each element back to its node in movieList.

```
<html>
  <head>
    <title>Guilty Pleasures</title>
  </head>
  <body>
    <article>
        <h1>Some Guilty Pleasures</h1>
        <p>These are <strong>a few</strong> of my guilty pleasures</p>
        <ul>
            <li>Crank (2006)</li>
            <li>Starship Troopers (1997)</li>
            <li>RoboCop (1987)</li>
        </ul>
    </article>
  </body>
</html>
```

Replacing Type Abbreviations

Single-case discriminated unions can be a useful alternative to type abbreviations, which, while nice for aliasing existing types, don't provide any additional type safety. For instance, suppose you've defined UserId as an alias for System.Guid and you have a function UserId -> User. Although the function accepts UserId, nothing prevents you from sending in an arbitrary Guid, no matter what that Guid actually represents.

Let's extend the markup examples from the previous section to show how single-case discriminated unions can solve this problem. If you wanted to display the generated HTML in a browser, you could define a function like this:

```
open System.IO

❶ type HtmlString = string

let displayHtml (html ❷: HtmlString) =
  let fn = Path.Combine(Path.GetTempPath(), "HtmlDemo.htm")
  let bytes = System.Text.UTF8Encoding.UTF8.GetBytes html
  using (new FileStream(fn, FileMode.Create, FileAccess.Write))
      (fun fs -> fs.Write(bytes, 0, bytes.Length))
  System.Diagnostics.Process.Start(fn).WaitForExit()
  File.Delete fn
```

The actual mechanics of the displayHtml function aren't important for this discussion. Instead, focus your attention on ❶ the HtmlString type abbreviation and ❷ the type annotation explicitly stating that the html parameter is an HtmlString.

It's clear from the signature that the displayHtml function expects the supplied string to contain HTML, but because HtmlString is merely a type abbreviation there's nothing ensuring that it actually is HTML. As written, both movieList |> toHtml |> displayHtml and "abc123" |> displayHtml are valid.

To introduce a bit more type safety, we can replace the HtmlString definition with a single-case discriminated union, like this:

```
type HtmlString = | HtmlString of string
```

Now that HtmlString is a discriminated union, we need to change the displayHtml function to extract the associated string. We can do this in one of two ways. The first option requires us to change the function's signature to include an Identifier pattern. Alternatively, we can leave the signature alone and introduce an intermediate binding (also using an Identifier pattern) for the associated value. The first option is cleaner, so that's the approach we'll use.

```
let displayHtml (HtmlString(html)) =
  let fn = Path.Combine(Path.GetTempPath(), "HtmlDemo.htm")
  let bytes = System.Text.UTF8Encoding.UTF8.GetBytes html
  using (new FileStream(fn, FileMode.Create, FileAccess.Write))
      (fun fs -> fs.Write(bytes, 0, bytes.Length))
  System.Diagnostics.Process.Start(fn).WaitForExit()
  File.Delete fn
```

To call the `displayHtml` function, we only need to wrap the string from the `toHtml` function in an `HtmlString` instance and pass it to `displayHtml` as follows:

```
HtmlString(movieList |> toHtml) |> displayHtml
```

Finally, we can further simplify this code by revising the `toHtml` function to return an `HtmlString` instead of a string. One approach would look like this:

```
let rec toHtml markup =
  match markup with
  | ContentElement (tag, children) ->
      use w = new System.IO.StringWriter()
      children
        |> Seq.map toHtml
        |> Seq.iter (fun ❶(HtmlString(html)) -> w.Write(html))
      HtmlString (sprintf "<%s>%s</%s>" tag (w.ToString()) tag)
  | EmptyElement (tag) -> HtmlString (sprintf "<%s />" tag)
  | Content (c) -> HtmlString (sprintf "%s" c)
```

In this revised version, we've wrapped each case's return value in an `HtmlString` instance. Less trivial, though, is ❶, which now uses an Identifier pattern to extract the HTML from the recursive result in order to write the raw text to the `StringWriter`.

With the `toHtml` function now returning an `HtmlString`, passing its result to `displayHtml` is simplified to this:

```
movieList |> toHtml |> displayHtml
```

Single-case discriminated unions can't guarantee that any associated values are actually correct, but they do offer a little extra safety in that they force developers to make conscious decisions about what they're passing to a function. Developers could create an `HtmlString` instance with an arbitrary string, but if they do they'll be forced to think about whether the data is correct.

Additional Members

Like record types, discriminated unions also allow additional members. For example, we could redefine the `toHtml` function as a method on the `Markup` discriminated union as follows:

```
type Markup =
| ContentElement of string * Markup list
| EmptyElement of string
| Content of string
```

```
member x.toHtml() =
  match x with
  | ContentElement (tag, children) ->
      use w = new System.IO.StringWriter()
      children
        |> Seq.map (fun m -> m.toHtml())
        |> Seq.iter (fun (HtmlString(html)) -> w.Write(html))
      HtmlString (sprintf "<%s>%s</%s>" tag (w.ToString()) tag)
  | EmptyElement (tag) -> HtmlString (sprintf "<%s />" tag)
  | Content (c) -> HtmlString (sprintf "%s" c)
```

Calling this method is like calling a method on any other type:

```
movieList.toHtml() |> displayHtml
```

Lazy Evaluation

By default, F# uses *eager evaluation*, which means that expressions are evaluated immediately. Most of the time, eager evaluation will be fine in F#, but sometimes you can improve perceived performance by deferring execution until the result is actually needed, through *lazy evaluation*.

F# supports a few mechanisms for enabling lazy evaluation, but one of the easiest and most common ways is through the use of the lazy keyword. Here, the lazy keyword is used in conjunction with a series of expressions that includes a delay to simulate a long-running operation.

```
> let lazyOperation = lazy (printfn "evaluating lazy expression"
                            System.Threading.Thread.Sleep(1000)
                            42);;

val lazyOperation : Lazy<int> = Value is not created.
```

You can see the lazy keyword's impact. If this expression had been eagerly evaluated, evaluating lazy expression would have been printed and there would have been an immediate one-second delay before it returned 42. Instead, the expression's result is an instance of the built-in Lazy<'T> type. In this case, the compiler inferred the return type and created an instance of Lazy<int>.

NOTE *Be careful using the lazy type across language boundaries. Prior to F# 3.0, the Lazy<'T> class was located in the FSharp.Core assembly. In .NET 4.0, Lazy<'T> was moved to mscorlib.*

The `Lazy<'T>` instance created by the lazy keyword can be passed around like any other type, but the underlying expression won't be evaluated until you force that evaluation by either calling the `Force` method or accessing its `Value` property, as shown next. Convention generally favors the `Force` method, but it doesn't really matter whether you use it or the `Value` property to force evaluation. Internally, `Force` is just an extension method that wraps the `Value` property.

```
> lazyOperation.Force() |> printfn "Result: %i";;
evaluating lazy expression
Result: 42
val it : unit = ()
```

Now that we've forced evaluation, we see that the underlying expression has printed its message, slept, and returned 42. The `Lazy<'T>` type can also improve application performance through memoization. Once the associated expression is evaluated, its result is cached within the `Lazy<'T>` instance and used for subsequent requests. If the expression involves an expensive or time-consuming operation, the result can be dramatic.

To more effectively observe memoization's impact, we can enable timing in FSI and repeatedly force evaluation as follows:

```
> let lazyOperation = lazy (System.Threading.Thread.Sleep(1000); 42)
#time "on";;

val lazyOperation : Lazy<int> = Value is not created.


--> Timing now on

> lazyOperation.Force() |> printfn "Result: %i";;
Result: 42
Real: ❶00:00:01.004, CPU: 00:00:00.000, GC gen0: 0, gen1: 0, gen2: 0
val it : unit = ()
> lazyOperation.Force() |> printfn "Result: %i";;
Result: 42
Real: ❷00:00:00.001, CPU: 00:00:00.000, GC gen0: 0, gen1: 0, gen2: 0
val it : unit = ()
> lazyOperation.Force() |> printfn "Result: %i";;
Result: 42
Real: ❸00:00:00.001, CPU: 00:00:00.000, GC gen0: 0, gen1: 0, gen2: 0
val it : unit = ()
```

As you can see at ❶, the first time `Force` is called we incur the expense of putting the thread to sleep. The subsequent calls at ❷ and ❸ complete instantaneously because the memoization mechanism has cached the result.

Summary

As you've seen in this chapter, functional programming requires a different mindset than object-oriented programming. While object-oriented programming emphasizes managing system state, functional programming is more concerned with program correctness and predictability through the application of side-effect-free functions to data. Functional languages like F# treat functions as data. In doing so, they allow for greater composability within systems through concepts like higher-order functions, currying, partial application, pipelining, and function composition. Functional data types like tuples, record types, and discriminated unions help you write correct code by letting you focus on the problem you're trying to solve instead of attempting to satisfy the compiler.

6

GOING TO COLLECTIONS

Programming tasks often require working with collections of data. The .NET Framework has always supported this scenario with constructs such as *arrays* and the `ArrayList` class, but it wasn't until generics were introduced in .NET 2.0 that collection support really matured.

F# builds upon .NET's legacy by not only supporting all of the existing collection types but also bringing a few of its own to the party. In this chapter, we'll see the role a few of the classic collection types play in F# and then explore the F#-specific types. Along the way, we'll see how the built-in collection modules add some functional flair and make working with both the traditional and F#-specific types a breeze.

Sequences

In .NET, *sequence* is an all-encompassing term for a collection of values that share a common type. More specifically, a sequence is any type that implements `IEnumerable<'T>`.

Nearly all of the major collection types in .NET are sequences. For instance, the generic collection types (like `Dictionary<'TKey, 'TValue>` and `List<'T>`) and even some types (like `String`) that aren't typically thought of as collections implement `IEnumerable<'T>`. Conversely, the legacy collection types (like `ArrayList` and `Hashtable`) predate generics, so they implement only the nongeneric `IEnumerable` interface. Accordingly, they don't enforce a single, common type, and they're generally regarded as enumerable collections rather than sequences.

In F#, `IEnumerable<'T>` is often expressed as `seq<'T>` or `'T seq`. Type annotations like `values : 'A seq` compile to `IEnumerable<'A>`, and any type that implements `IEnumerable<'T>` can be used wherever a sequence is expected. Because `IEnumerable<'T>` defines only the overloaded `GetEnumerator` method, sequences are inherently immutable. Be careful when using the specific collection types directly, however, because underlying implementations may be mutable.

Creating Sequences

Today's .NET developers take working with sequences for granted, but before LINQ's introduction, programming directly against `IEnumerable<'T>` was relatively rare. Instead, developers typically coded against specific collection types. LINQ's `IEnumerable<'T>` extension methods brought the abstraction to the forefront, though, and taught developers that they didn't always need to know anything about a collection other than that it implements the `GetEnumerator` method. Even with all of the goodness that LINQ gives us, it provides only a framework for working with `IEnumerable<'T>`; creating arbitrary sequences in LINQ still requires a method to create an instance of a specific sequence type.

F# takes the abstraction even further than LINQ by codifying sequence creation into the language through concepts like sequence and range expressions. While each sequence is ultimately still an implementation of `IEnumerable<'T>`, the compiler is free to provide its own implementations. The Seq module also includes several functions for creating new sequences.

Sequence Expressions

Sequence expressions allow you to create new sequences by iteratively applying other F# expressions and *yielding* (returning) the results into a new sequence. In some situations, particularly when you are working with large or computationally expensive collections, the sequence types used internally by sequence expressions are preferable to other collection types because they create values only as needed. These sequence types typically also hold only one value in memory at a time, making them ideal for large data sets.

Sequence expressions are technically a built-in workflow called a computation expression. *We'll cover these constructs in detail in Chapter 12.*

You create a sequence expression by enclosing one or more expressions within a sequence builder and using a do binding in conjunction with the yield keyword. For example, say you have a file named *ArnoldMovies.txt* that contains the following data:

```
The Terminator,1984
Predator,1987
Commando,1985
The Running Man,1987
True Lies,1994
Last Action Hero,1993
Total Recall,1990
Conan the Barbarian,1982
Conan the Destroyer,1984
Hercules in New York,1969
```

You can read each line of the text file into a sequence with a sequence expression like this:

```
let lines = seq { use r = new System.IO.StreamReader("ArnoldMovies.txt")
                  while not r.EndOfStream do yield r.ReadLine() }
```

Here, a while loop is used to iteratively read lines from a StreamReader, yielding a line for each iteration. (In some simpler sequence expressions—such as those using an enumerable for loop—do yield can be replaced with the -> operator, but for consistency I usually stick with do yield.)

If you wanted to write this sequence to the console, you could send it to the printfn function and use the default formatter (via the %A token), but only the first four values are included in the output, as shown here:

```
> lines |> printfn "%A";;
seq ["The Terminator,1984"; "Predator,1987"; "Commando,1985"; "The Running Man,1987"; ...]
val it : unit = ()
```

To print every value in the sequence, you need to force enumeration over the entire construct.

Range Expressions

Although *range expressions* resemble the slice expressions you learned about in Chapter 4 in that they use the .. operator, they're actually specialized sequence expressions that allow you to create sequences over a range of values. Range expressions are similar to the `Enumerable.Range` method but are a bit more powerful because they're not restricted to integers. For instance, you can easily create a sequence containing the integers 0 through 10 like this:

```
seq { 0..10 }
```

Or you could create a sequence containing 0 through 10 as floats this way:

```
seq { 0.0..10.0 }
```

Likewise, you could create a sequence containing the characters *a* through *z* like this:

```
seq { 'a'..'z' }
```

In most cases, you can also include a value that identifies how many items to skip between values when generating the sequence. Creating a sequence containing the integral multiples of 10 from 0 through 100 is easy with the following expression:

```
seq { 0..10..100 }
```

This range expression form works only with numeric types, so you can't use it with character data. For example, the following expression results in an error.

```
seq { 'a'..2..'z' }
```

Finally, you can create sequences with declining values by using a negative step value like this:

```
seq { 99..-1..0 }
```

Empty Sequences

When you need a sequence without any elements, you can turn to the `Seq` module's generic empty function to create one for you. For instance, to create an empty string sequence, you could call `Seq.empty` like this:

```
> let emptySequence = Seq.empty<string>;;

val emptySequence : seq<string>
```

Alternatively, if you don't need any particular type, you can let the compiler automatically generalize the sequence by omitting the type argument:

```
> let emptySequence = Seq.empty;;

val emptySequence : seq<'a>
```

Initializing a Sequence

Another module function, Seq.init, creates a sequence with up to a specified number of elements. For example, to create a sequence containing 10 random numbers, you could write:

```
> let rand = System.Random();;

val rand : System.Random

> Seq.init 10 (fun _ -> rand.Next(100));;
val it : seq<int> = seq [22; 34; 73; 42; ...]
```

Working with Sequences

The Seq module provides a number of functions for working with any sequence. The list of functions covered next is a sampling of the most useful functions in the Seq module, but it is by no means comprehensive.

While each of the functions discussed in the coming sections belongs to the Seq module, many have specialized counterparts in the other collection modules. In the interest of space, I'll cover the common functions only once, but I strongly encourage you to explore the other modules and discover the right tools for your task.

WHEN IS A FUNCTION NOT A FUNCTION?

You may have noticed in both of the empty sequence examples that Seq.empty was invoked without any arguments. Seq.empty differs from every function we've encountered so far in that it behaves more like a basic value binding than a function. In fact, if you were to call Seq.empty with an argument, you'd get a compiler error telling you that the value (Seq.empty) is not a function and cannot be applied.

Why is Seq.empty called a function when the compiler claims otherwise? Because it, along with some other functions (such as Operators.typeof and Operators.typedefof), is a special-case value called a *type function*. Type functions are generally reserved for pure functions that compute values based on their type arguments, and therefore—despite being represented as methods in the compiled assemblies—they are treated as values within F# code.

Finding Sequence Length

You use `Seq.length` to determine how many elements a sequence contains like this:

```
seq { 0..99 } |> Seq.length
```

Be careful with `Seq.length`, though, because, depending on the underlying collection type, it can force enumeration of the entire sequence or otherwise impair performance. Consider the following code, which checks if a sequence is empty using `Seq.length = 0`:

```
seq { for i in 1..10 do
    printfn "Evaluating %i" i
    yield i }
|> Seq.length = 0
```

To determine the sequence's length, the system must iterate over the sequence by calling the enumerator's `MoveNext` method until it returns `false`. Each invocation of `MoveNext` involves doing whatever work is necessary to obtain the next value. In this case, getting the next value involves writing a string to the console, as shown here:

```
Evaluating 1
Evaluating 2
Evaluating 3
-- snip --
Evaluating 10
val it : bool = false
```

Writing some text to the console is trivial, but even so, it is unnecessary work since the result isn't actually being used for anything. Going beyond this simple example, you can easily imagine each call to `MoveNext` triggering an expensive computation or database call. If you just need to determine whether the sequence has any elements, you should use the `Seq.isEmpty` function instead.

`Seq.isEmpty` checks whether a sequence contains any elements without forcing enumeration of the entire sequence. Consider the following code, which replaces `Seq.length = 0` with `Seq.isEmpty`:

```
seq { for i in 1..10 do
    printfn "Evaluating %i" i
    yield i }
|> Seq.isEmpty
```

Because `Seq.isEmpty` returns `false` as soon as it finds an element, `MoveNext` is called only once, resulting in:

```
Evaluating 1
val it : bool = false
```

As you can see, although the sequence expression defines 10 elements, only the first one was printed because evaluation stopped as soon as the function found a value.

Iterating over Sequences

The Seq.iter function is the functional equivalent of the enumerable for loop in that it iterates over a sequence, applying a function to each element. For example, to print each element of a sequence containing the values 0 through 99, you could write:

```
> seq { 0..99 } |> Seq.iter (printfn "%i");;
0
1
2
-- snip --
97
98
99
val it : unit = ()
```

Transforming Sequences

Seq.map is similar to Seq.iter in that it applies a function to every element in a sequence, but unlike Seq.iter, it builds a new sequence with the results. For instance, to create a new sequence containing the squares of elements from a sequence, you could write:

```
> seq { 0..99 } |> Seq.map (fun i -> i * i);;
val it : seq<int> = seq [0; 1; 4; 9; ...]
```

Sorting Sequences

The Seq module defines several functions for sorting sequences. Each sorting function creates a new sequence, leaving the original unchanged.

The simplest sorting function, Seq.sort, orders the elements using a default comparison based on the IComparable<'T> interface. For instance, you can apply Seq.sort to a sequence of random integer values like this:

```
> let rand = System.Random();;

val rand : System.Random

> Seq.init 10 (fun _ -> rand.Next 100) |> Seq.sort;;
val it : seq<int> = seq [0; 11; 16; 19; ...]
```

For more complex sorting needs, you can use the Seq.sortBy function. In addition to the sequence to be sorted, it accepts a function that returns the value to sort upon for each element in the sequence.

For example, each movie listed in *ArnoldMovies.txt* in "Sequence Expressions" on page 134 included the release year. If you wanted to sort the movies by their release years, you could revise the sequence expression to isolate the individual values as follows:

```
let movies =
  seq { use r = new System.IO.StreamReader("ArnoldMovies.txt")
        while not r.EndOfStream do
          let l = r.ReadLine().Split(',')
          yield ❶l.[0], int l.[1] }
```

At ❶ the sequence expression now yields *tuples* containing each movie title and release year. We can send the sequence to Seq.sortBy along with the snd function (to get the year) like this:

```
> movies |> Seq.sortBy snd;;
val it : seq<string * int> =
  seq
    [("Hercules in New York", 1969); ("Conan the Barbarian", 1982);
     ("The Terminator", 1984); ("Conan the Destroyer", 1984); ...]
```

Alternatively, to sort the movies by title, you can replace snd with fst.

```
> seq { use r = new System.IO.StreamReader(fileName)
        while not r.EndOfStream do
          let l = r.ReadLine().Split(',')
          yield l.[0], int l.[1] }
|> Seq.sortBy fst;;
val it : seq<string * int> =
  seq
    [("Commando", 1985); ("Conan the Barbarian", 1982);
     ("Conan the Destroyer", 1984); ("Hercules in New York", 1969); ...]
```

Filtering Sequences

When you want to work only with elements that meet certain criteria, you can use the Seq.filter function to create a new sequence containing only those elements. For example, continuing with the movie theme, you can get the movies released prior to 1984 like this:

```
> movies |> Seq.filter (fun (_, year) -> year < 1985);;
val it : seq<string * int> =
  seq
    [("The Terminator", 1984); ("Conan the Barbarian", 1982);
     ("Conan the Destroyer", 1984); ("Hercules in New York", 1969)]
```

Aggregating Sequences

The Seq module provides a number of functions for aggregating the elements in a sequence. The most flexible (and complex) of the aggregation functions is Seq.fold, which iterates over a sequence, applying a function to each element and returning the result as an accumulator value. For example, Seq.fold makes it easy to compute the sum of a sequence's elements:

```
> seq { 1 .. 10 } |> Seq.fold ❶(fun s c -> s + c) ❷0;;
val it : int = 55
```

This example shows just one way to add the values 1 through 10. The function that Seq.fold uses for aggregation ❶ accepts two values: an aggregation value (essentially a running total), and the current element. We also need to give the fold function an initial aggregation value ❷, which we do with 0. As fold executes, it applies the aggregation function to each element in the sequence and returns the new aggregation value for use in the next iteration.

Because the addition operator function itself satisfies the requirements for the aggregation function, we can simplify the previous expression like this:

```
> seq { 1..10 } |> Seq.fold (+) 0;;
val it : int = 55
```

A slightly more specialized aggregation function is Seq.reduce. The reduce function is very much like the fold function except that the aggregation value that's passed through the computation is always the same type as the sequence's elements, whereas fold can transform the data to another type. The reduce function also differs from fold in that it doesn't accept an initial aggregation value. Instead, reduce initializes the aggregation value to the first value in the sequence. To see Seq.reduce in action, we can rewrite the previous expression as follows:

```
> seq { 1 .. 10 } |> Seq.reduce (+);;
val it : int = 55
```

As expected, the result of adding the items in the sequence is the same regardless of whether we use Seq.fold or Seq.reduce.

Seq.fold and Seq.reduce aren't the only ways to calculate aggregate values from a sequence; some common aggregations like summations and averages have functions of their own. For example, rather than using Seq.reduce to calculate the sum of the elements like we did previously, we can use Seq.sum:

```
> seq { 1..10 } |> Seq.sum;;
val it : int = 55
```

Similarly, to compute the average, you can use Seq.average like this:

```
> seq { 1.0..10.0 } |> Seq.average;;
val it : float = 5.5
```

One thing to note about `Seq.average` is that it works only with types that support division by an integer. If you try to use it with a sequence of integers, you'll receive the following error:

```
> seq { 1..10 } |> Seq.average;;

  seq { 1..10 } |> Seq.average;;
  -----------------^^^^^^^^^^^

stdin(2,18): error FS0001: The type 'int' does not support the operator 'DivideByInt'
```

Like `Seq.sort`, the `Seq.sum` and `Seq.average` functions have the `Seq.sumBy` and `Seq.averageBy` counterparts that accept a function that lets you identify which value should be used in the calculation. The syntax for these functions is the same as `Seq.sortBy`, so I'll leave it to you to experiment a bit more with the Seq module.

Arrays

F# arrays are the same construct as traditional .NET arrays. They contain a fixed number of values (each of the same type) and are zero-based. Although an array binding itself is immutable, individual array elements are mutable, so you need to be careful that you don't introduce unwanted side effects. That said, the mutable nature of arrays makes them more desirable in some situations than other collection constructs because no further allocations are required to change element values.

Creating Arrays

F# provides a number of ways to create new arrays and control each element's initial value, using both native syntax and module functions.

Array Expressions

One of the most common ways to create an array is with an *array expression*. Array expressions consist of a semicolon-delimited list of values enclosed between the [| and |] tokens. For instance, you can create an array of strings like this (if you place each value on a separate line, you can omit the semicolons):

```
> let names = [| "Rose"; "Martha"; "Donna"; "Amy"; "Clara" |];;

val names : string [] = [|"Rose"; "Martha"; "Donna"; "Amy"; "Clara"|]
```

Finally, you can generate an array by enclosing a sequence expression between [| and |]. Unlike with the sequence builder, however, the array will be fully constructed when the array expression is evaluated. Compare this example with the corresponding one from the sequence expression discussion:

```
> let lines = [| use r = new System.IO.StreamReader("ArnoldMovies.txt")
                 while not r.EndOfStream do yield r.ReadLine() |];;

val lines : string [] =
  [|"The Terminator,1984"; "Predator,1987"; "Commando,1985";
    "The Running Man,1987"; "True Lies,1994"; "Last Action Hero,1993";
    "Total Recall,1990"; "Conan the Barbarian,1982";
    "Conan the Destroyer,1984"; "Hercules in New York,1969"|]
```

As you can see, the default array print formatter prints every element (it caps the output at 100 elements) rather than printing only the first four.

Empty Arrays

Should you need to create an empty array, you can use an empty pair of square brackets:

```
let emptyArray = [| |]
```

The downside of this approach is that, depending on context, you may need to include a type annotation to ensure that the compiler doesn't automatically generalize the array. Such a definition would look something like this:

```
let emptyArray : int array = [| |];;
```

In the preceding example, the type annotation, int array, is an English-like syntax. If you prefer a more traditional form, you could use int[] instead. Without the type annotation, the compiler would define the array as 'a [].

Another way to create an empty array is with the Array.empty function. Just like its counterpart in the Seq module, Array.empty is a type function, so you invoke it without any arguments to create a zero-length array. To create an empty string array with this function, you simply write:

```
Array.empty<string>
```

If you prefer to let the compiler infer the underlying type or automatically generalize it, you can omit the type parameter.

Initializing Arrays

To quickly create an array where all elements are initialized to the underlying type's default value, you can use `Array.zeroCreate`. Suppose you know that you need an array of five strings, but you don't yet know what values will be stored in each element. You could create the array like this:

```
> let stringArray = Array.zeroCreate<string> 5;;

val stringArray : string [] = [|null; null; null; null; null|]
```

Because `Array.zeroCreate` uses the underlying type's default value, it's possible that the elements will be initialized to `null` like they were here. If `null` is valid for the type and you're creating arrays like this, you'll need to code against `NullReferenceExceptions`.

Alternatively, `Array.init` lets you initialize each element to a specific value. `Array.init` is the array-specific equivalent of `Seq.init`. Its syntax is the same, but it creates and returns an array instead. For instance, to create a new array where the elements are initialized to the empty string, you could write:

```
> let stringArray = Array.init 5 (fun _ -> "");;

val stringArray : string [] = [|""; ""; ""; ""; ""|]
```

Here, the supplied function only returns the empty string, but your initialization function could easily have more complicated logic, allowing you to compute a different value for each element.

Working with Arrays

Working with arrays in F# is similar to working with them in other .NET languages, but F# extends their usefulness with constructs like slice expressions and the `Array` module.

Accessing Elements

Individual array elements are accessible through an indexed property. For instance, to retrieve the fourth element from the `lines` array defined previously, you'd write:

```
> lines.[3];;
val it : string = "The Running Man,1987"
```

You can combine the indexer syntax with the assignment operator to change individual elements of an array. For instance, to replace *Last Action Hero*, you could write:

```
lines.[5] <- "Batman & Robin,1997"
```

If you prefer a more functional approach to retrieving and mutating array elements, the `Array` module has you covered with the get and set functions. In the following example we'll create an array, change the second element's value, retrieve the new value, and write it to the console.

```
> let movies = [| "The Terminator"; "Predator"; "Commando" |];;

val movies : string [] = [|"The Terminator"; "Predator"; "Commando"|]

> Array.set movies 1 "Batman & Robin"
Array.get movies 1 |> printfn "%s";;
Batman & Robin

val it : unit = ()
```

Finally, arrays also support slice expressions. As noted in Chapter 4, slice expressions let you easily retrieve a range of values from a collection like this:

```
> lines.[1..3];;
val it : string [] =
  [|"Predator,1987"; "Commando,1985"; "The Running Man,1987"|]
```

Copying Arrays

You can easily copy the elements from one array to a new array with `Array.copy`. Here, we create an array containing the numbers 1 through 10 and immediately copy them to another.

```
[| 1..10 |] |> Array.copy
```

Behind the scenes, `Array.copy` is a wrapper around the CLR's `Array.Clone` method, which creates a shallow copy of the source array. `Array.copy` offers the added benefit of automatically downcasting the object instance returned by `Clone` to the appropriate array type; that is, passing an integer array directly to `Array.Clone` will give you an `obj` instance, whereas passing that same array to `Array.copy` will give you an instance of `int array`.

Sorting Arrays

Arrays can be sorted like any other sequence, but the `Array` module provides a few specialized sorting functions to take advantage of the fact that individual array elements are mutable. Unfortunately, each of these functions returns `unit` instead of the sorted array, so they're not particularly effective in pipelining or composition chains.

The first in-place sorting function, `sortInPlace`, sorts an array with the default comparison mechanism. The following snippet shows how to sort an array of random integers.

```
> let r = System.Random()
let ints = Array.init 5 (fun _ -> r.Next(-100, 100));;

val r : System.Random
val ints : int [] = [|-94; 20; 13; -99; 0|]

> ints |> Array.sortInPlace;;
val it : unit = ()
> ints;;
val it : int [] = [|-99; -94; 0; 13; 20|]
```

If you need more control over how sorting is performed, you can turn to the sortInPlaceBy or sortInPlaceWith functions. The sortInPlaceBy function lets you provide a transformation function that's used in the sorting process. The sortInPlaceWith function accepts a comparison function that returns an integer where less than zero means the first value is greater than the second, greater than zero means that the first value is less than the second value, and zero means the first and second values are equal.

To better understand both approaches, consider the following array containing some movies and their release years as tuples.

```
let movies = [| ("The Terminator", "1984")
                ("Predator", "1987")
                ("Commando", "1985")
                ("Total Recall", "1990")
                ("Conan the Destroyer", "1984") |]
```

The easiest way to sort by year is to just project the year value via sortInPlaceBy like this:

```
> movies |> Array.sortInPlaceBy (fun (_, y) -> y)
movies;;

val it : (string * string) [] =
  [|("The Terminator", "1984"); ("Conan the Destroyer", "1984");
    ("Commando", "1985"); ("Predator", "1987"); ("Total Recall", "1990")|]
```

Alternatively, we can directly compare two elements with sortInPlaceWith:

```
> movies |> Array.sortInPlaceWith (fun (_, y1) (_, y2) -> if y1 < y2 then -1
                                                          elif y1 > y2 then 1
                                                          else 0)
movies;;

val it : (string * string) [] =
  [|("The Terminator", "1984"); ("Conan the Destroyer", "1984");
    ("Commando", "1985"); ("Predator", "1987"); ("Total Recall", "1990")|]
```

As you can see, `sortInPlaceBy` allows you to sort according to the default equality semantics for a particular element's underlying type, whereas `sortInPlaceWith` allows you to essentially define your own equality semantics for each element in the array.

Multidimensional Arrays

All of the arrays we've looked at so far have been one-dimensional. While it's also possible to create multidimensional arrays, it's a bit more complicated because there's no direct syntactic support. For two-dimensional arrays, you can pass a sequence of sequences (typically either arrays or lists) to the `array2D` operator. To create arrays with more than two dimensions, you need to use either the `Array3D.init` or `Array4D.init` functions. Multidimensional arrays have modules (like `Array2D` and `Array3D`) that contain specialized subsets of those defined in the `Array` module.

NOTE   *The maximum number of dimensions F# supports is four.*

Suppose you wanted to represent the movies from the previous sections as a two-dimensional array instead of as an array of tuples. You could write something like the following, which passes an array of arrays to the `array2D` operator:

```
let movies = array2D [| [| "The Terminator"; "1984" |]
                        [| "Predator"; "1987" |]
                        [| "Commando"; "1985" |]
                        [| "The Running Man"; "1987" |]
                        [| "True Lies"; "1994" |]
                        [| "Last Action Hero"; "1993" |]
                        [| "Total Recall"; "1990" |]
                        [| "Conan the Barbarian"; "1982" |]
                        [| "Conan the Destroyer"; "1984" |]
                        [| "Hercules in New York"; "1969" |] |]
```

You can access any value in the two-dimensional array with the familiar indexer syntax. For instance, to get *Commando*'s release year you'd write `movies.[2, 1]`, which would return 1985. Much more interesting, though, is what you can do with slice expressions.

Slice expressions make it easy to create new arrays containing subsets of data from the source. For instance, you can slice the `movies` array vertically to create new arrays containing only the movie titles or release years like this:

```
> movies.[0..,0..0];;
val it : string [,] = [["The Terminator"]
                       ["Predator"]
                       ["Commando"]
                       ["The Running Man"]
                       -- snip --]
```

```
> movies.[0..,1..1];;
val it : string [,] = [["1984"]
                       ["1987"]
                       ["1985"]
                       ["1987"]
                       -- snip --]
```

You can also slice arrays horizontally to create new arrays containing only a few rows:

```
> movies.[1..3,0..];;
val it : string [,] = [["Predator"; "1987"]
                       ["Commando"; "1985"]
                       ["The Running Man"; "1987"]]
```

Multidimensional arrays are useful when the data has a nice, rectangular shape, but they don't work when even a single row has a different number of items. Consider what happens if we try to include a director name in the two-dimensional movies array (for brevity, we'll just work with three titles here).

```
> let movies = array2D [| [| "The Terminator"; "1984"; "James Cameron" |]
                          [| "Predator"; "1987"; "John McTiernan" |]
                          [| "Commando"; "1985" |] |];;
System.ArgumentException: The arrays have different lengths.
Parameter name: vals
-- snip --
Stopped due to error
```

Of course, one possible solution would be to provide an empty string as the third element in the row that's missing the director name. Alternatively, you can use a jagged array.

Jagged Arrays

Jagged arrays are arrays of arrays. Unlike multidimensional arrays, jagged arrays don't require a rectangular structure. To convert the preceding failing example, we just need to remove the call to the array2D function.

```
> let movies = [| [| "The Terminator"; "1984"; "James Cameron" |]
                 [| "Predator"; "1987"; "John McTiernan" |]
                 [| "Commando"; "1985" |] |];;

val movies : string [] [] =
  [|[|"The Terminator"; "1984"; "James Cameron"|];
    [|"Predator"; "1987"; "John McTiernan"|]; [|"Commando"; "1985"|]|]
```

As you might expect, since movies is now a jagged array, you need to use a different syntax to access each element. You also need to code a bit more defensively when using jagged arrays because there's no guarantee that a particular index will be valid for any given row. That said, you can get the director name from the second row like this:

```
> movies.[1].[2];;
val it : string = "John McTiernan"
```

ANY WAY YOU SLICE IT

F# 3.1 features a few extensions to array slicing that aren't covered here but do prove useful. Array slicing in F# 3.0 requires slices to have the same dimensions as the source array. Under F# 3.1 this restriction has been removed, so you can create a one-dimensional slice from a two-dimensional array, and so on.

Lists

Lists are used extensively in F# development. When .NET developers discuss lists, they typically mean the generic List<'T> class. Although it's possible (and sometimes even desirable) to use the generic list in F#, the language defines another immutable construct based on singly linked lists. In F#, lists created with the list syntax compile to instances of the FSharpList<'T> class found in the Microsoft.FSharp.Collections namespace, and that's the kind of list we'll be covering in this section.

Aside from both List<'T> and FSharpList<'T> being generic sequence types (they both implement IEnumerable<'T>), they have little in common and cannot be used interchangeably. You need to be careful to not mix list types when working in multilanguage solutions.

NOTE   *You can use the generic* List<'T> *class directly by opening the* System.Collections .Generic *namespace or through the built-in* ResizeArray<'T> *type abbreviation.*

Creating Lists

Creating lists in F# is so similar to creating arrays that I won't spend much time explaining the various forms here. The only notable syntactic difference between creating arrays and lists is the brace style. To create a new list, you enclose semicolon-delimited values, range expressions, or list sequence expressions between square brackets ([]) like this:

```
> let names = [ "Rose"; "Martha"; "Donna"; "Amy"; "Clara" ];;

val names : string list = ["Rose"; "Martha"; "Donna"; "Amy"; "Clara"]
```

```
> let numbers = [ 1..11 ];;

val numbers : int list = [1; 2; 3; 4; 5; 6; 7; 8; 9; 10; 11]
```

To create an empty list, you can use either `List.empty` or a pair of empty brackets.

Working with Lists

Although there are some similarities between working with F# lists and `List<'T>`, they're mostly syntactic and deal with accessing individual known elements. Beyond that, F# lists are quite unique, especially because of their head and tail structure, which lends itself well to functional programming and to recursive techniques in particular.

Accessing Elements

When you want to get the element at a particular position, you can use the familiar indexer syntax just like you would with an array. Alternatively, you can use `List.nth` to get the same result:

```
> List.nth [ 'A'..'Z' ] 3;;
val it : char = 'D'
```

What's more interesting (and often more useful) than accessing a particular element by index is a list's *head* and *tail*. A list's head is simply its first element, whereas its tail is all elements except the head. You can get a list's head and tail through the `Head` or `Tail` properties or the `List.head` or `List.tail` module functions. Here's an example using the module functions:

```
> let names = [ "Rose"; "Martha"; "Donna"; "Amy"; "Clara" ];;

val names : string list = ["Rose"; "Martha"; "Donna"; "Amy"; "Clara"]

> List.head names;;
val it : string = "Rose"
> List.tail names;;
val it : string list = ["Martha"; "Donna"; "Amy"; "Clara"]
```

NOTE   *Pattern matching is another way to get the head and tail, but we'll save that discussion for Chapter 7.*

Why would you want to get only the first element or everything else? Recursion. If you had to iterate over a list using indexes, you'd need to track both the list and the current position. By separating a list into head and tail components, you're free to operate against the head and then iterate with the tail.

Consider this function, which returns a Boolean value indicating whether a list contains a particular value (much like the List.exists module function).

```
let rec contains fn l =
  if l = [] then false
  else fn(List.head l) || contains fn (List.tail l)
```

The contains function accepts both a function for testing the elements and a list to scan. The first thing contains does is check whether the supplied list is empty. If the list is empty, contains immediately returns false; otherwise, it tests the list's head with the provided function or recursively calls contains with both the function and the list's tail.

Now let's test for a few values, starting with an empty list:

```
> [] |> contains (fun n -> n = "Rose");;
val it : bool = false
```

You can see that contains correctly returns false when the list is empty, but what about a populated list?

```
> let names = [ "Rose"; "Martha"; "Donna"; "Amy"; "Clara" ];;

val names : string list = ["Rose"; "Martha"; "Donna"; "Amy"; "Clara"]

> names |> contains (fun n -> n = "Amy");;
val it : bool = true
> names |> contains (fun n -> n = "Rory");;
val it : bool = false
```

The contains function recursively walked the list, examining each element with the supplied function and passing the tail to contains if the element didn't match.

Combining Lists

Even though F# lists are immutable, we can still construct new lists from existing ones. F# provides two primary mechanisms: the cons operator (::) and list concatenation with the @ operator.

The cons operator (so named because it *cons*tructs a new list) essentially prepends an item to an existing list like this:

```
> let names = [ "Rose"; "Martha"; "Donna"; "Amy"; "Clara" ]
let newNames = "Ace" :: names;;

val names : string list = ["Rose"; "Martha"; "Donna"; "Amy"; "Clara"]
val newNames : string list =
  ["Ace"; "Rose"; "Martha"; "Donna"; "Amy"; "Clara"]
```

The cons operator doesn't make any changes to the existing list. Instead, it simply creates a new list with its head set to the new value and tail set to the existing list. The cons operator can add only a single item to the list, but since it's at the beginning of the list it's a quick operation. If you want to combine two lists, you'll need to turn to list concatenation.

To concatenate two lists, you can use either the list concatenation operator (@) or the List.append module function, as follows:

```
> let classicNames = [ "Susan"; "Barbara"; "Sarah Jane" ]
let modernNames = [ "Rose"; "Martha"; "Donna"; "Amy"; "Clara" ];;

val classicNames : string list = ["Susan"; "Barbara"; "Sarah Jane"]
val modernNames : string list = ["Rose"; "Martha"; "Donna"; "Amy"; "Clara"]

> classicNames @ modernNames;;
val it : string list =
  ["Susan"; "Barbara"; "Sarah Jane"; "Rose"; "Martha"; "Donna"; "Amy"; "Clara"]
> List.append classicNames modernNames;;
val it : string list =
  ["Susan"; "Barbara"; "Sarah Jane"; "Rose"; "Martha"; "Donna"; "Amy"; "Clara"]
```

There's no difference between the list created with the concatenation operator and the list created by List.append. Internally, List.append wraps the append operator so they're functionally equivalent.

To combine more than two lists at once, you can pass a sequence of lists to List.concat like this:

```
> List.concat [[ "Susan"; "Sarah Jane" ]
               [ "Rose"; "Martha" ]
               ["Donna"; "Amy"; "Clara"]];;
val it : string list =
  ["Susan"; "Sarah Jane"; "Rose"; "Martha"; "Donna"; "Amy"; "Clara"]
```

Now, what started as three independent lists was combined into a single list containing each item.

Sets

In F#, a *set* is an immutable collection of unique values whose order is not preserved. F# sets closely correlate to mathematical sets (think Venn diagrams) and provide a number of operations useful for comparing sets.

Creating Sets

There are no syntactic niceties like special bracket formats for creating sets, so if you want to use one, you'll need to rely on either the type constructor or some of the Set module functions (like Set.ofList, which creates a set from an F# list). For instance, to create a set containing the letters of the alphabet, you could write:

```
> let alphabet = [ 'A'..'Z' ] |> Set.ofList;;

val alphabet : Set<char> =
  set ['A'; 'B'; 'C'; 'D'; 'E'; 'F'; 'G'; 'H'; 'I'; ...]
```

The Set<'T> class defines methods to add and remove values from a set, but because F# sets are immutable, both of these methods return new sets and leave the original intact. The Add method can be useful for populating a new set from an empty one, like so:

```
> let vowels = Set.empty.Add('A').Add('E').Add('I').Add('O').Add('U');;

val vowels : Set<char> = set ['A'; 'E'; 'I'; 'O'; 'U']
```

Of course, creating sets in this manner is a more object-oriented approach than is typical in F#.

Working with Sets

Because sets are so closely related to mathematical sets, the Set module provides several functions for performing a variety of set operations like finding unions, intersections, and differences, and even determining if two sets are related as subsets or supersets.

Unions

To find the union of two sets—that is, those elements contained within either the first or second set—you use the Set.union function as follows:

```
> let set1 = [ 1..5 ] |> Set.ofList
let set2 = [ 3..7 ] |> Set.ofList
Set.union set1 set2;;

val set1 : Set<int> = set [1; 2; 3; 4; 5]
val set2 : Set<int> = set [3; 4; 5; 6; 7]
val it : Set<int> = set [1; 2; 3; 4; 5; 6; 7]
```

Here, set1 contains the integers one through five, while set2 contains the integers three through seven. Because the union of two sets contains each distinct value found in either set, the union of set1 and set2 is the range of integers from one through seven.

The Set<'T> class also defines a custom + operator you can use to find the union of two sets:

```
> set1 + set2;;
val it : Set<int> = set [1; 2; 3; 4; 5; 6; 7]
```

Intersections

The Set.intersect function returns a new set containing only the elements found in both sets. For example, if you have a set containing the values one through five, and another set containing the values three through seven, you'd find the intersection like this:

```
> let set1 = [ 1..5 ] |> Set.ofList
let set2 = [ 3..7 ] |> Set.ofList
Set.intersect set1 set2;;

val set1 : Set<int> = set [1; 2; 3; 4; 5]
val set2 : Set<int> = set [3; 4; 5; 6; 7]
val it : Set<int> = set [3; 4; 5]
```

The resulting intersection set contains only the three values common to both set1 and set2—in this case, 3, 4, and 5.

Differences

While the intersection contains all elements common to both sets, the difference contains those elements found only in the first set. You can find the difference between two sets with the Set.difference function.

```
> let set1 = [ 1..5 ] |> Set.ofList
let set2 = [ 3..7 ] |> Set.ofList
Set.difference set1 set2;;

val set1 : Set<int> = set [1; 2; 3; 4; 5]
val set2 : Set<int> = set [3; 4; 5; 6; 7]
val it : Set<int> = set [1; 2]
```

Here, the first set contains two elements not found in the second, 1 and 2; therefore, the difference set contains only those values.

Just as with intersections, the Set<'T> class defines a custom - operator that returns a set containing the difference between two sets.

```
> set1 - set2;;
val it : Set<int> = set [1; 2]
```

Subsets and Supersets

The Set module makes it easy to determine whether two sets are related as subsets or supersets through four functions: isSubset, isProperSubset, isSuperset, and isProperSuperset. The difference between basic subset/superset and proper subset/supersets is that proper subsets/supersets require at least one additional element not present in the opposite set. The following sets illustrate:

```
> let set1 = [ 1..5 ] |> Set.ofList
let set2 = [ 1..5 ] |> Set.ofList;;
```

```
val set1 : Set<int> = set [1; 2; 3; 4; 5]
val set2 : Set<int> = set [1; 2; 3; 4; 5]
```

Because both set1 and set2 contain the same values, set1 can be considered a superset of set2. Conversely, set2 can be considered a subset of set1. For the same reason, however, set2 cannot be a proper subset of set1, as shown in the following snippet.

```
> Set.isSuperset set1 set2;;
val it : bool = true
> Set.isProperSuperset set1 set2;;
val it : bool = false
> Set.isSubset set2 set1;;
val it : bool = true
> Set.isProperSubset set2 set1;;
val it : bool = false
```

To make set2 a proper subset of set1, we need to redefine set1 to include at least one more value.

```
> let set1 = [ 0..5 ] |> Set.ofList;;

val set1 : Set<int> = set [0; 1; 2; 3; 4; 5]
```

Now, if we test for subsets and supersets again, we should see that set2 is both a subset and proper subset of set1.

```
> Set.isSuperset set1 set2;;
val it : bool = true
> Set.isProperSuperset set1 set2;;
val it : bool = true
> Set.isSubset set2 set1;;
val it : bool = true
> Set.isProperSubset set2 set1;;
val it : bool = true
```

Maps

The Map type represents an unordered, immutable dictionary (a map of keys to values) and provides many of the same capabilities as the generic Dictionary<'TKey, 'TValue> class.

NOTE *Although the Map<'Key, 'Value> class and the associated Map module provide methods for adding and removing entries, as an immutable construct, maps make sense only when the underlying entries won't change. Adding and removing entries from a map requires creating a new map instance and copying the data from the source instance, so it is significantly slower than modifying a mutable dictionary.*

Creating Maps

As with sets, F# doesn't provide any direct syntactic support for creating maps, so the type constructor or Map module functions are required to create them, too. Regardless of the approach you choose, maps are always based on a sequence of tuples consisting of both the key and the mapped value. Here, a list of states and their respective capitals is passed to the type's constructor:

```
> let stateCapitals =
  Map [("Indiana", "Indianapolis")
       ("Michigan", "Lansing")
       ("Ohio", "Columbus")
       ("Kentucky", "Frankfort")
       ("Illinois", "Springfield")];;

val stateCapitals : Map<string,string> =
  map
    [("Illinois", "Springfield"); ("Indiana", "Indianapolis");
     ("Kentucky", "Frankfort"); ("Michigan", "Lansing"); ("Ohio", "Columbus")]
```

Working with Maps

Because maps are like immutable dictionaries, interacting with them is similar to Dictionary<'TKey, 'TValue>.

Finding Values

Like the generic dictionary, the Map type provides an indexed property for accessing a value via a known key. For instance, using the stateCapitals map, we can find Indiana's capital like this:

```
> stateCapitals.["Indiana"];;
val it : string = "Indianapolis"
```

The Map.find function lets us do the same thing functionally.

```
> stateCapitals |> Map.find "Indiana";;
val it : string = "Indianapolis"
```

The biggest problem with both of the preceding approaches is that they'll throw a KeyNotFoundException when the key isn't present in the map. To avoid the exception, you can see if the map contains a particular key with the Map.containsKey function. If you wanted to test whether stateCapitals included Washington, you could write this:

```
> stateCapitals |> Map.containsKey "Washington";;
val it : bool = false
```

Finally, if you prefer to test for the key and get the mapped value in a single operation you can turn to the `Map.tryFind` function, which returns an option indicating whether the key was found and the associated value, as shown here:

```
> stateCapitals |> Map.tryFind "Washington";;
val it : string option = None
> stateCapitals |> Map.tryFind "Indiana";;
val it : string option = Some "Indianapolis"
```

Finding Keys

Occasionally, you may need to find a key based on its mapped value. The `Map` module provides two functions for this: `findKey` and `tryFindKey`. Like their value-finding counterparts, the difference between `findKey` and `tryFindKey` is that `findKey` throws `KeyNotFoundException` when it can't find a value that satisfies the criteria, whereas `tryFindKey` does not.

To look up a key, you pass a function that accepts both the key and its mapped value and returns a Boolean indicating whether the value matches your criteria. For instance, to find a state by its capital using `Map.tryFindKey`, you could write:

```
> stateCapitals |> Map.tryFindKey (fun k v -> v = "Indianapolis");;
val it : string option = Some "Indiana"
> stateCapitals |> Map.tryFindKey (fun k v -> v = "Olympia");;
val it : string option = None
```

As you can see, `tryFindKey` returns an option, so you'll need to test for `Some` and `None` accordingly.

Converting Between Collection Types

Sometimes you'll have an instance of one collection type but you really need a different one. For instance, you might be working with an F# list but want to apply a function that works only with arrays. Each of the collection modules includes several functions that make converting between many of the other collection types easy.

In each module, the conversion functions are named according to the conversion direction and target type. For instance, to convert a sequence to an array, you could pass the sequence to either `Seq.toArray` or `Array.ofSeq` like this:

```
> seq { 1..10 } |> Seq.toArray;;
val it : int [] = [|1; 2; 3; 4; 5; 6; 7; 8; 9; 10|]
> seq { 1..10 } |> Array.ofSeq;;
val it : int [] = [|1; 2; 3; 4; 5; 6; 7; 8; 9; 10|]
```

Similarly, to convert from a list to a sequence, you could pass the list to either `List.toSeq` or `Seq.ofList`. The `Set` and `Map` modules let you convert to and from sequences, arrays, and maps according to the same conventions.

Although most of the conversion functions create a new collection, some of them work by casting. For example, `Seq.ofList` simply casts the source list to `seq<'t>` (remember, `FSharpList<'T>` implements `IEnumerable<'T>`, so it's a valid conversion), whereas `List.ofArray` creates a new array and populates it with the list's values. If there's ever a question as to whether the resulting collection is a type conversion or a new object, you can inspect them with the static `obj.ReferenceEquals` method as shown here:

```
> let l = [ 1..10 ]
obj.ReferenceEquals(l, Seq.ofList l);;

val l : int list = [1; 2; 3; 4; 5; 6; 7; 8; 9; 10]
val it : bool = ❶true

> let a = [| 1..10 |]
obj.ReferenceEquals(a, List.ofArray a);;

val a : int [] = [|1; 2; 3; 4; 5; 6; 7; 8; 9; 10|]
val it : bool = ❷false
```

The preceding snippet shows the result of calling both `Seq.ofList` and `List.ofArray`. You can see that ❶ `Seq.ofList` returns the same object, whereas `List.ofArray` ❷ returns a new object.

Summary

Working with data collections is something virtually every nontrivial application must do. F# lets you work with all of the traditional .NET collections like arrays and generic lists but also adds several other types like the F# list, sets, and maps, which are more suitable for functional programming.

In many regards, working with data collections in F# is more streamlined than in traditional .NET development because language features like sequence expressions, range expressions, and slice expressions make it easier to not only create collections, but also get at individual elements.

Finally, the various collection modules like `Seq`, `Array`, and `List` provide an easy mechanism for performing many common tasks with their respective collection types.

7

PATTERNS, PATTERNS, EVERYWHERE

Pattern matching is one of F#'s most powerful features. Patterns are so ingrained within the language that they're employed by many of the constructs you've already seen, like let bindings, try...with expressions, and lambda expressions. In this chapter, you'll learn about match expressions, predefined pattern types, and creating your own patterns with active patterns.

Match Expressions

Although F# allows imperative style branching through if expressions, they can be difficult to maintain, particularly as the conditional logic's complexity increases. Match expressions are F#'s primary branching mechanism.

On the surface, many match expressions resemble C#'s switch or Visual Basic's Select Case statements, but they're significantly more powerful. For instance, while switch and Select Case operate against only constant values, match expressions select an expression to evaluate according to which pattern matches the input. At their most basic, match expressions take the following form:

```
match ❶test-expression with
  | ❷pattern1 -> ❸result-expression1
  | ❹pattern2 -> ❺result-expression2
  | ...
```

In the preceding syntax, the expression at ❶ is evaluated and sequentially compared to each pattern in the expression body until a match is found. For example, if the result satisfies the pattern at ❷, the expression at ❸ is evaluated. Otherwise, the pattern at ❹ is tested and, if it matches, the expression at ❺ is evaluated, and so on. Because match expressions also return a value, each result expression must be of the same type.

The fact that patterns are matched sequentially has consequences for how you structure your code; you must organize your match expressions such that the patterns are listed from most to least specific. If a more general pattern is placed ahead of more specific patterns in a way that prevents any subsequent patterns from being evaluated, the compiler will issue a warning for each affected pattern.

Match expressions can be used with a wide variety of data types including (but not limited to) numbers, strings, tuples, and records. For example, here's a function with a simple match expression that works with a discriminated union:

```
let testOption opt =
  match opt with
  | Some(v) -> printfn "Some: %i" v
  | None -> printfn "None"
```

In this snippet, opt is inferred to be of type int option, and the match expression includes patterns for both the Some and None cases. When the match expression evaluates, it first tests whether opt matches Some. If so, the pattern binds the value from Some into v, which is then printed when the result expression is evaluated. Likewise, when None matches, the result expression simply prints out "None".

Guard Clauses

In addition to matching disparate values against patterns, you can further refine each case through *guard clauses*, which allow you to specify additional criteria that must be met to satisfy a case. For instance, you can use guard clauses (by inserting when followed by a condition) to distinguish between positive and negative numbers like so:

```
let testNumber value =
  match value with
  | ❶v when v < 0 -> printfn "%i is negative" v
  | ❷v when v > 0 -> printfn "%i is positive" v
  | _ -> printfn "zero"
```

In this example, we have two cases with identical patterns but different guard clauses. Even though any integer will match any of the three patterns, the guard clauses on patterns ❶ and ❷ cause matching to fail unless the captured value meets their criteria.

You can combine multiple guard clauses with Boolean operators for more complex matching logic. For instance, you could construct a case that matches only positive, even integers as follows:

```
let testNumber value =
  match value with
  | v when v > 0 && v % 2 = 0 -> printfn "%i is positive and even" v
  | v -> printfn "%i is zero, negative, or odd" v
```

Pattern-Matching Functions

There is an alternative match expression syntax called a *pattern-matching function*. With the pattern-matching function syntax, the match...with portion of the match expression is replaced with function like this:

```
> let testOption =
  function
  | Some(v) -> printfn "Some: %i" v
  | None -> printfn "None";;

val testOption : _arg1:int option -> unit
```

As you can see from the signature in the output, by using the pattern-matching function syntax, we bind testOption to a function that accepts an int option (with the generated name _arg1) and returns unit. Using the function keyword this way is a convenient shortcut for creating a pattern-matching lambda expression and is functionally equivalent to writing:

```
fun x ->
  match x with
  | Some(v) -> printfn "Some: %i" v
  | None -> printfn "None";;
```

Because pattern-matching functions are just a shortcut for lambda expressions, passing match expressions to higher-order functions is trivial. Suppose you want to filter out all of the None values from a list of optional integers. You might consider passing a pattern-matching function to the List.filter function like this:

```
[ Some 10; None; Some 4; None; Some 0; Some 7 ]
|> List.filter (function | Some(_) -> true
                         | None -> false)
```

When the filter function is executed, it will invoke the pattern-matching function against each item in the source list, returning true when the item is Some(_), or false when the item is None. As a result, the list created by filter will contain only Some 10, Some 4, Some 0, and Some 7.

Exhaustive Matching

When a match expression includes patterns such that every possible result of the test expression is accounted for, it is said to be *exhaustive*, or *covering*. When a value exists that isn't covered by a pattern, the compiler issues a warning. Consider what happens when we match against an integer but cover only a few cases.

```
> let numberToString =
  function
  | 0 -> "zero"
  | 1 -> "one"
  | 2 -> "two"
  | 3 -> "three";;

    function
  --^^^^^^^^

stdin(4,3): warning FS0025: Incomplete pattern matches on this expression. For
example, the value '4' may indicate a case not covered by the pattern(s).

val numberToString : _arg1:int -> string
```

Here you can see that if the integer is ever anything other than 0, 1, 2, or 3, it will never be matched. The compiler even provides an example of a value that might not be covered—four, in this case. If numberToString is called with a value that isn't covered, the call fails with a MatchFailureException:

```
> numberToString 4;;
Microsoft.FSharp.Core.MatchFailureException: The match cases were incomplete
   at FSI_0025.numberToString(Int32 _arg1)
   at <StartupCode$FSI_0026>.$FSI_0026.main@()
Stopped due to error
```

To address this problem, you could add more patterns, trying to match every possible value, but many times (such as with integers) matching every possible value isn't feasible. Other times, you may care only about a few cases. In either scenario, you can turn to one of the patterns that match any value: the Variable pattern or the Wildcard pattern.

Variable Patterns

Variable patterns are represented with an identifier and are used whenever you want to match any value and bind that value to a name. Any names defined through Variable patterns are then available for use within guard clauses and the result expression for that case. For example, to make `numberToString` exhaustive, you could revise the function to include a Variable pattern like this:

```
let numberToString =
  function
  | 0 -> "zero"
  | 1 -> "one"
  | 2 -> "two"
  | 3 -> "three"
❶ | n -> sprintf "%O" n
```

When you include a Variable pattern at ❶, anything other than 0, 1, 2, or 3 will be bound to n and simply converted to a string.

The identifier defined in a Variable pattern should begin with a lowercase letter to distinguish it from an Identifier pattern. Now, invoking `numberToString` with 4 will complete without error, as shown here:

```
> numberToString 4;;
val it : string = "4"
```

The Wildcard Pattern

The *Wildcard pattern*, represented as a single underscore character (_), works just like a Variable pattern except that it discards the matched value rather than binding it to a name.

Here's the previous `numberToString` implementation revised with a Wildcard pattern. Note that because the matched value is discarded, we need to return a general string instead of something based on the matched value.

```
let numberToString =
  function
  | 0 -> "zero"
  | 1 -> "one"
  | 2 -> "two"
  | 3 -> "three"
  | _ -> "unknown"
```

Matching Constant Values

Constant patterns consist of hardcoded numbers, characters, strings, and enumeration values. You've already seen several examples of Constant patterns, but to reiterate, the first four cases in the `numberToString` function that follows are all Constant patterns.

```
let numberToString =
  function
  | 0 -> "zero"
  | 1 -> "one"
  | 2 -> "two"
  | 3 -> "three"
  | _ -> "..."
```

Here, the numbers 0 through 3 are explicitly matched and return the number as a word. All other values fall into the wildcard case.

Identifier Patterns

When a pattern consists of more than a single character and begins with an uppercase character, the compiler attempts to resolve it as a name. This is called an *Identifier pattern* and typically refers to discriminated union cases, identifiers decorated with `LiteralAttribute`, or exception names (as seen in a `try...with` block).

Matching Union Cases

When the identifier is a discriminated union case, the pattern is called a *Union Case pattern*. Union Case patterns must include a wildcard or identifier for each data item associated with that case. If the case doesn't have any associated data, the case label can appear on its own.

Consider the following discriminated union that defines a few shapes:

```
type Shape =
| Circle of float
| Rectangle of float * float
| Triangle of float * float * float
```

From this definition, it's trivial to define a function that uses a match expression to calculate the perimeter of any of the included shapes. Here is one possible implementation:

```
let getPerimeter =
  function
  | Circle(r) -> 2.0 * System.Math.PI * r
  | Rectangle(w, h) -> 2.0 * (w + h)
  | Triangle(l1, l2, l3) -> l1 + l2 + l3
```

As you can see, each shape defined by the discriminated union is covered, and the data items from each case are extracted into meaningful names like r for the radius of a circle or w and h for the width and height of a rectangle, respectively.

Matching Literals

When the compiler encounters an identifier defined with LiteralAttribute used as a case, it is called a *Literal pattern* but is treated as though it were a Constant pattern.

Here is the numberToString function revised to use a few Literal patterns instead of Constant patterns:

```
[<LiteralAttribute>]
let Zero = 0
[<LiteralAttribute>]
let One = 1
[<LiteralAttribute>]
let Two = 2
[<LiteralAttribute>]
let Three = 3

let numberToString =
  function
  | Zero -> "zero"
  | One -> "one"
  | Two -> "two"
  | Three -> "three"
  | _ -> "unknown"
```

Matching Nulls

When performing pattern matching against types where null is a valid value, you'll typically want to include a *Null pattern* to keep any nulls as isolated as possible. Null patterns are represented with the null keyword.

Consider this matchString pattern-matching function:

```
> let matchString =
  function
  | "" -> None
  | v -> Some(v.ToString());;

val matchString : _arg1:string -> string option
```

The matchString function includes two cases: a Constant pattern for the empty string and a Variable pattern for everything else. The compiler was happy to create this function for us without warning about incomplete pattern matches, but there's a potentially serious problem: null is a valid value for strings, but the Variable pattern matches any value, including null!

Should a null string be passed to matchString, a NullReferenceException will be thrown when the ToString method is called on v because the Variable pattern matches null and therefore sets v to null, as shown here:

```
> matchString null;;
System.NullReferenceException: Object reference not set to an instance of an object.
   at FSI_0070.matchString(String _arg1) in C:\Users\Dave\AppData\Local\Temp\~vsE434.fsx:line 68
   at <StartupCode$FSI_0071>.$FSI_0071.main@()
Stopped due to error
```

Adding a Null pattern before the Variable pattern will ensure that the null value doesn't leak into the rest of the application. By convention, Null patterns are typically listed first, so that's the approach shown here with the null and empty string patterns combined with an OR pattern:

```
let matchString =
  function
  | null
  | "" -> None
  | v -> Some(v.ToString())
```

Matching Tuples

You can match and decompose a tuple to its constituent elements with a *Tuple pattern*. For instance, a two-dimensional point represented as a tuple can be decomposed to its individual x- and y-coordinates with a Tuple pattern within a let binding like this:

```
let point = 10, 20
let x, y = point
```

In this example, the values 10 and 20 are extracted from point and bound to the x and y identifiers, respectively.

Similarly, you can use several Tuple patterns within a match expression to perform branching based upon the tupled values. In keeping with the point theme, to determine whether a particular point is located at the origin or along an axis, you could write something like this:

```
let locatePoint p =
  match p with
  | ❶(0, 0) -> sprintf "%A is at the origin" p
  | ❷(_, 0) -> sprintf "%A is on the x-axis" p
  | ❸(0, _) -> sprintf "%A is on the y-axis" p
  | ❹(x, y) -> sprintf "Point (%i, %i)" x y
```

The `locatePoint` function not only highlights using multiple Tuple patterns but also shows how multiple pattern types can be combined to form more complex branching logic. For instance, ❶ uses two Constant patterns within a Tuple pattern, while ❷ and ❸ each use a Constant pattern and a Wildcard pattern within a Tuple pattern. Finally, ❹ uses two Variable patterns within a Tuple pattern.

Remember, the number of items in a Tuple pattern must match the number of items in the tuple itself. For instance, attempting to match a Tuple pattern containing two items with a tuple containing three items will result in a compiler error because the underlying types are incompatible.

Matching Records

Record types can participate in pattern matching through Record patterns. With *Record patterns*, individual record instances can be matched and decomposed to their individual values.

Consider the following record type definition based on a typical American name:

```
type Name = { First : string; Middle : string option; Last : string }
```

In this record type, both the first and last names are required, but the middle name is optional. You can use a match expression to format the name according to whether a middle name is specified like so:

```
let formatName =
  function
  | { First = f; Middle = Some(m); Last = l } -> sprintf "%s, %s %s" l f m
  | { First = f; Middle = None; Last = l } -> sprintf "%s, %s" l f
```

Here, both patterns bind the first and last names to the identifiers f and l, respectively. But more interesting is how the patterns match the middle name against union cases for Some(m) and None. When the match expression is evaluated against a Name that includes a middle name, the middle name is bound to m. Otherwise, the match fails and the None case is evaluated.

The patterns in the `formatName` function extract each value from the record, but Record patterns can operate against a subset of the labels, too. For instance, if you want to determine only whether a name includes a middle name, you could construct a match expression like this:

```
let hasMiddleName =
  function
  | { Middle = Some(_) } -> true
  | { Middle = None } -> false
```

Many times, the compiler can automatically resolve which record type the pattern is constructed against, but if it can't, you can specify the type name as follows:

```
let hasMiddleName =
  function
  | { Name.Middle = Some(_) } -> true
  | { Name.Middle = None } -> false
```

Qualifying the pattern like this will typically be necessary only when there are multiple record types with conflicting definitions.

Matching Collections

Pattern matching isn't limited to single values or structured data like tuples and records. F# includes several patterns for matching one-dimensional arrays and lists, too. If you want to match against another collection type, you'll typically need to convert the collection to a list or array with List.ofSeq, Array.ofSeq, or a comparable mechanism.

Array Patterns

Array patterns closely resemble array definitions and let you match arrays with a specific number of elements. For example, you can use Array patterns to determine the length of an array like this:

```
let getLength =
  function
  | null -> 0
  | [| |] -> 0
  | [| _ |] -> 1
  | [| _; _; |] -> 2
  | [| _; _; _ |] -> 3
  | a -> a |> Array.length
```

Ignoring the fact that to get the length of an array you'd probably forego this contrived pattern-matching example and inspect the Array.length property directly, the getLength function shows how Array patterns can match individual array elements from fixed-size arrays.

List Patterns

List patterns are similar to Array patterns except that they look like and work against F# lists. Here's the getLength function revised to work with F# lists instead of arrays.

```
let getLength =
  function
  | [ ] -> 0
  | [ _ ] -> 1
```

```
  | [ _; _; ] -> 2
  | [ _; _; _ ] -> 3
  | lst -> lst |> List.length
```

Note that there's no `null` case because `null` is not a valid value for an F# list.

Cons Patterns

Another way to match F# lists is with the *Cons pattern*. In pattern matching, the cons operator (::) works in reverse; instead of prepending an element to a list, it separates a list's head from its tail. This allows you to recursively match against a list with an arbitrary number of elements.

In keeping with our theme, here's how you could use a Cons pattern to find a collection's length through pattern matching:

```
let getLength n =
  ❶let rec len c l =
    match l with
    | ❷[] -> c
    | ❸_ :: t -> len (c + 1) t
  len 0 n
```

This version of the `getLength` function is very similar to the F# list's internal `length` property implementation. It defines `len` ❶, an internal function that recursively matches against either an empty pattern ❷ or a Cons pattern ❸. When the empty list is matched, `len` returns the supplied count value (`c`); otherwise, it makes a recursive call, incrementing the count and passing along the tail. The Cons pattern in `getLength` uses the Wildcard pattern for the head value because it's not needed for subsequent operations.

Matching by Type

F# has two ways to match against particular data types: Type-Annotated patterns and Dynamic Type-Test patterns.

Type-Annotated Patterns

Type-Annotated patterns let you specify the type of the matched value. They are especially useful in pattern-matching functions where the compiler needs a little extra help determining the expected type of the function's implicit parameter. For example, the following function is supposed to check whether a string begins with an uppercase character:

```
// Does not compile
let startsWithUpperCase =
  function
  | ❶s when ❷s.Length > 0 && s.[0] = System.Char.ToUpper s.[0] -> true
  | _ -> false
```

As written, though, the `startsWithUpperCase` function won't compile. Instead, it will fail with the following error:

```
~vsD607.fsx(83,12): error FS0072: Lookup on object of indeterminate type based
on information prior to this program point. A type annotation may be needed
prior to this program point to constrain the type of the object. This may
allow the lookup to be resolved.
```

The reason this fails to compile is that the guard conditions at ❷ rely on string properties, but those properties aren't available because the compiler has automatically generalized the function's implicit parameter. To fix the problem, we could either revise the function to have an explicit string parameter or we can include a type annotation in the pattern at ❶ like this (note that the parentheses are required):

```
let startsWithUpperCase =
  function
  | (s : string) when s.Length > 0 && s.[0] = System.Char.ToUpper s.[0] ->
    true
  | _ -> false
```

With the type annotation in place, the parameter is no longer automatically generalized, making the string's properties available within the guard condition.

Dynamic Type-Test Patterns

Dynamic Type-Test patterns are, in a sense, the opposite of Type-Annotated patterns. Where Type-Annotated patterns force each case to match against the same data type, Dynamic Type-Test patterns are satisfied when the matched value is an instance of a particular type; that is, if you annotate a pattern to match strings, every case must match against strings. Dynamic Type-Test patterns are therefore useful for matching against type hierarchies. For instance, you might match against an interface instance but use Dynamic Type-Test patterns to provide different logic for specific implementations. Dynamic Type-Test patterns resemble the dynamic cast operator (:?>) except that the > is omitted.

The following `detectColorSpace` function shows you how to use Dynamic Type-Test patterns by matching against three record types. If none of the types are matched, the function raises an exception.

```
type RgbColor = { R : int; G : int; B : int }
type CmykColor = { C : int; M : int; Y : int; K : int }
type HslColor = { H : int; S : int; L : int }

let detectColorSpace (cs : obj) =
  match cs with
  | :? RgbColor -> printfn "RGB"
  | :? CmykColor -> printfn "CMYK"
  | :? HslColor -> printfn "HSL"
  | _ -> failwith "Unrecognized"
```

As Patterns

The *As pattern* lets you bind a name to the whole matched value and is particularly useful in let bindings that use pattern matching and pattern-matching functions where you don't have direct named access to the matched value.

Normally, a let binding simply binds a name to a value, but as you've seen, you can also use patterns in a let binding to decompose a value and bind name to each of its constituent parts like this:

```
> let x, y = (10, 20);;

val y : int = 20
val x : int = 10
```

If you want to bind not only the constituent parts but also the whole value, you could explicitly use two let bindings like this:

```
> let point = (10, 20)
let x, y = point;;

val point : int * int = (10, 20)
val y : int = 20
val x : int = 10
```

Having two separate let bindings certainly works, but it's more succinct to combine them into one with an As pattern like so:

```
> let x, y as point = (10, 20);;

val point : int * int = (10, 20)
val y : int = 20
val x : int = 10
```

The As pattern isn't restricted to use within let bindings; you can also use it within match expressions. Here, we include an As pattern in each case to bind the matched tuple to a name.

```
let locatePoint =
  function
  | (0, 0) as p -> sprintf "%A is at the origin" p
  | (_, 0) as p -> sprintf "%A is on the X-Axis" p
  | (0, _) as p -> sprintf "%A is on the Y-Axis" p
  | (x, y) as p -> sprintf "Point (%i, %i)" x y
```

Combining Patterns with AND

With *AND patterns*, sometimes called *Conjunctive patterns*, you match the input against multiple, compatible patterns by combining them with an ampersand (&). For the case to match, the input must satisfy each pattern.

Generally speaking, AND patterns aren't all that useful in basic pattern-matching scenarios because the more expressive guard clauses are usually better suited to the task. That said, AND patterns are still useful for things like extracting values when another pattern is matched. (AND patterns are also used heavily with active patterns, which we'll look at later.) For example, to determine whether a two-dimensional point is located at the origin or along an axis, you could write something like this:

```
let locatePoint =
  function
  | (0, 0) as p -> sprintf "%A is at the origin" p
  | ❶(x, y) & (_, 0) -> sprintf "(%i, %i) is on the x-axis" x y
  | ❷(x, y) & (0, _) -> sprintf "(%i, %i) is on the y-axis" x y
  | (x, y) -> sprintf "Point (%i, %i)" x y
```

The locatePoint function uses AND patterns at ❶ and ❷ to extract the x and y values from a tuple when the second or first value is 0, respectively.

Combining Patterns with OR

If a number of patterns should execute the same code when they're matched, you can combine them using an OR, or *Disjunctive*, pattern. An *OR pattern* combines multiple patterns with a vertical pipe character (|). In many ways, OR patterns are similar to fall-through cases in C#'s switch statements.

Here, the locatePoint function has been revised to use an OR pattern so the same message can be printed for points on either axis:

```
let locatePoint =
  function
  | (0, 0) as p -> sprintf "%A is at the origin" p
  | ❶(_, 0) | ❷(0, _) as p -> ❸sprintf "%A is on an axis" p
  | p -> sprintf "Point %A" p
```

In this version of locatePoint, the expression at ❸ is evaluated when either the pattern at ❶ or ❷ is satisfied.

Parentheses in Patterns

When combining patterns, you can establish precedence with parentheses. For instance, to extract the x and y values from a point and also match whether the point is on either axis, you could write something like this:

```
let locatePoint =
  function
  | (0, 0) as p -> sprintf "%A is at the origin" p
  | (x, y) & ❶((_, 0) | (0, _)) -> sprintf "(%i, %i) is on an axis" x y
  | p -> sprintf "Point %A" p
```

Here, you match three patterns, establishing associativity at ❶ by wrapping the two axis-checking patterns in parentheses.

Active Patterns

When none of the built-in pattern types do quite what you need, you can turn to active patterns. *Active patterns* are a special type of function definition, called an *active recognizer*, where you define one or more case names for use in your pattern-matching expressions.

Active patterns have many of the same characteristics of the built-in pattern types; they accept an input value and can decompose the value to its constituent parts. Unlike basic patterns, though, active patterns not only let you define what constitutes a match for each named case, but they can also accept other inputs.

Active patterns are defined with the following syntax:

```
let (|CaseName1|CaseName2|...|CaseNameN|) [parameters] -> expression
```

As you can see, the case names are enclosed between (| and |) (called *banana clips*) and are pipe-delimited. The active pattern definition must always include at least one parameter for the value to match and, because active recognizer functions are curried, the matched value must be the final parameter in order to work correctly with match expressions. Finally, the expression's return value must be one of the named cases along with any associated data.

There are plenty of uses for active patterns, but a good example lies in a possible solution to the famed FizzBuzz problem. For the uninitiated, FizzBuzz is a puzzle that employers sometimes use during interviews to help screen candidates. The task at the heart of the problem is simple and often phrased thusly:

> Write a program that prints the numbers from 1 to 100. But for multiples of three, print "Fizz" instead of the number; for the multiples of five, print "Buzz". For numbers that are multiples of both three and five, print "FizzBuzz".

To be clear, active patterns certainly aren't the only (or necessarily even the best) way to solve the FizzBuzz problem. But the FizzBuzz problem—with its multiple, overlapping rules—allows us to showcase how powerful active patterns are.

We can start by defining the active recognizer. From the preceding description, we know that we need four patterns: Fizz, Buzz, FizzBuzz, and a default case for everything else. We also know the criteria for each case, so our recognizer might look something like this:

```
let (|Fizz|Buzz|FizzBuzz|Other|) n =
  match ❶(n % 3, n % 5) with
  | ❷0, 0 -> FizzBuzz
  | ❸0, _ -> Fizz
```

```
| ❹_, 0 -> Buzz
| ❺_  -> Other n
```

Here we have an active recognizer that defines the four case names. The recognizer's body relies on further pattern matching to select the appropriate case. At ❶, we construct a tuple containing the modulus of *n* and 3 and the modulus of *n* and 5. We then use a series of Tuple patterns to identify the correct case, the most specific being ❷, where both elements are 0. The cases at ❸ and ❹ match when *n* is divisible by 3 and *n* is divisible by 5, respectively. The final case, ❺, uses the Wildcard pattern to match everything else and return Other along with the supplied number. The active pattern gets us only partway to the solution, though; we still need to print the results.

The active recognizer identifies only which case a given number meets, so we still need a way to translate each case to a string. We can easily map the cases with a pattern-matching function like this:

```
let fizzBuzz =
  function
  | Fizz -> "Fizz"
  | Buzz -> "Buzz"
  | FizzBuzz -> "FizzBuzz"
  | Other n -> n.ToString()
```

The preceding fizzBuzz function uses basic pattern matching, but instead of using the built-in patterns, it uses cases defined by the active recognizer. Note how the Other case includes a Variable pattern, n, to hold the number associated with it.

Finally, we can complete the task by printing the results. We could do this in an imperative style, but because a functional approach is more fun let's use a sequence like this:

```
seq { 1..100 }
|> Seq.map fizzBuzz
|> Seq.iter (printfn "%s")
```

Here, we create a sequence containing the numbers 1 through 100 and pipe it to Seq.map, which creates a new sequence containing the strings returned from fizzBuzz. The resulting sequence is then piped on to Seq.iter to print each value.

Partial Active Patterns

As convenient as active patterns are, they do have a few drawbacks. First, each input must map to a named case. Second, active patterns are limited to seven named cases. If your situation doesn't require mapping every possible input or you need more than seven cases, you can turn to partial active patterns.

Partial active patterns follow the same basic structure as complete active patterns, but instead of a list of case names they include only a single case name followed by an underscore. The basic syntax for a partial active pattern looks like this:

```
let (|CaseName|_|) [parameters] = expression
```

The value returned by a partial active pattern is a bit different than complete active patterns, too. Instead of returning the case directly, partial active patterns return an option of the pattern's type. For example, if you have a partial active pattern for `Fizz`, the expression needs to return either `Some(Fizz)` or `None`. As far as your match expressions are concerned, though, the option is transparent, so you need to deal only with the case name.

NOTE   *If you're following along in FSI, you'll want to reset your session before proceeding with the next examples to avoid any potential naming conflicts between the active patterns.*

To see partial active patterns in action, we can return to the FizzBuzz problem. Using partial active patterns lets us rewrite the solution more succinctly. We can start by defining the partial active patterns like this:

```
let (|Fizz|_|) n = if n % 3 = 0 then Some Fizz else None
let (|Buzz|_|) n = if n % 5 = 0 then Some Buzz else None
```

The first thing you probably thought after reading the preceding snippet is "Why are there only two cases when the problem specifically defines three?" The reason is that partial active patterns are evaluated independently. So, to meet the requirements, we can construct a match expression such that a single case matches both `Fizz` and `Buzz` with an AND pattern, as shown here:

```
let fizzBuzz =
  function
  | Fizz & Buzz -> "FizzBuzz"
  | Fizz -> "Fizz"
  | Buzz -> "Buzz"
  | n -> n.ToString()
```

Now all that's left is to print the required values just like we did before:

```
seq { 1..100 }
|> Seq.map fizzBuzz
|> Seq.iter (printfn "%s")
```

Parameterized Active Patterns

All of the active patterns we've seen so far have accepted only the single match value; we haven't seen any that accept additional arguments that aid in matching. Remember, active recognizer functions are curried, so to include additional parameters in your active pattern definition you'll need to list them before the match input argument.

It's possible to construct yet another solution to the FizzBuzz problem using only a single *Parameterized partial active pattern*. Consider this definition:

```
let (|DivisibleBy|_|) d n = if n % d = 0 then Some DivisibleBy else None
```

This partial active pattern looks just like the `Fizz` and `Buzz` partial active patterns we defined in the previous section except that it includes the `d` parameter, which it uses in the expression. We can now use this pattern to resolve the correct word from any input, like so:

```
let fizzBuzz =
  function
  | DivisibleBy 3 & DivisibleBy 5 -> "FizzBuzz"
  | DivisibleBy 3 -> "Fizz"
  | DivisibleBy 5 -> "Buzz"
  | n -> n.ToString()
```

Now, instead of specialized cases for `Fizz` and `Buzz`, we simply match whether the input is divisible by three or five through the parameterized pattern. Printing out the results is no different than before:

```
seq { 1..100 }
|> Seq.map fizzBuzz
|> Seq.iter (printfn "%s")
```

Summary

Pattern matching is one of F#'s most powerful and versatile features. Despite some superficial similarities to case-based branching structures in other languages, F#'s match expressions are a completely different animal. Not only does pattern matching offer an expressive way to match and decompose virtually any data type, but it even returns values as well.

In this chapter, you learned how to compose match expressions directly using `match...with` and indirectly using the `function` keyword. You also saw how the simple pattern types like the Wildcard, Variable, and Constant patterns can be used independently or in conjunction with other more complex patterns like those for records and lists. Finally, you saw how you can create your own custom patterns with complete and partial active patterns.

8

MEASURING UP

It is all too easy to mix up units of measurement in a long, intricate computer program. When such a mix-up occurs, the consequences can be extremely costly, even tragic. One of the most famous examples is the crash of NASA's *Mars Climate Orbiter* in 1999. Investigation into the accident revealed that the crash was caused by a unit mismatch; pound-force seconds were used instead of newton seconds. This error led to an incorrect trajectory calculation and ultimately to the vehicle's demise.

One can argue that proper testing should have detected the calculation error and thus prevented the crash, but a bigger question is whether the error would have even occurred if the programming language had enforced the proper units through its type system.

Over the years, people have tried enforcing units of measure in software systems, usually through external libraries, to varying degrees of success. F# is one of the first languages to include units of measure as a native part of its static type checking system. In addition to providing an extra level of safety beyond the basic type system, F#'s units of measure can enhance code readability by removing ambiguity about what is actually expected in the code without resorting to longer identifiers.

Defining Measures

To enable static measure checking, you first need to define a measure. *Measures* are type-like constructs that are decorated with the Measure attribute to represent real-world measurements. They can include an optional *measure formula* that describes the measure in terms of other measures. For example, the following definition creates a named unit of measure for a foot:

```
[<Measure>] type foot
```

INTERNATIONAL SYSTEM OF UNITS

F# 3.0 includes predefined measure types for the International System of Units (SI) units, including meters, kilograms, and amperes, among many others. You can find each SI unit in the Microsoft.FSharp.Data.UnitSystems namespace. Prior to F# 3.0, the SI units are included in the F# PowerPack and can be found in the Microsoft.FSharp.Math namespace.

Measure Formulas

Measure formulas allow you to define derivative measures based on one or more previously defined measures. At their most basic, formulas serve as an easy way to create synonyms for types. For instance, if you've defined a measure named foot and want to abbreviate it as ft, you could write this:

```
[<Measure>] type ft = foot
```

Measure formulas aren't always quite so simple, though; they can also be used to describe more complex relationships between types, such as a measurement of distance over time. For example, miles per hour could be defined as m / h (assuming that m and h were previously defined to represent miles and hours, respectively).

Here are some of the most notable guidelines to follow when composing measure formulas:

- You can multiply measures by separating two measures with a space or an asterisk (*) to create a *product measure*. For instance, torque is sometimes measured in pound-feet and could be represented in F# as:

```
[<Measure>] type lb
[<Measure>] type ft
[<Measure>] type lbft = lb ft
```

- You can divide measures by separating two measures with a forward slash (/) to create a *quotient measure*. For instance, a distance over time, such as miles per hour, could be expressed like this:

```
[<Measure>] type m
[<Measure>] type h
[<Measure>] type mph = m / h
```

- Positive and negative integral values can be used to express an exponential relationship between two measures. For instance, square feet can be expressed like this:

```
[<Measure>] type ft
[<Measure>] type sqft = ft ^ 2
```

Applying Measures

Once you've defined some measures you can apply them to values. Out of the box, F# defines measure-aware variations of the sbyte, int16, int32, int64, float, float32, and decimal primitive types. Values without measure annotations are said to be *measureless* or *dimensionless*.

To apply a measure to a constant value, you simply need to annotate the value as if the measure were a generic type parameter. For instance, you could define a length in feet and an area in square feet as follows:

```
> let length = 10.0<ft>
let area = 10.0<sqft>;;

val length : float<ft> = 10.0
val area : float<sqft> = 10.0
```

As you can see, length is bound to float<ft> while area is bound to float<sqft>.

Measure annotations are great for constant values, but how can we apply measures to external data (such as something read from a database)? The easiest way to convert a measureless value to a measured one is to multiply it by a measured value, like this:

```
[<Measure>] type dpi
let resolution = 300.0 * 1.0<dpi>
```

Here, we define a measure representing dots per inch (dpi) and create a resolution by multiplying 300.0 by 1.0<dpi>.

For a more verbose alternative, you can use one of the seven typed WithMeasure functions from the LanguagePrimitives module. Each WithMeasure function corresponds to one of the measured primitives. Here's how to create a new measured value using the FloatWithMeasure function:

```
[<Measure>] type dpi
let resolution = LanguagePrimitives.FloatWithMeasure<dpi> 300.0
```

The WithMeasure functions are a bit more explicit in their intent and are definitely more verbose. Typically, their use is reserved for when type inference fails.

Stripping Measures

The vast majority of functions do not accept unitized values, so you may need to strip measures from values. Luckily, like applying measures, stripping measures is easy.

The typical way to strip measures is to simply divide the value by a measured 1, like this:

```
[<Measure>] type dpi
300.0<dpi> / 1.0<dpi>
```

Alternatively, you can use the corresponding type conversion operator to achieve the same effect. For instance, we can strip the units from 300.0<dpi> by calling the float function as follows:

```
[<Measure>] type dpi
float 300.0<dpi>
```

Enforcing Measures

Because units of measure are part of F#'s type system, you can enforce that values passed to a function use the correct units through type annotations on the parameters. Here we define a getArea function that requires the supplied width and height to be measured in feet:

```
> let getArea (w : float<ft>) (h : float<ft>) = w * h;;

val getArea : w:float<ft> -> h:float<ft> -> float<ft ^ 2>
```

If you were to call getArea with measureless arguments as shown here, you'd receive the following error:

```
> getArea 10.0 10.0;;

  getArea 10.0 10.0;;
  --------^^^^

C:\Users\Dave\AppData\Local\Temp\stdin(9,9): error FS0001: This expression was expected to have type
    float<ft>
but here has type
    float
```

Similarly, calling getArea with arguments annotated with the wrong measure (or no measure at all) will result in a compiler error. To correctly call the getArea function, you must provide values in the proper units, like this:

```
> getArea 10.0<ft> 10.0<ft>;;
val it : float<ft ^ 2> = 100.0
```

Notice that the function's return value is float<ft ^ 2> despite our having defined sqft as ft ^ 2. The compiler doesn't automatically convert the measures unless explicitly instructed to do so through a return type annotation, as shown here:

```
> let getArea (w : float<ft>) (h : float<ft>) : float<sqft> = w * h;;

val getArea : w:float<ft> -> h:float<ft> -> float<sqft>

> getArea 10.0<ft> 10.0<ft>;;
val it : float<sqft> = 100.0
```

Ranges

Measured units are permissible in range expressions, but there's a catch: You must provide a step value. To create a measured range, you could write something like this:

```
> let measuredRange = [1.0<ft>..1.0<ft>..10.0<ft>];;

val measuredRange : float<ft> list =
  [1.0; 2.0; 3.0; 4.0; 5.0; 6.0; 7.0; 8.0; 9.0; 10.0]
```

Without an explicit step value, the compiler will try to create the range with the underlying type's default, measureless value and will raise an error.

Converting Between Measures

While measure formulas allow you to create derivative units, they really aren't flexible enough to allow arbitrary conversions between measures. To work around this limitation, you can define measure types with static members for both conversion factors and functions.

Static Conversion Factors

Defining a conversion factor on a measure type takes the same syntax as a static property. For instance, since there are 12 inches per foot, you could write something like this:

```
[<Measure>] type ft
[<Measure>] type inch = static member perFoot = 12.0<inch/ft>
```

The perFoot conversion can be accessed through the inch type like any static property. To convert from feet to inches, you would multiply a value measured in feet by inch.perFoot, as follows:

```
> 2.0<ft> * inch.perFoot;;
val it : float<inch> = 24.0
```

Notice how the compiler inferred through the multiplication operation that the result should be measured in inches. Similarly, we can convert from inches to feet by dividing a value measured in inches by inch.perFoot:

```
> 36.0<inch> / inch.perFoot;;
val it : float<ft> = 3.0
```

Static Conversion Functions

When you need more than a conversion factor, you can define static conversion functions (and their reciprocal conversions) directly on the measure types. Consistently defining the conversion functions on both measure types can help avoid confusion about where they're defined.

To maximize code reuse, you can define the measure types as mutually recursive types by joining them together with the and keyword. Here, we define Fahrenheit and Celsius measures as mutually recursive types:

```
[<Measure>]
type f =
  static member toCelsius (t : float<f>) = ((float t - 32.0) * (5.0/9.0)) * 1.0<c>
  static member fromCelsius (t : float<c>) = ((float t * (9.0/5.0)) + 32.0) * 1.0<f>
and
  [<Measure>]
  c =
    static member toFahrenheit = f.fromCelsius
    static member fromFahrenheit = f.toCelsius
```

The Fahrenheit measure includes functions for converting to and from Celsius. Likewise, the Celsius measure includes functions for converting to and from Fahrenheit, but through the mutually recursive definition it can reuse the functions defined on the Fahrenheit type.

Depending on the complexity of your measure definitions or the conversion functions, you may find it cleaner to define the types independently and add the static methods later with intrinsic type extensions. This snippet shows one possible approach:

```
[<Measure>] type f
[<Measure>] type c

let fahrenheitToCelsius (t : float<f>) =
  ((float t - 32.0) * (5.0/9.0)) * 1.0<c>

let celsiusToFahrenheit (t : float<c>) =
  ((float t * (9.0/5.0)) + 32.0) * 1.0<f>

type f with static member toCelsius = fahrenheitToCelsius
           static member fromCelsius = celsiusToFahrenheit

type c with static member toFahrenheit = celsiusToFahrenheit
           static member fromFahrenheit = fahrenheitToCelsius
```

Here, the measure types are defined on their own (without mutual recursion) and immediately followed by the conversion functions. Since neither of the conversion functions has been attached to the measure types, we follow their definition by extending the measure types with static properties that expose the conversion functions.

Generic Measures

You've already seen numerous examples of how to write measure-aware functions for specific measure types, but it's also possible to write functions against arbitrary measures using *generic measures*. Writing such a function is the same as for specific measure types, except that instead of using a concrete unit value you use an underscore character (_). Alternatively, or when your function accepts multiple parameters that must use the same generic measure type, you can use a generic identifier (such as 'U) instead of an underscore.

You might use generic measures when you need to perform the same operation against a variety of measures. For instance, you could write a function that computes the square of any measured float like this:

```
let square (v : float<_>) = v * v
```

Because square is defined to use a generic measure, its argument can accept any measured type. In fact, its argument can even be measureless. Here we use the square function to compute square inches, square feet, and a measureless square:

```
> square 10.0<inch>;;
val it : float<inch ^ 2> = 100.0
> square 10.0<ft>;;
val it : float<ft ^ 2> = 100.0
> square 10.0;;
val it : float = 100.0
```

Custom Measure-Aware Types

You can create your own measure-aware type by defining a generic type with a type parameter decorated with the Measure attribute. Consider the following record type:

```
type Point< ❶[<Measure>] 'u > = { X : ❷float<'u>; Y : ❸float<'u> } with
  member ❹this.FindDistance other =
    let deltaX = other.X - this.X
    let deltaY = other.Y - this.Y
    sqrt ((deltaX * deltaX) + (deltaY * deltaY))
```

The Point type behaves just like any other record type, except that its members are defined as generic measures. Rather than working only with measureless floats, Point includes a single measure, 'u ❶, that is used by X ❷ and Y ❸. Point also defines a FindDistance function ❹ that performs a measure-safe calculation to find the distance between two points. Here we create a `Point` instance and invoke the `FindDistance` function against another `Point`:

```
> let p = { X = 10.0<inch>; Y = 10.0<inch> }
p.FindDistance { X = 20.0<inch>; Y = 15.0<inch> };;

val p : Point<inch> = {X = 10.0;
                       Y = 10.0;}
val it : float<inch> = 11.18033989
```

If you try calling `FindDistance` with a `Point` that uses a different measure, the compiler will raise a type mismatch error like this:

```
> p.FindDistance { X = 20.0<ft>; Y = 15.0<ft> };;

  p.FindDistance { X = 20.0<ft>; Y = 15.0<ft> };;
  --------------------^^^^^^^^

C:\Users\Dave\AppData\Local\Temp\stdin(5,22): error FS0001: Type mismatch. Expecting a
    float<inch>
but given a
    float<ft>
The unit of measure 'inch' does not match the unit of measure 'ft'
```

Custom measure-aware types aren't restricted to record types, either. For instance, you could define an equivalent measure-aware class like this:

```
type Point< [<Measure>] 'u > (x : float<'u>, y : float<'u>) =
  member this.X = x
  member this.Y = y
  member this.FindDistance (other : Point<'u>) =
    let deltaX = other.X - this.X
    let deltaY = other.Y - this.Y
    sqrt ((deltaX * deltaX) + (deltaY * deltaY))
```

Summary

Most programming languages rely on programmer discipline to ensure that measures are used correctly and consistently. One of the unique ways that F# helps developers produce more correct code is by including a rich syntax for units of measure directly within its type system.

F# not only includes predefined measure types for the International System of Units, but it also lets you define your own. You can enforce that the proper units are used in your calculations by annotating individual constant values with the appropriate measure or including them in type annotations in function definitions. Finally, you can define your own measure-aware types using a generic-like syntax.

9

CAN I QUOTE YOU ON THAT?

Another feature introduced to the .NET Framework with LINQ is expression trees. Often using the same syntax as lambda expressions, *expression trees* compile not to executable code but instead into a tree structure that describes the code and can be parsed for translation to other forms. This type of programming is often called *metaprogramming*. Just as we can think of metadata as data that describes data, we can think of metaprogramming as code that describes code.

This chapter isn't about expression trees, though; it's about a similar construct in F# called a *quoted expression*, also known as a *code quotation*. Quoted expressions address the same basic problem as expression trees, but they take a fundamentally different approach. Let's quickly compare expression trees to quoted expressions before diving into how to compose and parse quoted expressions within your F# code.

Comparing Expression Trees and Quoted Expressions

Expression trees are commonly used with LINQ providers to translate certain C# or Visual Basic expressions into SQL, but they aren't only useful for translating code between languages. Sometimes expression trees are employed to add an extra degree of safety or readability to code that would otherwise be confusing or error-prone. Consider the INotifyPropertyChanged interface commonly used in WPF and Silverlight.

INotifyPropertyChanged defines a single member: an event with a string parameter, PropertyName, that identifies the property that changed and triggered the event. You raise the PropertyChanged event by creating a PropertyChangedEventArgs instance and passing the property name to the constructor as a string. This approach is error prone, though: Because there are no inherent checks around the string passed to the PropertyChangedEventArgs constructor, it's possible to provide an invalid name. Expression trees can help avoid problems like this, as shown in the following C# class, which employs an expression tree to safely identify the changed property without resorting to obscene amounts of reflection code:

```
// C#
public class PropertyChangedExample
  : INotifyPropertyChanged
{
  public event PropertyChangedEventHandler PropertyChanged;

  private string _myProperty = String.Empty;

  public string MyProperty
  {
    get { return _myProperty; }
    set
    {
      _myProperty = value;
      RaisePropertyChangedEvent(❶() => MyProperty);
    }
  }

  protected void RaisePropertyChangedEvent<TValue>(
    ❷Expression<Func<TValue>> propertyExpr)
  {
    if(PropertyChanged == null) return;

    var memberExpr = ❸(MemberExpression)propertyExpr.Body;
    var ea = new PropertyChangedEventArgs(❹memberExpr.Member.Name);

    PropertyChanged(this, ea);
  }
}
```

The preceding example shows a twist on the typical pattern for implementing INotifyPropertyChanged. Instead of passing a magic string to the RaisePropertyChangedEvent method ❶, it uses a lambda expression. This lambda expression isn't compiled to a delegate, however. Instead, the C# compiler infers through the signature that it should compile the lambda expression to an expression tree ❷. Inside the method, we then cast the expression's body to MemberExpression at ❸ so we can extract the property name and pass it to PropertyChangedEventArgs at ❹.

Quoted expressions serve a similar purpose in F#, but unlike expression trees, they were designed with an emphasis on functional programming, not only with how they're constructed but also with how they're parsed. Furthermore, expression trees don't support many important F# concepts. By contrast, quoted expressions are fully aware of concepts like currying, partial application, and recursive declarations (let rec). Finally, quoted expressions are designed for recursive parsing, which makes it almost trivial to walk the entire quoted structure.

You can rewrite the preceding C# class in F# using quoted expressions as follows:

```
// F#
open Microsoft.FSharp.Quotations
open Microsoft.FSharp.Quotations.Patterns
open System.ComponentModel

type PropertyChangedExample() as x =
  let pce = Event<_, _>()
  let mutable _myProperty = ""
❶ let triggerPce =
    function
    | ❷PropertyGet(_, pi, _) ->
        let ea = PropertyChangedEventArgs(pi.Name)
        pce.Trigger(x, ea)
    | _ -> failwith "PropertyGet quotation is required"
  interface INotifyPropertyChanged with
    [<CLIEvent>]
    member x.PropertyChanged = pce.Publish
  member x.MyProperty with get() = _myProperty
                      and set(value) = _myProperty <- value
                                       triggerPce(❸<@@ x.MyProperty @@>)
```

This revised version of the PropertyChangedExample class is structured much like the C# version. As in the C# version, PropertyChangedEvent isn't published directly. Instead, the triggerPce function at ❶ accepts a quoted expression and uses pattern matching to determine whether the supplied quoted expression represents getting the value of a property at ❷. Finally, instead of a lambda expression in the call to triggerPce at ❸, the quoted expression is represented as a property reference enclosed within <@@ and @@>. By using a quoted expression, we allow the compiler to determine whether the supplied property is valid, rather than crossing our fingers and hoping we've entered the correct name. Using a quoted expression in this manner also protects us against future refactorings where we remove or rename a property but forget to update the string.

Despite their many similarities, quoted expressions and expression trees aren't quite the same. First, there's no built-in way to evaluate quoted expressions, nor is there any built-in way to translate between quoted expressions and expression trees. Should you need to perform either task, you'll need to turn to the F# PowerPack, or another library that provides these capabilities. With the inclusion of query expressions (Chapter 10) in F# 3.0, however, these needs should be diminished.

Composing Quoted Expressions

Quoted expressions can take one of two forms: strongly typed and weakly typed. The distinction between the two forms is a bit of a misnomer because all quotation expressions are ultimately based upon either the Expr<'T> or Expr types found in the Microsoft.FSharp.Quotations namespace. In this context, strong and weak typing really indicates whether the quotation carries information about the expression type as opposed to describing the expression through its constituent parts. You can get a weakly typed quoted expression from a strongly typed one through its Raw property.

In addition to the Expr and Expr<'T> types, the Microsoft.FSharp.Quotations namespace also includes the Var type. The Var type is used inside quoted expressions to describe binding information including a binding name, its data type, and whether the binding is mutable.

Regardless of whether a quoted expression is strongly or weakly typed, all quoted expressions are subject to a few constraints. First, object expressions are forbidden within quotations. Next, the quotation cannot resolve to a generic expression. Finally, the quotation must be a complete expression; that is, a quotation must do more than define a let binding. Attempting to create a quoted expression that violates any of these criteria will result in a compiler error.

Quoted Literals

To create a quoted expression, you simply need to enclose an expression within <@ and @> or <@@ and @@>, where the first form creates a strongly typed quoted expression and the second creates a weakly typed quoted expression. For example, to create a strongly typed quoted expression that represents multiplying two values, you could write something like this:

```
> open Microsoft.FSharp.Quotations
let x, y = 10, 10
let expr = <@ x * y @>;;

val x : int = 10
val y : int = 10
val expr : ❶Expr<int> =
  Call (None, op_Multiply, [PropertyGet (None, x, []), PropertyGet (None, y, [])])
```

In the preceding snippet, the underlying type of the quoted expression is ❶ Expr<int>. In this case, the compiler infers the quoted expression's type as int and carries that type along with the expression. The expression's value is a listing of the source expression's constituent elements. We'll dive into what the pieces mean and how to use them to decompose quoted expressions a bit later in this chapter.

Quoted expressions can be simple like the one in the preceding example, but they can also represent more complex expressions including lambda expressions. For instance, a lambda expression that multiplies two integers could be quoted like this:

```
> open Microsoft.FSharp.Quotations
let expr = <@ fun a b -> a * b @>;;

val expr : Expr<(int -> int -> int)> =
  Lambda (a, Lambda (b, Call (None, op_Multiply, [a, b])))
```

Similarly, you can include multiple expressions in a single quoted expression. Here, a let bound function is defined and applied to two integer values:

```
> let expr = <@ let mult x y = x * y
                mult 10 20 @>;;

val expr : Quotations.Expr<int> =
  Let (mult, Lambda (x, Lambda (y, Call (None, op_Multiply, [x, y])))),
    Application (Application (mult, Value (10)), Value (20)))
```

.NET Reflection

Another way to create a quoted expression is through standard .NET reflection. Normally, quoted expressions are created from nonexecutable code, but on occasion you may find that you've already defined a function that includes the code you want to quote. Rather than duplicating the code, you can decorate the function with the ReflectedDefinition attribute:

```
type Calc =
  [<ReflectedDefinition>]
  static member Multiply x y = x * y
```

Here, Multiply is compiled normally so it can be invoked directly, but the ReflectedDefinition attribute instructs the compiler to also generate a weakly typed quoted expression and embed the result within the compiled assembly. To access the generated quoted expression, you need to obtain a standard reflection MethodInfo object that represents the compiled method and pass it to the Expr class's static TryGetReflectedDefinition method:

```
> let expr =
  typeof<Calc>
    .GetMethod("Multiply")
  |> Expr.TryGetReflectedDefinition;;

val expr : Expr option =
  Some Lambda (x, Lambda (y, Call (None, op_Multiply, [x, y])))
```

When you need to quote multiple values within a type, decorating each one with the `ReflectedDefinition` attribute can get tedious. Fortunately, you can also apply the attribute to modules and types to generate quoted expressions for each of their values or members, respectively.

Manual Composition

The final way to compose a quoted expression is to manually construct one by chaining the results of calls to the `Expr` type's static methods. The `Expr` type defines over 40 methods that create new `Expr` instances, each representing the various constructs that can appear in a quoted expression.

The `Expr` methods are defined such that their purpose should be clear now that you know about the data structures and language constructs available to you in F#, so I won't go into detail about each of them. There are two important things to note about the methods, though.

First, the method parameters are tupled so instead of currying multiple parameters, they must be provided in tupled form. Second, many of the methods—nearly 50 percent of them—use .NET reflection to construct the corresponding expression.

Building quoted expressions manually can be tedious, but it gives you the most control over how expressions are constructed. Perhaps more important, however, is that these methods allow you to build quoted expressions based on code that you don't control and therefore can't decorate with the `ReflectedDefinition` attribute.

To demonstrate the process of manually constructing a quoted expression, let's walk through constructing a method that multiplies two values using the multiplication operator. To begin, we need to use reflection to access the `Operators` module where the multiplication operator is defined, like this:

```
let operators =
    System.Type.GetType("Microsoft.FSharp.Core.Operators, FSharp.Core")
```

This binding uses a partially qualified name to identify the type we're looking for. (We had to use reflection here because typeof<'T> and typedefof<'T> don't work on modules.) Now that we have a reference to the `Operators` module, we can obtain a reference to the multiplication operator method by its name, `op_Multiply`, with the `GetMethod` method:

```
let multiplyOperator = operators.GetMethod("op_Multiply")
```

Next, we inspect the returned `MethodInfo` to retrieve each of the operator's parameters. To include these parameters in our expression, we need to create `Var` instances from the corresponding `PropertyInfo` instances. We can easily perform this transformation by mapping each parameter through the `Array.map` function. For convenience, we can also use an Array pattern to convert the resulting array into a tuple, as shown here:

```
let varX, varY =
  multiplyOperator.GetParameters()
  |> Array.map (fun p -> Var(p.Name, p.ParameterType))
  |> (function | [| x; y |] -> x, y
               | _ -> failwith "not supported")
```

We now have enough information to construct the quoted expression:

```
let call = Expr.Call(multiplyOperator, [ Expr.Var(varX); Expr.Var(varY) ])
let innerLambda = Expr.Lambda(varY, call)
let outerLambda = Expr.Lambda(varX, innerLambda)
```

The preceding bindings incrementally construct a quoted expression representing a curried function that multiplies two values. As you can see, the quoted expression contains a method call for the multiplication operator, an inner lambda expression that applies the y value, and an outer lambda expression that applies the x value. If you were to inspect the value of outerLambda, you should see the resulting expression represented like this:

```
val outerLambda : Expr =
  Lambda (x, Lambda (y, Call (None, op_Multiply, [x, y])))
```

After all this work, we finally have a quoted expression that's equivalent to this weakly typed expression:

```
<@@ fun x y -> x * y @@>
```

For your convenience, I'm including the previous examples in their entirety here so you can see all the parts working together.

```
let operators =
  System.Type.GetType("Microsoft.FSharp.Core.Operators, FSharp.Core")
let multiplyOperator = operators.GetMethod("op_Multiply")
let varX, varY =
  multiplyOperator.GetParameters()
  |> Array.map (fun p -> Var(p.Name, p.ParameterType))
  |> (function | [| x; y |] -> x, y
               | _ -> failwith "not supported")

let call = Expr.Call(multiplyOperator, [ Expr.Var(varX); Expr.Var(varY) ])
let innerLambda = Expr.Lambda(varY, call)
let outerLambda = Expr.Lambda(varX, innerLambda)
```

Splicing Quoted Expressions

If you need to combine multiple quoted expressions, you could manually construct a new quoted expression by passing each one to the appropriate static method on the Expr class (typically Call), but there's a much easier way: You can create a new literal quoted expression by splicing them together using the splicing operators. For example, suppose you have the following sequence and strongly typed quoted expressions:

```
let numbers = seq { 1..10 }
let sum = <@ Seq.sum numbers @>
let count = <@ Seq.length numbers @>
```

You can combine sum and count into a third quoted expression that represents calculating the average from a sequence using the strongly typed splice operator (%) like this:

```
let avgExpr = <@ %sum / %count @>
```

Weakly typed quoted expressions can be spliced, too. If sum and count had been defined as weakly typed quoted expressions (via the <@@ ... @@> syntax), you could splice them with the weakly typed splice operator (%%) like this:

```
let avgExpr = <@@ %%sum / %%count @@>
```

Decomposing Quoted Expressions

While code quotations can be useful for helping you understand the structure of code, most of their power comes from decomposition. F# includes three modules, also within the Microsoft.FSharp.Quotations namespace, that define a plethora of complete and partial active patterns that you can use to decompose a quoted expression to its constituent parts at varying degrees of granularity.

Pattern module The partial active patterns in the Pattern module match the elementary F# language features such as function calls, function applications, looping constructs, raw values, binding definitions, and object creation. They correspond nearly one-to-one with the functions defined on the Expr type, helping you identify which pattern to use for the most common expressions.

DerivedPatterns module The DerivedPatterns module includes partial active patterns that primarily match quoted expressions representing primitive literals, basic Boolean operators such as && and ||, and constructs decorated with ReflectedDefinition.

ExprShape module   The ExprShape module defines a complete active pattern with three cases: ShapeVar, ShapeLambda, and ShapeCombination. It's designed for use in recursive pattern matching so you can easily traverse a quoted expression, matching every expression along the way.

Parsing Quoted Expressions

Rather than going into detail about the specific active patterns defined in each module, I think it's more helpful to see how they work together. We'll start with a typical example, where a sampling of patterns from each module is used to build a string that represents the quoted F# syntax.

```
open System.Text
open Microsoft.FSharp.Quotations.Patterns
open Microsoft.FSharp.Quotations.DerivedPatterns
open Microsoft.FSharp.Quotations.ExprShape

let rec showSyntax =
  function
  | Int32 v ->
      sprintf "%i" v
  | Value (v, _) ->
      sprintf "%s" (v.ToString())
  | SpecificCall <@@ (+) @@> (_, _, exprs) ->
      let left = showSyntax exprs.Head
      let right = showSyntax exprs.Tail.Head
      sprintf "%s + %s" left right
  | SpecificCall <@@ (-) @@> (_, _, exprs) ->
      let left = showSyntax exprs.Head
      let right = showSyntax exprs.Tail.Head
      sprintf "%s - %s" left right
  | Call (opt, mi, exprs) ->
      let owner = match opt with
                  | Some expr -> showSyntax expr
                  | None -> sprintf "%s" mi.DeclaringType.Name
      if exprs.IsEmpty then
        sprintf "%s.%s ()" owner mi.Name
      else
        let sb = StringBuilder(showSyntax exprs.Head)
        exprs.Tail
        |> List.iter (fun expr ->
                      sb
                        .Append(",")
                        .Append(showSyntax expr) |> ignore)
        sprintf "%s.%s (%s)" owner mi.Name (sb.ToString())
  | ShapeVar var ->
      sprintf "%A" var
  | ShapeLambda (p, body) ->
      sprintf "fun %s -> %s" p.Name (showSyntax body)
  | ShapeCombination (o, exprs) ->
      let sb = StringBuilder()
      exprs |> List.iter (fun expr -> sb.Append(showSyntax expr) |> ignore)
      sb.ToString()
```

The preceding example may look intimidating, but despite including a number of match cases, it's really not particularly complicated when you break it down. The first thing to note is that the showSyntax function is recursive, which allows us to traverse the tree with any nested expressions we encounter. Each of the match cases belongs to one of the three quoted expression modules and matches a particular type of expression. I won't go into detail about the bodies of each case since they don't introduce any new concepts, but I encourage you to experiment with them.

The first two cases, Int32 and Value, match individual literal values. The Int32 pattern is a derived pattern that matches only integer values, whereas Value is a basic pattern that matches any literal value. As you can see from the definitions, both of these patterns extract the literal value. The Value pattern also extracts the corresponding data type, but since we're not using it here we simply discard it with the Wildcard pattern.

Following the Value case are two SpecificCall cases and a generalized Call case. The SpecificCall cases are derived patterns that match calls to the addition and subtraction operators (as inline weakly typed quoted expressions), respectively. The Call case, on the other hand, is a basic pattern that matches any function call. The SpecificCall cases are much simpler than the Call case because we can make certain assumptions about the code given that we know more about what constitutes a match. The Call case needs to do more work to expand the expression.

Finally, we reach the last three cases: ShapeVar, ShapeLambda, and ShapeCombination. The simplest of these, ShapeVar, matches any variable definition. (Note that the term *variable* is preferable to *binding* here because it represents a placeholder within the code.) The value captured by ShapeVar includes information such as the variable name, its data type, and mutability. ShapeLambda matches any lambda expression, capturing its parameter definition and body as a nested expression. The last case, ShapeCombination, matches any other expression and is included here for completeness.

To see the showSyntax function in action, you can pass in any quoted expression. Just remember that this implementation hardly covers every possible case, so with more complex expressions your results will probably be less than stellar. For starters, though, here are a few sample inputs and results:

```
> showSyntax <@ fun x y -> x + y @>;;
val it : string = "fun x -> fun y -> x + y"
> showSyntax <@ fun x y -> x - y @>;;
val it : string = "fun x -> fun y -> x - y"
> showSyntax <@ 10 * 20 @>;;
val it : string = "Operators.op_Multiply (10,20)"
> showSyntax <@@ System.Math.Max(10, 20) @@>;;
val it : string = "Math.Max (10,20)"
```

Substituting Reflection

Just as you can use expression trees to enable reflection-like capabilities (as you saw at the beginning of this chapter), you can use quoted expressions to achieve a similar effect. To demonstrate, I'll use an adapted version of a sample I found extremely helpful when I was first learning about quoted expressions.

This example, found in its original form at *http://fssnip.net/eu/*, defines a module that makes extensive use of higher-order functions, partial application, and quoted expressions, letting you define ad hoc validation functions for your types. We'll start with the full listing and break it down after you've had a chance to digest it.

```
module Validation =
  open System
  open Microsoft.FSharp.Quotations
  open Microsoft.FSharp.Quotations.Patterns

  type Test<'e> = | Test of ('e -> (string * string) option)

❶ let private add (quote : Expr<'x>) message args validate (xs : Test<'e> list) =
    let propName, eval =
      match quote with
      | PropertyGet (_, p, _) -> p.Name, fun x -> p.GetValue(x, [|||])
      | Value (_, ty) when ty = typeof<'e> -> "x", box
      | _ -> failwith "Unsupported expression"
    let test entity =
      let value = eval entity
      if validate (unbox value) then None
      else Some (propName, String.Format(message, Array.ofList (value :: args)))
    Test(test) :: xs

❷ let notNull quote =
    let validator = (fun v -> v <> null)
    add quote "Is a required field" [] validator

❸ let notEmpty quote =
    add quote "Cannot be empty" [] (String.IsNullOrWhiteSpace >> not)

❹ let between quote min max =
    let validator = (fun v -> v >= min && v <= max)
    add quote "Must be at least {2} and greater than {1}" [min; max] validator

❺ let createValidator (f : 'e -> Test<'e> list -> Test<'e> list) =
    let entries = f Unchecked.defaultof<_> []
    fun entity -> List.choose (fun (Test test) -> test entity) entries
```

The Validation module's heart is the private add function at ❶. This function accepts five parameters that each participate in the validation. Of primary interest are the first parameter, quote; the third parameter, validate; and the final parameter, xs. These represent the quotation that identifies the property being validated, a validation function, and a list of test functions, respectively.

Inside add, we first attempt to match quote against the PropertyGet and Value active patterns to appropriately extract the value from the source object so it can be passed to the validation function later. Next, we define a function, test, that invokes the supplied validate function and returns an option indicating whether the extracted value is valid. Finally, the test function is wrapped inside the Test union case and prepended to xs, and the entire list is returned.

With the add function in place, we define a variety of functions that return partially applied versions of add, giving us an expressive validation syntax. In this example, we've defined notNull ❷, notEmpty ❸, and between ❹. Each of these functions accepts a quoted expression that's applied to add along with the next three parameters, resulting in new functions that accept only a list of Test union cases and return the same.

The createValidator ❺ function is the primary entry point into the Validation module. createValidator accepts a curried function whose arguments include a generic value and a list of Test union cases (of the same generic type), and ultimately returns another list of Test union cases. Notice how the second parameter and return value correspond to the functions returned by the notNull, notEmpty, and between functions. The implication here is that we can compose a validation function to pass into createValidator for arbitrary invocation later.

Now that the Validation module is fully defined, we can see how to use it. Let's begin by opening the Validation module and defining a simple record type definition that we can validate against.

```
open Validation
type TestType = { ObjectValue : obj
                  StringValue : string
                  IntValue : int }
```

There's nothing particularly notable about this type; it merely includes three labels we can reference for validation. Now we can create a validation method by calling createValidator like this:

```
let validate =
  createValidator <| fun x -> notNull <@ x.ObjectValue @> >>
                              notEmpty <@ x.StringValue @> >>
                              between <@ x.IntValue @> 1 100
```

Here, we've chained together calls to notNull, notEmpty, and between using the composition operator within the function we pass to createValidator. The resulting function (returned from createValidator) is then bound to validate. Each of the chained calls includes a quoted expression that identifies one of TestType's labels. You can even see here how F#'s type inference has played a role in determining the type of x in this expression.

All we need to do now is invoke the `validate` function by passing it instances of `TestType`. When all values satisfy the validation, `validate` simply returns an empty list like this:

```
> { ObjectValue = obj(); StringValue = "Sample"; IntValue = 35 }
|> validate;;
val it : (string * string) list = []
```

On the other hand, when one or more values fail validation, the `validate` function returns a list including the name of the member that failed along with a failure message, as shown here where all three values fail:

```
> { ObjectValue = null; StringValue = ""; IntValue = 1000 }
|> validate;;
val it : (string * string) list =
  [("IntValue", "Must be at least 100 and greater than 1");
   ("StringValue", "Cannot be empty"); ("ObjectValue", "Is a required field")]
```

Summary

Although quoted expressions serve much the same purpose as the expression trees introduced with LINQ, F#'s quoted expressions are more finely tuned for functional programming. As you've seen, you can construct quoted expressions as literal expressions, directly through reflection with the `ReflectedDefinition` attribute, or programmatically with reflection and the static methods on the `Expr` class. Quoted expressions derive their true power from their decomposition, however. By using the active patterns defined in the `Patterns`, `DerivedPatterns`, and `ExprShape` modules, you can decompose a quoted expression at varying degrees of granularity to accomplish a variety of tasks such as language translation or even flexible validation.

10

SHOW ME THE DATA

Virtually every application written today requires robust mechanisms to both access and manipulate data. While the full gamut of data access technologies across the .NET Framework is available to you in F#, this chapter focuses on two specific areas: query expressions and type providers.

Query Expressions

When LINQ was added to .NET, it revolutionized the way we access data by providing a unified syntax for querying data from disparate data sources. Upon LINQ's introduction, C# and Visual Basic were extended to include the *query syntax*, a SQL-like syntax with context-sensitive keywords that were really syntactic sugar over several language features, such as extension methods and lambda expressions. In this regard, F# was a little late to the party because, prior to F# 3.0, the only way to use LINQ in F# was to directly call the LINQ extension methods.

Despite their foundations in functional programming, using the LINQ methods directly has a highly object-oriented feel due to their fluent interface; sequences are passed to methods that return new sequences and the methods are typically chained with dot notation. Consider the following query, which uses the LINQ extension methods directly against an F# list to filter out odd numbers, and then sorts the results in descending order (remember to open the System.Linq namespace):

```
[ 1..100 ]
  .Where(fun n -> n % 2 = 0)
  .OrderByDescending(fun n -> n)
```

As you can see, chaining the method calls in this manner is much more object-oriented than functional. *Query expressions*, introduced with F# 3.0, changed that by providing a convenient SQL-like syntax that resembles the query syntax from C# and Visual Basic. They really are LINQ for F#.

Query expressions take the form of query { ... }. Inside the braces we identify a series of operations we want to apply to a sequence, thereby forming a query. For instance, we could rewrite the previous query as a query expression like this (explicitly opening System.Linq isn't required for query expressions):

```
query { for n in [ 1..100 ] do
        where (n % 2 = 0)
        sortByDescending n }
```

Now, filtering and sorting the list looks and feels more functional. Instead of chaining method calls directly, we're expressing the query in a more idiomatic manner that uses expression composition and function calls. Because query expressions are a wrapper around the LINQ technologies, you can use them with any sequence.

Given this simple example, one could argue that the Seq and List module functions could be used to similar effect, and in many cases, that's true. For instance, we could easily replace the where operator with a call to Seq.filter. Likewise, we can often sort using Seq.sortBy instead of the sortBy operator. What's not immediately apparent is that by being built upon LINQ, query expressions can offer additional optimizations, such as generating a WHERE clause in a SQL query to prevent retrieving a large data set from a database.

In the interest of simplicity, unless otherwise noted, each query expression example in this chapter will use the types and collections defined in the following QuerySource module.

```
module QuerySource =
  open System

  type film = { id : int; name : string; releaseYear : int; gross : Nullable<float> }
           override x.ToString() = sprintf "%s (%i)" x.name x.releaseYear
  type actor = { id : int; firstName : string; lastName : string }
              override x.ToString() = sprintf "%s, %s" x.lastName x.firstName
  type filmActor = { filmId : int; actorId : int }

  let films =
    [ { id = 1; name = "The Terminator"; releaseYear = 1984; gross = Nullable 38400000.0 }
      { id = 2; name = "Predator"; releaseYear = 1987; gross = Nullable 59735548.0 }
      { id = 3; name = "Commando"; releaseYear = 1985; gross = Nullable<float>() }
      { id = 4; name = "The Running Man"; releaseYear = 1987; gross = Nullable 38122105.0 }
      { id = 5; name = "Conan the Destroyer"; releaseYear = 1984; gross = Nullable<float>() } ]

  let actors =
    [ { id = 1; firstName = "Arnold"; lastName = "Schwarzenegger" }
      { id = 2; firstName = "Linda"; lastName = "Hamilton" }
      { id = 3; firstName = "Carl"; lastName = "Weathers" }
      { id = 4; firstName = "Jesse"; lastName = "Ventura" }
      { id = 5; firstName = "Vernon"; lastName = "Wells" } ]

  let filmActors =
    [ { filmId = 1; actorId = 1 }
      { filmId = 1; actorId = 2 }
      { filmId = 2; actorId = 1 }
      { filmId = 2; actorId = 3 }
      { filmId = 2; actorId = 4 }
      { filmId = 3; actorId = 1 }
      { filmId = 3; actorId = 5 }
      { filmId = 4; actorId = 1 }
      { filmId = 4; actorId = 4 }
      (* Intentionally omitted actor for filmId = 5 *) ]
```

There's nothing particularly interesting about the QuerySource module, but the types and collections defined here sufficiently represent a basic data model we can query in a variety of ways. The film and actor types also include overrides of ToString to simplify the query output.

Basic Querying

In their most basic form, query expressions consist of an enumerable for loop and a projection. The enumerable for loop defines a name for items in a source sequence. The projection identifies the data that will be returned by the query.

One of the most common projection operators is select, which equates to LINQ's Select method and defines the structure of each item in the resulting sequence (much like Seq.map). At their most basic, select operations simply project each data item directly, like this:

```
query { for f in QuerySource.films do select f }
```

which results in:

```
val it : seq<QuerySource.film> =
  seq
    [{id = 1;
      name = "The Terminator";
      releaseYear = 1984;
      gross = 38400000.0;};
      -- snip -- ]
```

select operations aren't limited to projecting only the source data item; they can also transform the source sequence to project more complex types like tuples, records, or classes. For instance, to project a tuple containing the film's name and its release year, you could write:

```
query { for f in QuerySource.films do
        select (f.name, f.releaseYear) }
```

which gives:

```
val it : seq<string * int> =
  seq
    [("The Terminator", 1984); ("Predator", 1987); ("Commando", 1985);
     ("The Running Man", 1987); ...]
```

In these simple examples, we've explicitly included a select operation to transform the source sequence. As query complexity grows, projecting the raw, nontransformed data items is often implied, so the select operation can often be safely omitted. In the interest of space, I'll generally project results with ToString, but I encourage you to experiment with different projections to familiarize yourself with the query behavior.

Filtering Data

Queries often involve specifying some criteria to filter out unwanted data. There are two primary approaches to filtering with query expressions: predicate-based filters and distinct item filters.

Predicate-Based Filters

Predicate-based filters allow you to filter data by specifying the criteria that each item in the source sequence must satisfy in order to be included in the projected sequence. To create a predicate-based filter, simply include F#'s equivalent of LINQ's Where method, the where operator, followed by a Boolean expression (often called a *predicate*) in your query. (Note that parentheses are typically required around the expression.) For example, to select only the films released in 1984, you could write this:

```
query { for f in QuerySource.films do
        where (f.releaseYear = 1984)
        select (f.ToString()) }
```

to get:

```
val it : seq<string> =
  seq ["The Terminator (1984)"; "Conan the Destroyer (1984)"]
```

When composing predicate-based filters, you must be aware of the source sequence's underlying type. For the simple examples you've seen so far it hasn't been an issue, but in many cases, particularly when you are working with IQueryable<'T> instances, you might have to deal with null values.

Null values can pose a problem in query expressions because the standard comparison operators don't handle them. For example, if you were to query for all films that grossed no more than $40 million using the standard equality operator like this:

```
query { for f in QuerySource.films do
        where (f.gross <= 40000000.0)
        select (f.ToString()) }
```

you'd receive the following error because gross is defined as Nullable<float>:

```
QueryExpressions.fsx(53,16): error FS0001: The type 'System.Nullable<float>'
does not support the 'comparison' constraint. For example, it does not support
the 'System.IComparable' interface
```

To work around this limitation, you need to use the nullable operators defined in the Microsoft.FSharp.Linq.NullableOperators module. These operators look like the standard operators except that they begin with a question mark (?) when the left operand is Nullable<_>, end with a question mark when the right operand is Nullable<_>, or are surrounded by question marks when both operands are Nullable<_>. Table 10-1 lists each of the nullable operators.

Table 10-1: Nullable Operators

Operator	Left Side Nullable	Right Side Nullable	Both Sides Nullable
Equality	?=	=?	?=?
Inequality	?<>	<>?	?<>?
Greater than	?>	>?	?>?
Greater than or equal	?>=	>=?	?>=?
Less than	?<	<?	?<?
Less than or equal	?<=	<=?	?<=?
Addition	?+	+?	?+?
Subtraction	?-	-?	?-?
Multiplication	?*	*?	?*?
Division	?/	/?	?/?
Modulus	?%	%?	?%?

Now we can rewrite the previous query using the appropriate nullable operator like this:

```
open Microsoft.FSharp.Linq.NullableOperators

query { for f in QuerySource.films do
        where (f.gross ?<= 40000000.0)
        select (f.ToString()) }
```

to get:

```
val it : seq<string> = seq ["The Terminator (1984)"; "The Running Man (1987)"]
```

As you can see, the query resulted in two matches despite the underlying sequence containing some null values.

It's possible to chain multiple predicates together with Boolean operators. For instance, to get only the films released in 1987 that grossed no more than $40 million, you could write:

```
query { for f in QuerySource.films do
        where (f.releaseYear = 1987 && f.gross ?<= 40000000.0)
        select (f.ToString()) }
```

which gives:

```
val it : seq<string> = seq ["The Running Man (1987)"]
```

Distinct-Item Filters

Query expressions can produce a sequence containing only the distinct values from the underlying sequence by filtering out duplicates. To achieve this, you need only include the distinct operator in your query.

The distinct operator corresponds to LINQ's Distinct method, but unlike in C# or VB, query expressions allow you to include it directly within the query rather than as a separate method call. For example, to query for distinct release years, you could write this:

```
query { for f in QuerySource.films do
        select f.releaseYear
        distinct }
```

Here, we've projected the distinct release years to a new sequence:

```
val it : seq<int> = seq [1984; 1987; 1985]
```

Accessing Individual Items

It's quite common for a sequence to contain multiple items when you really care about only one in particular. Query expressions include several operators for accessing the first item, the last item, or arbitrary items from a sequence.

Getting the First or Last Item

To get the first item from a sequence, you can use the `head` or `headOrDefault` operators. These operators respectively correspond to the parameterless overloads of the `First` and `FirstOrDefault` LINQ methods but use the more functional nomenclature of "head" to identify the first item (just like with F# lists). The difference between `head` and `headOrDefault` is that `head` raises an exception when the source sequence is empty, whereas `headOrDefault` returns `Unchecked.defaultof<_>`.

To get the first item from a sequence, simply project a sequence to one of the head operators like this:

```
query { for f in QuerySource.films do headOrDefault }
```

In this case, the result is:

```
val it : QuerySource.film = {id = 1;
                             name = "The Terminator";
                             releaseYear = 1984;
                             gross = 38400000.0;}
```

Similarly, you can get the last item in a sequence using either the `last` or `lastOrDefault` operators. These operators behave the same way as their head counterparts in that `last` raises an exception when the sequence is empty, whereas `lastOrDefault` does not. Depending on the underlying sequence type, getting the last item may require enumerating the entire sequence, so exercise some care because the operation could be expensive or time consuming.

Getting an Arbitrary Item

When you want to get a specific item by its index you can use the `nth` operator, which is equivalent to LINQ's `ElementAt` method. For instance, to get the third element from the `films` sequence, you could structure a query like this:

```
query { for f in QuerySource.films do nth 2 }
```

Here, the result is:

```
val it : QuerySource.film = {id = 3;
                             name = "Commando";
                             releaseYear = 1985;
                             gross = null;}
```

Although the nth operator is useful when you already know the index, it's more common to want the first item that matches some criteria. In those cases, you'll want to use the find operator instead.

The find operator is equivalent to calling LINQ's First method with a predicate. It is also similar to the where operator except that it returns only a single item instead of a new sequence. For example, to get the first film listed for 1987, you could write:

```
query { for f in QuerySource.films do find (f.releaseYear = 1987) }
```

Executing this query will give you:

```
val it : QuerySource.film = {id = 2;
                             name = "Predator";
                             releaseYear = 1987;
                             gross = 59735548.0;}
```

The find operator is useful for locating the first item that matches some criteria, but it doesn't guarantee that the first match is the only match. When you want to return a single value but also need to be certain that a query result contains one and only one item (such as when you are finding an item by a key value), you can use the exactlyOne operator, which corresponds to the parameterless overload of LINQ's Single method. For example, to get a film by its id while enforcing uniqueness, you could write:

```
query { for f in QuerySource.films do
        where (f.id = 4)
        exactlyOne }
```

In this case, the query yields:

```
val it : QuerySource.film = {id = 4;
                             name = "The Running Man";
                             releaseYear = 1987;
                             gross = 38122105.0;}
```

When the source sequence doesn't contain exactly one item, the exactlyOne operator raises an exception. Should you want a default value when the source sequence is empty, you can use the exactlyOneOrDefault operator instead. Be warned, though, that if the source sequence includes more than one item, exactlyOneOrDefault will still raise an exception.

NOTE   *Query expression syntax does not include operators equivalent to the predicate-based overload of* Single *or* SingleOrDefault.

Sorting Results

Query expressions make sorting data easy, and, in some ways, they are more flexible than the sorting functions in the various collection modules. The sorting operators allow you to sort in ascending or descending order on both nullable and non-nullable values. You can even sort by multiple values.

Sorting in Ascending Order

Sorting a sequence in ascending order requires either the sortBy or sortByNullable operators. Both of these operators are built upon LINQ's OrderBy method. Internally, these methods differ only by the generic constraints applied to their arguments. As their names imply, the sortBy operator is used with non-nullable values, whereas sortByNullable is used with Nullable<_> values.

With both of these operators, you need to specify the value on which to sort. For example, to sort the films by name, you could write:

```
query { for f in QuerySource.films do
        sortBy f.name
        select (f.ToString()) }
```

This returns the following sequence:

```
val it : seq<string> =
  seq
    ["Commando (1985)"; "Conan the Destroyer (1984)"; "Predator (1987)";
     "The Running Man (1987)"; ...]
```

Sorting in Descending Order

To sort a sequence in descending order, you use either the sortByDescending or sortByNullableDescending operators. These operators are based on LINQ's OrderByDescending method and, like their ascending counterparts, internally differ only by the generic constraints applied to their parameters.

To sort the films sequence in descending order by name, you could write:

```
query { for f in QuerySource.films do
        sortByDescending f.name
        select (f.ToString()) }
```

which returns:

```
val it : seq<string> =
  seq
    ["The Terminator (1984)"; "The Running Man (1987)"; "Predator (1987)";
     "Conan the Destroyer (1984)"; ...]
```

Sorting by Multiple Values

To sort on multiple values, first sort with one of the sortBy or sortByDescending operators and then supply subsequent sort values with one of the thenBy operators. As with the primary sort operators, there are variations of thenBy that allow you to sort in ascending or descending order using both nullable and non-nullable values.

The four thenBy variations, which can appear only after one of the sortBy variations, are:

- thenBy
- thenByNullable
- thenByDescending
- thenByNullableDescending

These operators are based upon LINQ's ThenBy and ThenByDescending methods. To see these in action, let's sort the films sequence by releaseYear and then in descending order by gross:

```
query { for f in QuerySource.films do
        sortBy f.releaseYear
        thenByNullableDescending f.gross
        select (f.releaseYear, f.name, f.gross) }
```

This query results in the following sorted sequence:

```
val it : seq<int * string * System.Nullable<float>> =
  seq
    [(1984, "The Terminator", 38400000.0); (1984, "Conan the Destroyer", null);
     (1985, "Commando", null); (1987, "Predator", 59735548.0); ...]
```

You can chain additional thenBy operators to create even more complex sorting scenarios.

Grouping

Another common query operation is grouping. Query expressions provide two operators, both based on LINQ's GroupBy method, to do just that. Both operators produce an intermediate sequence of IGrouping<_,_> instances that you refer to later in your query.

The first operator, groupBy, lets you specify the key value by which the items in the source sequence will be grouped. Each IGrouping<_,_> produced by groupBy includes the key value and a child sequence containing any items from the source sequence that matches the key. For example, to group the films by release year, you could write:

```
query { for f in QuerySource.films do
        groupBy f.releaseYear into g
        sortBy g.Key
        select (g.Key, g) }
```

This query produces the result (formatted and abbreviated for readability):

```
val it : seq<int * IGrouping<int, QuerySource.film>> =
  seq
    [(1984, seq [{id = 1; -- snip --};
                 {id = 5; -- snip --}]);
     (1985, seq [{id = 3; -- snip --}]);
     (1987, seq [{id = 2; -- snip --};
                 {id = 4; -- snip --}])]
```

It isn't always necessary to include the full source item in the resulting IGrouping<_,_> like the groupBy operator does. Instead, you can use the groupValBy operator to specify what to include, be it a single value from the source or some other transformation. Unlike the other operators we've seen so far, groupValBy takes two arguments: the value to include in the result, and the key value.

To demonstrate the groupValBy operator, let's group the films by releaseYear again, but this time we'll include a tuple of the film name and its gross earnings:

```
query { for f in QuerySource.films do
        groupValBy (f.name, f.gross) f.releaseYear into g
        sortBy g.Key
        select (g.Key, g) }
```

This gives us:

```
val it : seq<int * IGrouping<int,(string * System.Nullable<float>)>> =
  seq
    [(1984,
      seq [("The Terminator", 38400000.0); ("Conan the Destroyer", null)]);
     (1985, seq [("Commando", null)]);
     (1987, seq [("Predator", 59735548.0); ("The Running Man", 38122105.0)])]
```

Now, instead of the full film instance, the resulting groupings include only the data we explicitly requested.

Paginating

Query expressions allow you to easily paginate a sequence. Think about your typical search results page, where items are partitioned into some number of items (say, 10) per page. Rather than having to manage placeholders that identify which partition a user should see, you can use query expressions, which provide the skip, skipWhile, take, and takeWhile operators to help you get to the correct partition in the query itself. Each of these operators shares its name with its underlying LINQ method.

The skip and take operators both accept an integer indicating how many items to bypass or include, respectively. For example, you could compose a function to get a particular page, like this:

```
let getFilmPageBySize pageSize pageNumber =
  query { for f in QuerySource.films do
          skip (pageSize * (pageNumber - 1))
          take pageSize
          select (f.ToString()) }
```

Now, getting a particular page is only a matter of invoking the getFilmPage function. For instance, to get the first page of three items, you would write:

```
getFilmPageBySize 3 1
```

which yields:

```
val it : seq<string> =
  seq ["The Terminator (1984)"; "Predator (1987)"; "Commando (1985)"]
```

Likewise, you would get the second result page as follows:

```
getFilmPageBySize 3 2
```

which gives us:

```
val it : seq<string> =
  seq ["The Running Man (1987)"; "Conan the Destroyer (1984)"]
```

It's okay to specify more items than are present in the sequence. If the end of the sequence is reached, the skip and take operators return what has been selected so far and no exceptions are thrown.

The skipWhile and takeWhile operators are very similar to skip and take except that instead of working against a known number of items, they skip or take items as long as a condition is met. This is useful for paging over a variable number of items according to some criteria. For example, the following function returns the films released in a given year:

```
let getFilmPageByYear year =
  query { for f in QuerySource.films do
          sortBy f.releaseYear
          skipWhile (f.releaseYear < year)
          takeWhile (f.releaseYear = year)
          select (f.ToString()) }
```

Invoking this function with a year will generate a sequence containing zero or more items. For instance, invoking it with 1984 returns:

```
val it : seq<string> =
  seq ["The Terminator (1984)"; "Conan the Destroyer (1984)"]
```

whereas invoking it with 1986 returns no items because the source sequence doesn't include any films released in 1986.

If you're wondering whether this simple example of paging by releaseYear could be simplified with a single where operator, it can. This example simply demonstrates takeWhile's effect. where and takeWhile serve similar purposes, but distinguishing between them is important, particularly for more complex predicates. The difference between the two operators is that takeWhile stops looking as soon as it finds something that doesn't match, but where does not.

Aggregating Data

As often as we need to present or otherwise work with tabular data, sometimes what we're really after is an aggregated view of the data. Aggregations such as counting the number of items in a sequence, totaling some values, or finding an average are all commonly sought-after values that can be exposed through built-in query operators.

Counting the items in a sequence is easy; simply project the sequence to the count operator.

```
query { for f in QuerySource.films do count }
```

Evaluating this query tells us that five items are present in the films sequence. Be warned, though, that counting the items in a sequence can be an expensive operation; it typically requires enumerating the entire sequence, which could have a negative impact on performance. That said, the Count method on which this operator is based is smart enough to short-circuit some sequences (like arrays). If you're counting items only to determine whether the sequence contains any data, you should instead consider using the exists operator, discussed in "Detecting Items" on page 214.

The remaining aggregation operators allow you to easily perform mathematical aggregations against a sequence according to a selector. The operators—minBy, maxBy, sumBy, and averageBy—allow you to calculate the minimum value, maximum value, total, or average for the values, respectively. Internally, the minBy and maxBy operators use LINQ's Min and Max methods, respectively, but sumBy and averageBy provide their own implementations and are completely independent of LINQ.

Each of these four operators also have nullable counterparts that work against nullable values much like the sorting operators introduced in "Sorting Results" on page 209. To demonstrate, we'll query the films sequence using the nullable forms.

To find the highest grossing film, we could write:

```
query { for f in QuerySource.films do maxByNullable f.gross }
```

As expected, running this query returns 59735548.0. Replacing maxByNullable with minByNullable returns 38122105.0, and sumByNullable returns 136257653.0. The averageByNullable operator doesn't behave quite as you might expect, however.

Averaging the gross earnings using averageByNullable results in 27251530.6. What happens is that although the operator skips null values during the summation phase, it divides the sum by the count of items in the sequence regardless of how many null items were skipped. This means that the null values are effectively treated as zero, which may or may not be desirable. Later in this chapter, we'll look at how to define a new query operator that truly ignores null values when calculating an average.

Detecting Items

Thus far, we've explored the many ways you can structure query expressions to transform, filter, sort, group, and aggregate sequences. Sometimes, though, you don't really care to obtain specific items from a sequence but rather want to inspect a sequence to determine whether it contains data that matches some criterion. Instead of returning a new sequence or a specific item, the operators discussed in this section return a Boolean value indicating whether the sequence contains the desired data. Like the distinct operator, these operators are part of the query expression itself, which is another feature that distinguishes F#'s query expressions from query syntax in C# and Visual Basic.

When you want to see if a known item is contained within a sequence, you use the contains operator. Built upon LINQ's Contains method, the contains operator accepts the item you are looking for as its argument. For instance, if we want to detect whether *Kindergarten Cop* is present in the films collection, we could write:

```
open System
open QuerySource

let kindergartenCop =
  { id = 6; name = "Kindergarten Cop"; releaseYear = 1990; gross = Nullable 91457688.0 }

query { for f in films do
        contains kindergartenCop }
```

Invoking this query will inform you that *Kindergarten Cop* is not present in the collection (much to my relief). As you can see, though, the contains operator is really suitable only when you already have a reference to an item that may already be part of the collection. If you know only part of the value you're looking for, such as the name of the film, you can revise the query to project each name and pass the name you're looking for to contains, like this:

```
query { for f in QuerySource.films do
        select f.name
        contains "Kindergarten Cop" }
```

Projecting the values like this, however, isn't particularly efficient because it involves enumerating the entire sequence prior to locating the specified item. Instead, you can turn to another operator, exists, which is based on LINQ's Any method. The exists operator is like where except that it stops enumerating the sequence and returns true or false as soon as an item that matches its predicate is found. For example, the previous query could be expressed with exists like this:

```
query { for f in QuerySource.films do
        exists (f.name = "Kindergarten Cop") }
```

Of course, the predicate supplied to exists doesn't have to look for a specific item. We can easily determine if any films grossed at least $50 million with the following query:

```
open Microsoft.FSharp.Linq.NullableOperators

query { for f in QuerySource.films do
        exists (f.gross ?>= 50000000.0) }
```

Because *Predator* grossed nearly $60 million, the previous query returns true. If you want to check whether every item in a sequence satisfies some condition, you can use the all operator. Based on LINQ's All method, the all operator enumerates the sequence and returns true when each item matches the predicate. When an item that doesn't match the predicate is encountered, enumeration stops and all returns false. For example, to see if every film grossed at least $50 million, you could construct a query like this:

```
query { for f in QuerySource.films do
        all (f.gross ?>= 50000000.0) }
```

In our films collection, only one item satisfies the condition; therefore, the query returns false.

Joining Multiple Data Sources

Querying data from a single sequence is useful, but data is often spread across multiple sources. Query expressions carry forward LINQ's join capabilities, which allow you to query data from multiple sources within a single expression. Joins in query expressions resemble enumerable for loops in that they include an iteration identifier and the source sequence but begin with the appropriate join operator and also include join criteria.

The first type of join, the *inner join*, uses the join operator to correlate values from one sequence with values in a second sequence. Internally, the join operator uses LINQ's Join method to work its magic. Once the sequences are joined, values from both sequences can be referenced by subsequent operators like where or select.

Until now, all of the queries we've written have used only the films collection. Recall that when we created the QuerySource module at the beginning of the chapter, we also defined two other collections: actors and filmActors. Together, the films, actors, and filmActors collections model a many-to-many relationship between films and actors, with filmActors serving as the junction table. We can use the join operator to bring these three collections together in a single query like this:

```
query { for f in QuerySource.films do
        join fa in QuerySource.filmActors on (f.id = fa.filmId)
        join a in QuerySource.actors on (fa.actorId = a.id)
        select (f.name, f.releaseYear, a.lastName, a.firstName) }
```

Joining multiple sequences together merely requires us to include a join expression for each sequence and identify the relationship between them through their members and an equality operator. Invoking this query results in the following sequence (truncated per FSI):

```
val it : seq<string * int * string * string> =
  seq
    [("The Terminator", 1984, "Schwarzenegger", "Arnold");
     ("The Terminator", 1984, "Hamilton", "Linda");
     ("Predator", 1987, "Schwarzenegger", "Arnold");
     ("Predator", 1987, "Weathers", "Carl"); ...]
```

F# exposes LINQ's GroupJoin function through the groupJoin operator. This lets you join two sequences, but instead of selecting items that satisfy the join criterion individually, you project each item that satisfies the join criterion into another sequence you can subsequently reference within your query. You can use this intermediate sequence to create a hierarchical data structure that resembles the IGrouping<_,_> instances created by the groupBy operator.

Consider the following query, which creates a hierarchy where each actor is grouped by the films in which he or she appears:

```
query { for f in QuerySource.films do
        groupJoin fa in QuerySource.filmActors on (f.id = fa.filmId) into junction
        select (f.name, query { for j in junction do
                                join a in QuerySource.actors on (j.actorId = a.id)
                                select (a.lastName, a.firstName) } ) }
```

Here, we use the groupJoin operator to create an intermediate sequence named junction. Inside the projected tuple, we have a nested query where we join actors to junction and project individual actor names. This results in the following sequence, which I've formatted for readability:

```
val it : seq<string * seq<string * string>> =
  seq
    [("The Terminator", seq [("Schwarzenegger", "Arnold");
                              ("Hamilton", "Linda")]);
     ("Predator", seq [("Schwarzenegger", "Arnold");
                        ("Weathers", "Carl");
                        ("Ventura", "Jesse")]);
     ("Commando", seq [("Schwarzenegger", "Arnold");
                        ("Wells", "Vernon")]);
     ("The Running Man", seq [("Schwarzenegger", "Arnold");
                              ("Ventura", "Jesse")]);
     ...]
```

As you can see, the outer query (the films part) returns a single sequence of tuples. Nested within each item is another sequence containing the actors associated with that film. What isn't apparent from these truncated results is that when none of the items in the joined sequence satisfies the join criterion (as is the case for *Conan the Destroyer*), the sequence created by the groupJoin operation is empty.

If you prefer to flatten the results of a groupJoin rather than return them as a hierarchy, you can follow the groupJoin operation with another enumerable for loop, using the junction sequence as the loop source. Here, the previous query is restructured to return each actor inline with the film:

```
query { for f in QuerySource.films do
        groupJoin fa in QuerySource.filmActors on (f.id = fa.filmId) into junction
        for j in junction do
        join a in QuerySource.actors on (j.actorId = a.id)
        select (f.name, f.releaseYear, a.lastName, a.firstName) }
```

The result of this query is the same as for an inner join, so I won't repeat the output here. In most cases, you'd want to use the join operator to forego the overhead associated with creating the intermediate junction sequence, but there is one place where using a groupJoin like this makes sense: left outer joins.

By default, if no items satisfy the join criterion in a group join, the result is an empty sequence. However, if you use the DefaultIfEmpty method with the resulting sequence, you'll get a new sequence containing a single item that's the default value for the underlying type. To perform a left outer join in your query, you can use the groupJoin operator as we did in the previous query but include a call to DefaultIfEmpty in your enumerable for loop—for example, j.DefaultIfEmpty(). Alternatively, you can use the leftOuterJoin operator to achieve the same result.

Unfortunately, left outer joins are one area where the dissonance between F# and the rest of the .NET Framework can cause a lot of misery. But this is really a problem only when you're working with the core F# types. Consider the following query:

```
query { for f in QuerySource.films do
        leftOuterJoin fa in QuerySource.filmActors on (f.id = fa.filmId) into junction
        for j in junction do
        join a in QuerySource.actors on (j.actorId = a.id)
        select (f.name, f.releaseYear, a.lastName, a.firstName) }
|> Seq.iter (printfn "%O")
```

When this query enumerates (via Seq.iter), it raises a NullReferenceException as soon as it tries to join in the actors for *Conan the Barbarian*. Because there are no entries for that film in the filmActors sequence, the call to DefaultIfEmpty in the left outer join causes the sole entry in junction to be null.

Wait, what? Null? Isn't filmActor a record type? How can it possibly be null if null isn't a valid value for record types? The answer lies in the fact that by calling into .NET Framework methods we've left the confines of the F# sandbox. null may not be valid for record types in F#, but the Common Language Runtime has no notion of a record type; all it knows are value and reference types and, from its perspective, a record type is just a reference type. Therefore, null is a valid value. Unfortunately, because our code is all in F# and the F# compiler enforces the value constraints around the record type, we can't handle the null value with pattern matching or if...then expressions. We can't even use the AllowNullLiteral attribute on the type because the compiler doesn't allow that either.

Working around this issue is a bit of a pain. We can start by splitting the query into two parts: one that joins actors to filmActors and another that joins in films, like this:

```
let actorsFilmActors =
  query { for a in QuerySource.actors do
          join fa in QuerySource.filmActors on (a.id = fa.actorId)
          select (fa.filmId, a) }

query { for f in QuerySource.films do
        leftOuterJoin (id, a) in actorsFilmActors on (f.id = id) into junction
        for (_, a) in junction do
        select (f.name, a.lastName, a.firstName) }
```

This is a good start, but we'll still get a NullReferenceException with the Tuple pattern match in the enumerable for loop for junction because F# doesn't allow null for tuples either. There is yet another workaround we can use: an upcast to obj.

```
query { for f in QuerySource.films do
        leftOuterJoin (id, a) in actorsFilmActors on (f.id = id) into junction
        for x in junction do
        select (match (x :> obj) with
```

```
        | null -> (f.name, "", "")
        | _ -> let _, a = x
               (f.name, a.lastName, a.firstName))
}
```

null may not be a valid value for a tuple, but it certainly is for obj. By explicitly upcasting to obj, we can use pattern matching to detect the null value and return the appropriate tuple instead of raising the exception.

Extending Query Expressions

As you've seen in the previous sections, query expressions provide an easy and expressive way to work with data. Query expressions also offer another benefit that really sets them apart from query syntax in C# and Visual Basic: They're fully extensible. In this section, I'll show a few additional operators. We'll start by plugging a hole in the built-in operators by defining operators that expose the parameterized overloads of Single and SingleOrDefault. We'll then move on to a more complex example that allows us to calculate an average by disregarding all null values.

Example: ExactlyOneWhen

Recall from "Getting an Arbitrary Item" on page 207 that the exactlyOne and exactlyOneOrDefault operators expose the parameterless versions of LINQ's Single and SingleByDefault operators, but no such operators exist for the overloads that accept a predicate. We can easily define our own operators to expose these methods by leveraging the power of F# type extensions.

To create the custom operators, we need to extend the QueryBuilder class found within the Microsoft.FSharp.Linq namespace. This class defines the methods that ultimately serve as the query operators. Fundamentally, the type extension we'll define is no different than any other type extension; we need only to include a few attributes so the compiler knows how the functions should behave within a query expression.

Here is the code listing in full:

```
open System
open Microsoft.FSharp.Linq

type QueryBuilder with
❶ [<CustomOperation("exactlyOneWhen")>]
  member ❷ __.ExactlyOneWhen (❸source : QuerySource<'T,'Q>,
                             ❹[<ProjectionParameter>] selector) =
    System.Linq.Enumerable.Single (source.Source, Func<_,_>(selector))

  [<CustomOperation("exactlyOneOrDefaultWhen")>]
  member __.ExactlyOneOrDefaultWhen (source : QuerySource<'T,'Q>,
                                    [<ProjectionParameter>] selector) =
    System.Linq.Enumerable.SingleOrDefault (source.Source, Func<_,_>(selector))
```

This snippet defines two extension methods on the QueryBuilder class: exactlyOneWhen and exactlyOneOrDefaultWhen. Because these are so similar, we'll just focus on the exactlyOneWhen operator. The first item of interest is the CustomOperation attribute ❶ applied to the method itself. This attribute indicates that the method should be available within a query expression and the operator name.

Next, the method's this identifier is two underscore characters ❷ to be consistent with the other operator definitions. The source parameter at ❸, annotated as QuerySource<'T, 'Q>, identifies the sequence the operator will work against.

Immediately following source is the selector parameter ❹. This parameter is a function that will be applied against every item in source to determine whether it should be selected. The ProjectionParameter attribute applied to selector instructs the compiler that the function is implied to accept 'T (as inferred from source) so that you can write the selector function as if you were working directly with an instance; that is, if you're querying the films collection and have used f as your iteration identifier, you could write f.id = 4. Without ProjectionParameter, you'd have to use the full lambda syntax (or a formal function) instead of just the expression.

With the new operators defined, we can now write queries that use them. For instance, to use the exactlyOneWhen operator to find a film by id, you would write:

```
query { for f in QuerySource.films do
        exactlyOneWhen (f.id = 4) }
```

As you can see, with these operators you no longer need to include the where operator to filter the results before checking that the sequence contains only a single item.

Example: AverageByNotNull

For a more complex example of a custom operator, let's provide an alternative to the averageByNullable operator we used in "Aggregating Data" on page 213 to compute the average gross earnings for our films. The calculation resulted in the average being reported as 27251530.6 because the two null values were excluded from the sum but the divisor was still five. If you wanted to truly ignore the null values and divide the total by three, the averageByNullable operator wouldn't help you, but you could define a custom operator like this:

```
open System
open Microsoft.FSharp.Linq

type QueryBuilder with
    -- snip --
    [<CustomOperation("averageByNotNull")>]
    member inline __.AverageByNotNull< 'T, 'Q, 'Value
                    when 'Value :> ValueType
                    and 'Value : struct
                    and 'Value : (new : unit -> 'Value)
                    and 'Value : (static member op_Explicit : 'Value -> float)>
```

```
(source : QuerySource<'T, 'Q>,
 [<ProjectionParameter>] selector : 'T -> Nullable<'Value>) =
 source.Source
 |> Seq.fold
     (fun (s, c) v -> let i = v |> selector
                      if i.HasValue then
                        (s + float i.Value, c + 1)
                      else (s, c))
     (0.0, 0)
 |> (function
     | (_, 0) -> Nullable<float>()
     | (sum, count) -> Nullable(sum / float count))
```

Notice that the `AverageByNotNull` method incorporates many of the same principles as exactlyOneWhen and exactlyOneOrDefaultWhen; that is, they each involve the `CustomOperation` and `ProjectionParameter` attributes. Where `AverageByNotNull` differs is that it's defined as inline to ensure that the generic parameters can be resolved. Because they're so similar, I've based the signature and generic constraints for `AverageByNotNull` largely upon that of the averageByNullable operator, although I've simplified it a bit for demonstration purposes.

Now that we've defined the averageByNotNull operator, we can include it in a query like this:

```
query { for f in QuerySource.films do
        averageByNotNull f.gross }
```

Invoking this query returns `45419217.67`, a stark contrast from `27251530.6` as returned by averageByNullable.

Type Providers

Along with query expressions, the other "killer feature" of F# 3.0 is type providers. *Type providers* were developed to abstract away creation of the types, properties, and methods necessary to work with external data because this process is often tedious, error prone, and difficult to maintain.

Many type providers can be likened to traditional object-relational mapping (ORM) tools like NHibernate or Entity Framework, although their scope is potentially much greater. ORM tools typically require a great deal of configuration to be used effectively. Although there are tools that simplify this process for many of the more popular ORM technologies, they still require plenty of maintenance. ORM-like type providers aim to remove this overhead by automating type generation as part of the compilation process.

The other primary use for type providers is to simplify otherwise complex interfaces. Consider how cumbersome and error-prone something like matching strings with regular expressions can be. Regular expression syntax is confusing enough on its own, but getting named captures from the match collection requires using string keys to identify the values you're trying to access. A regular expression type provider can simplify the interface by generating types that correspond to the named captures in the regular expression.

Regardless of which need type providers satisfy, they all offer three primary benefits:

- Making data-centric exploratory programming more accessible by eliminating the need to manually create mappings and type definitions
- Eliminating the administrative burden of manually maintaining mappings or other type definitions
- Reducing the likelihood of errors caused by undetected changes to the underlying data structure

A full discussion of type providers goes well beyond the scope of this book. Instead, this section is intended to introduce many of the type providers that are available to you either as part of the core F# distribution or through some popular third-party libraries. After you've seen what's available, we'll discuss how to initialize and use a few type providers to easily get the data you care about.

Available Type Providers

F# 3.0 includes several type providers out of the box. Table 10-2 lists the built-in providers and a brief description of each.

Table 10-2: Built-in Type Providers

Provider	Description
DbmlFile	Provides the types that correspond to a SQL Server database as described in a Database Markup Language file (*.dbml*)
EdmxFile	Provides the types that correspond to a database as described by a LINQ-to-Entities mapping file (*.edmx*)
ODataService	Provides the types that correspond to those returned by an OData service
SqlDataProvider	Provides the types that correspond to a SQL Server database
SqlEntityProvider	Provides the types that correspond to a database according to a LINQ-to-Entities mapping
WsdlService	Provides the types that correspond to those returned by a WSDL-based web service

The list of built-in type providers is pretty sparse and is focused on database or database-like sources. Even so, what's provided covers a fairly large number of use cases. Should your data fall outside of the cases covered by the built-in types, you can define custom type providers, but doing so is outside the scope of this book.

Before you start down the path of building your own type providers, you should see if there are any third-party providers that will meet your needs. At the time of this writing, several popular libraries include a number of useful type providers, most notably: FSharpx and FSharp.Data. Table 10-3 lists several of the type providers in each library to give you an idea of what's readily available and the diversity of uses for type providers. This list is not meant to be exhaustive; there are definitely other libraries available.

Table 10-3: Some Available Third-Party Type Providers

Provider	Description	FSharpx	FSharp.Data
AppSettingsProvider	Provides types that correspond to the nodes in the AppSettings section of a configuration file	✓	
CsvProvider	Provides types that allow for easy parsing of comma-separated value (CSV) files		✓
ExcelProvider	Provides the types necessary for working with an Excel workbook	✓	
FileSystemProvider	Provides the types necessary for working with the filesystem	✓	
JsonProvider	Provides types that represent a JavaScript Object Notation (JSON) document		✓
RegexProvider	Provides types that allow for inspecting regular expression matches	✓	
XamlProvider	Provides types that allow for easy XAML parsing	✓	
XmlProvider	Provides types that represent an XML document		✓

Using Type Providers

Regardless of which type provider you need, initializing one always follows the same basic pattern:

```
type name = providerName<parameters>
```

In the preceding syntax, *name* is the name by which you'll access the provider's capabilities, *providerName* identifies the provider type itself, and *parameters* are the provider-specific arguments that control the provider's behavior. Parameters will typically include things like a connection string or the path to the data source, but ultimately each type provider is responsible for defining the parameters it accepts.

The first time a provider is used within Visual Studio, you'll be presented with a security dialog like the one pictured in Figure 10-1.

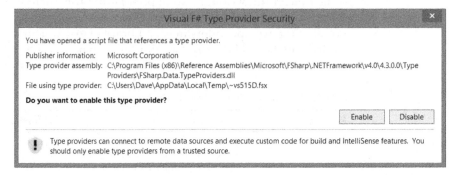

Figure 10-1: Type Provider Security dialog

As the dialog indicates, type providers can connect to remote data sources and execute custom code for build and IntelliSense features. Once you've enabled or disabled a type provider, you won't be prompted again. If you want to change your selection at a later time, you can find a listing of type providers under F# Tools in the Visual Studio Options dialog.

Example: Accessing an OData Service

This first example uses the ODataService type provider to query the publicly available Northwind sample OData service from *http://www.odata.org/*. To start, we need to reference two assemblies:

```
#r "System.Data.Services.Client"
#r "FSharp.Data.TypeProviders"
```

The first assembly includes several Windows Communication Foundation (WCF) classes required by the ODataService provider. Though we don't use the WCF types directly within this example, failure to add the reference will result in compilation errors. The second assembly contains the provider itself. With these assemblies referenced, we can now open the namespace that contains the ODataService provider:

```
open Microsoft.FSharp.Data.TypeProviders
```

Next, we include a type definition that references the appropriate type provider along with the address to the Northwind service:

```
type northwind =
  ODataService<"http://services.odata.org/V3/Northwind/Northwind.svc/">
```

The ODataService provider takes the supplied address, appends $metadata, and then proceeds to construct and import the types described by the service. In order to do anything with the service, we need to obtain a data context via the provider type like this:

```
let svc = northwind.GetDataContext()
```

With the data context established, we now have everything we need to query the data. Here we'll use a query expression to get some invoice information from the Northwind service.

```
let invoices =
    query { for i in svc.Invoices do
            sortByNullableDescending i.ShippedDate
            select (i.OrderDate, i.CustomerName, i.ProductName)
            take 5 }
```

There's nothing out of the ordinary with the preceding query; it uses standard query operators to select OrderDate, CustomerName, and ProductName from the five most recently shipped invoices. What *is* exceptional is that with no more effort than pointing the type provider at the OData service, we have a full type hierarchy that models the types exposed by the service.

NOTE *Not all of the standard query operators are supported by every data source. For example, join is not supported by OData, so including it in a query with two OData sources will result in an error.*

Although we've defined the invoices binding, the query execution is deferred until we actually enumerate the sequence. For simplicity, we can do so by piping the sequence to Seq.iter, which we'll use to print each item like this:

```
invoices |> Seq.iter (printfn "%A")
```

Invoking the preceding code printed the following items when I ran it, but your results may differ if the source data changes:

```
(5/4/1998 12:00:00 AM, "Drachenblut Delikatessen", "Jack's New England Clam Chowder")
(4/30/1998 12:00:00 AM, "Hungry Owl All-Night Grocers", "Sasquatch Ale")
(4/30/1998 12:00:00 AM, "Hungry Owl All-Night Grocers", "Boston Crab Meat")
(4/30/1998 12:00:00 AM, "Hungry Owl All-Night Grocers", "Jack's New England Clam Chowder")
(5/4/1998 12:00:00 AM, "Tortuga Restaurante", "Chartreuse verte")
```

So far, the ODataService provider has been a black box; as long as you give it a valid address, it usually just works and you don't have to think about how. This is particularly great when you're doing exploratory coding, but it can be frustrating when the provider isn't returning what you expect. Fortunately, there are a couple of events you can subscribe to in order to gain some insight into what the provider is doing: SendingRequest and ReadingEntity.

The `SendingRequest` event occurs whenever the provider creates a new `HttpWebRequest`, whereas `ReadingEntity` occurs after data has been read into an entity. For the purposes of this discussion, we'll focus on `SendingRequest` because it can show exactly what is being requested and help you refine your queries.

Probably the most helpful thing to do with `SendingRequest` is interrogate the `RequestUri` property of the `WebRequest` object that's associated with the `SendingRequestEventArgs`. `RequestUri` includes the full address of the OData request, so once you have it, you can paste it into a browser (or other diagnostic utility such as Fiddler) and refine it. One easy way to get the URI is to simply print it to the console like this:

```
svc.DataContext.SendingRequest.Add (fun args -> printfn "%O" args.Request.RequestUri)
```

So long as the preceding snippet is executed before the query is enumerated, the URI will be printed ahead of the results. In the case of the query described in this section, the printed URI is: http://services.odata.org/V3/ Northwind/Northwind.svc/Invoices()?$orderby=ShippedDate%20desc&$top=5&$select= OrderDate,CustomerName,ProductName.

For your convenience, the entire example from this section, including the subscription to `SendingRequest`, is reproduced in its entirety here:

```
#r "System.Data.Services.Client"
#r "FSharp.Data.TypeProviders"

open Microsoft.FSharp.Data.TypeProviders

type northwind =
  ODataService<"http://services.odata.org/V3/Northwind/Northwind.svc/">
let svc = northwind.GetDataContext()

let invoices =
  query { for i in svc.Invoices do
          sortByNullableDescending i.ShippedDate
          select (i.OrderDate, i.CustomerName, i.ProductName)
          take 5 }

svc.DataContext.SendingRequest.Add (fun args -> printfn "%O" args.Request.RequestUri)
invoices |> Seq.iter (printfn "%A")
```

Example: Parsing a String with RegexProvider

For this example, we'll look at how the `RegexProvider` from the FSharpx project can generate types that correspond to a regular expression, providing you with a remarkable degree of safety when working with matches. To use this provider, you'll need to obtain the `FSharpx.TypeProviders.Regex` package from NuGet or download the source from GitHub (*https://github.com/fsharp/ fsharpx/*).

As with the `ODataProvider` example, we'll start by referencing some assemblies and opening some namespaces:

```
#r "System.Drawing"
#r @"..\packages\FSharpx.TypeProviders.Regex.1.8.41\lib\40\FSharpx.TypeProviders.Regex.dll"

open System
open System.Drawing
```

Because I created this script as part of a project that included the `FSharp.TypeProviders.Regex` package from NuGet, I simply referenced the package directly via a relative path; the path to the assembly may be different on your machine depending on how you obtained the assembly and its version.

With the assemblies referenced and the common namespaces opened, we can now create the type provider. Creating a `RegexProvider` is similar to creating the `ODataService` except that, instead of a URI, `RegexProvider` takes a regular expression pattern. For this example, we'll create the `RegexProvider` with a simple pattern that matches hexadecimal RGB values. (The space before the verbatim string is significant. Without the space, the compiler would try to interpret the string as a quoted expression, which is definitely not what we want.)

```
type colorRegex =
    FSharpx.Regex< @"^#(?<Red>[\dA-F]{2})(?<Green>[\dA-F]{2})(?<Blue>[\dA-F]{2})$">
```

The `RegexProvider` works a bit differently than the `ODataService` in that it's not really intended for use as a query source. Instead, we'll write a function that uses the type provider to convert a hexadecimal string into a standard .NET `Color` instance if it matches the regular expression pattern.

```
let convertToRgbColor color =
    let inline hexToDec hex = Convert.ToInt32(hex, 16)
    let m = color |> ❶colorRegex().Match
    if m.Success then
        Some (Color.FromArgb(❷m.Red.Value |> hexToDec,
                             ❸m.Green.Value |> hexToDec,
                             ❹m.Blue.Value |> hexToDec))
    else None
```

In the preceding code, we push the supplied color string into the `Match` method of a new instance of the colorRegex ❶. The value returned by `Match` is similar to the `Match` object returned when we're using regular expressions directly (through the `Regex` class in `System.Text.RegularExpressions`), but as you can see at ❷, ❸, and ❹, it also includes named properties that match the named groups defined within the source regular expression! This means that you don't have to fumble with magic strings to access the individual named captures!

To test this, we merely need to pass some strings to the convertToRgbColor function. Here we invoke the function for each string in a list:

```
[ ""; "#FFFFFF"; "#000000"; "#B0C4DE" ]
|> List.iter
  (convertToRgbColor >>
  (function
   | None -> printfn "Not a color"
   | Some(c) -> printfn "%O" c))
```

Evaluating this code should result in the following:

```
Not a color
Color [A=255, R=255, G=255, B=255]
Color [A=255, R=0, G=0, B=0]
Color [A=255, R=176, G=196, B=222]
```

As you can see, the first string didn't match the color pattern so it was not converted, whereas the remaining three items were converted and written accordingly.

Summary

With the addition of query expressions and type providers in F# 3.0, F# took massive strides toward being an even better language for data-intensive development work.

Query expressions bring the power of LINQ to the language with an idiomatic flair. With them, you can easily compose complex queries for analyzing and presenting data from a variety of data sources. Furthermore, the extensible nature of query expressions makes them well suited for more complex needs.

Type providers further expand upon F#'s already rich data experience by abstracting away the details of creating types that map to different data sources. They greatly improve a developer's ability to perform exploratory programming in data-centric scenarios because the developer doesn't need to be as concerned about how to access the data. Finally, type providers can add an extra degree of safety to the code by detecting changes to the underlying data structures as part of the build process.

11

ASYNCHRONOUS AND PARALLEL PROGRAMMING

For most of computing's history, software developers have been spoiled by processor manufacturers that were constantly pushing the limits of their chips' clock speeds. If you needed your software to run faster (to process larger data sets, or because users were complaining about the system freezing when it was really just busy), often all you had to do was upgrade to the latest chip. Over the past decade or so something changed: Processor manufacturers began improving processor performance not by increasing clock speeds but by adding processing cores.

Although processor architecture has changed, software architecture has largely remained static. Multicore processors have become the norm, yet many applications are still written as though only one core is available to them and thus are not taking full advantage of the underlying hardware. Long-running tasks are still being executed on the UI thread, and large data sets are often processed synchronously. A big reason for this is that, traditionally, asynchronous and parallel programming have been sufficiently complex and error prone that they were typically the domain of expert developers working on highly specialized software.

Fortunately, software is starting to catch up. Programmers are learning that the days of solving performance issues by throwing faster hardware at the problem have passed and that it's increasingly important to consider concurrent processing needs at an architectural level.

Although they're closely related, asynchronous and parallel programming have different goals. Asynchronous programming aims to separate processing and reduce blocking so that longer-running tasks don't prevent the system from completing other tasks within the same process. By contrast, parallel processing aims to improve performance by partitioning work into chunks that can be distributed across processors and operated against independently.

Since its inception, the .NET Framework has supported both asynchronous and parallel programming through threads and a multitude of synchronization mechanisms such as monitors, mutexes, semaphores, and so on. The *Asynchronous Programming Model (APM)*, where classes define `BeginX` and `EndX` methods for operations that should be run asynchronously (such as the `BeginRead` and `EndRead` methods on the `System.IO.FileStream` class) has long been the preferred approach to asynchronous programming in .NET.

In this chapter, we'll explore several ways that F# makes asynchronous and parallel programming more accessible, thereby freeing you to focus on creating correct solutions. We'll begin with a brief introduction to the Task Parallel Library. Next, we'll discuss another F# construct: asynchronous workflows. Finally, we'll conclude with an introduction to the `MailboxProcessor`, F#'s agent-based model for asynchronous programming.

Task Parallel Library

As its name implies, the *Task Parallel Library (TPL)* excels at handling parallel programming scenarios and is the preferred mechanism for CPU-bound operations. It abstracts much of the complexity of managing threads, locks, callbacks, cancellations, and exception handling behind a uniform interface. Although the TPL is not specific to F#, a basic understanding of it is helpful especially if you need to interact with code from libraries that use it.

The TPL enables two types of parallelism: data parallelism and task parallelism.

Data parallelism   Involves performing a specific action against each value in a sequence by distributing the work effectively across available processing resources. Under the data parallelism model, you specify a sequence along with an action and the TPL determines how to partition the data and distributes the work accordingly.

Task parallelism   Focuses on executing independent tasks concurrently. With task parallelism, you are responsible for manually creating and managing tasks, but this model offers you more control. Through the various `Task` classes, you can easily initiate asynchronous processing, wait for tasks to complete, return values, set up continuations, or spawn additional tasks.

NOTE *This section is not intended to be a comprehensive guide to the TPL. Thus, it won't get into many of the intricacies of task creation, scheduling, management, or other associated topics. The intention here is to establish a baseline, providing you with enough information to make you immediately productive when writing code using the TPL.*

Potential Parallelism

One of the key differences between working directly with threads and using the TPL is that the TPL is task based rather than thread based. This difference is quite important in that the TPL tries to run tasks concurrently by pulling threads from the thread pool, but it does not guarantee parallelism. This is known as *potential parallelism.*

Whenever you create a thread directly, you incur the overhead of allocating and scheduling it. This overhead can be detrimental to overall system performance if there aren't enough system resources available to support it. The basic concurrency mechanisms, like thread pooling, help reduce the impact by reusing existing threads, but the TPL goes a step further by taking available system resources into account. If there aren't sufficient resources available or the TPL otherwise determines that running a task in parallel will be detrimental to performance, it will run the task synchronously. As resources fluctuate over time, the TPL's task scheduling and work partitioning algorithms help rebalance work to use the available resources effectively.

Data Parallelism

Data parallelism is achieved primarily through the use of the static `For` and `ForEach` methods of the `Parallel` class located in the `System.Threading.Tasks` namespace. As their names imply, these methods are essentially parallel versions of the simple and enumerable for loops, respectively.

NOTE *Data parallelism can also be achieved through PLINQ's (Parallel LINQ) `AsParallel` extension method. To simplify working with parallel sequences in F#, the `PSeq` module in the F# PowerPack exposes many of the `ParallelEnumerable` methods using the same nomenclature as the `Seq` module.*

For normal usage, `Parallel.For` and `Parallel.ForEach` differ only by their input; `Parallel.For` accepts range boundaries, whereas `Parallel.ForEach` accepts a sequence. Both methods also accept a function that serves as the loop body, and they implicitly wait for all iterations to complete before returning control to the caller. Since the methods are so similar, the examples in this section will use `Parallel.For` for consistency.

The simplest form, the parallel for loop, simply invokes an action for each value in the range. Here, we use a parallel for loop to write the numbers 0 through 99.

```
open System
open System.Threading.Tasks

Parallel.For(0, 100, printfn "%i")
```

This snippet is pretty self-explanatory. The first argument passed to Parallel.For identifies the inclusive beginning of the range, while the second identifies the exclusive end of the range. The third argument is a function that writes a number to the console.

Locking and Lock Avoidance

Now that we're dealing with concurrency, there's a subtle bug in the previous example. Internally, printfn incrementally sends its text to System.Console.Out as it parses the pattern. Hence, it's possible that as each parallel iteration executes, multiple calls to printfn will be invoked simultaneously, resulting in some items being interlaced.

NOTE *The example used for this discussion is less of an issue in F# 3.1, where printf and its related functions have been improved such that they run up to 40 times faster than in previous releases.*

We can address this problem a few ways. One approach is to control access to System.Console.Out with the lock operator. The lock operator serves the same purpose as the lock statement in C# (SyncLock in Visual Basic) in that it prevents additional threads from executing a block of code until the locked resource is freed. Here is the previous example reworked to use locking:

```
Parallel.For(0, 100, fun n -> lock Console.Out (fun () -> printfn "%i" n))
```

There are times when locking is appropriate, but using it like this is a horrible idea. By locking, we negate most of the benefits of parallelizing the loop because only one item can be written at a time! Instead, we want to try another approach that avoids locking and doesn't interlace the results.

One of the easiest ways to achieve a satisfactory result is with function composition. Here, we use the sprint function to format the number and send that result to Console.WriteLine:

```
Parallel.For(0, 100, (sprintf "%i") >> Console.WriteLine)
```

This approach works because each call to sprintf writes to an isolated StringBuilder rather than a shared TextWriter. This eliminates the need to lock, thereby eliminating a potential bottleneck in your application.

Short-Circuiting Parallel Loops

Unlike F#'s built-in for loops, parallel loops provide some short-circuiting mechanisms by means of the ParallelLoopState class's Break and Stop methods. The TPL handles creating and managing the loop state, so all you need to do to access either of these methods is use one of the overloads that exposes it. Consider the following shortCircuitExample function:

```
open System.Collections.Concurrent
open System.Threading.Tasks

let shortCircuitExample shortCircuit =
  let bag = ConcurrentBag<_>()
  Parallel.For(
    0,
    999999,
❶ fun i s -> if i < 10000 then bag.Add i else shortCircuit s) |> ignore
  (bag, bag.Count)
```

Like the previous examples, the shortCircuitExample function uses Parallel.For, but notice at ❶ that the supplied function accepts two parameters instead of one. The second parameter, s, is the loop state.

With shortCircuitExample in place we can now invoke it, passing a function that accepts a ParallelLoopState instance and calls either Stop or Break, like this:

```
shortCircuitExample (fun s -> s.Stop()) |> printfn "%A"
shortCircuitExample (fun s -> s.Break()) |> printfn "%A"
```

Both of the preceding lines will force the parallel loop to terminate before all iterations complete, but they have very different effects. Stop causes the loop to terminate at its earliest convenience but allows any iterations that are executing to continue. Break, on the other hand, causes the loop to terminate at its earliest convenience after the current iteration. You also need to take care that you do not call Stop and Break in succession to avoid an InvalidOperationException.

The difference between these two methods can be drastic. For example, in one run on my desktop, the Break version processed 10,000 items, whereas the Stop version processed only 975.

Cancelling Parallel Loops

Cancelling a parallel for loop is similar to short-circuiting, except that instead of using the Stop or Break methods to terminate the loop from within, you identify an external *cancellation token* that the loop monitors and responds to. Unlike the short-circuiting mechanism, cancellation forces all tasks configured with the same token to stop. Cancelling does raise an OperationCanceledException, so you'll want to handle that accordingly.

The following function demonstrates cancelling a parallel for loop:

```
open System
open System.Threading.Tasks

let parallelForWithCancellation (wait : int) =
  use tokenSource = new ❶System.Threading.CancellationTokenSource(wait)

  try
    Parallel.For(
      0,
      Int32.MaxValue,
      ❷ParallelOptions(❸CancellationToken = ❹tokenSource.Token),
      fun (i : int) -> Console.WriteLine i
    ) |> ignore
  with
  | :? ❺OperationCanceledException -> printfn "Cancelled!"
  | ex -> printfn "%O" ex
```

In the preceding code, we create a CancellationTokenSource at ❶. This object is initialized to automatically cancel after a provided number of milliseconds. Inside the try block, we use an overload of Parallel.For that accepts a ParallelOptions instance as shown at ❷. Through this ParallelOptions instance, we initialize the CancellationToken property ❸ to the token exposed by the CancellationTokenSource ❹. When the token source's internal timer expires, the parallel loop raises an exception, which is then caught and handled at ❺. Although we relied on a CancellationTokenSource that automatically cancelled, you can manually force cancellation by calling the Cancel method, typically from another task or thread.

Task Parallelism

Task parallelism gives you the most control over executing code in parallel while still abstracting many of the implementation details from you.

Creating and Starting Tasks

Tasks can be created and started in several ways. The easiest, but least flexible, way is the Parallel.Invoke method, which accepts one or more functions to execute concurrently and implicitly waits for them to finish, like this:

```
open System
open System.Threading.Tasks

Parallel.Invoke(
  (fun () -> printfn "Task 1"),
  (fun () -> Task.Delay(100).Wait()
             printfn "Task 2"),
  (fun () -> printfn "Task 3")
)

printfn "Done"
```

Here, `Parallel.Invoke` creates and starts three independent tasks. The first and third tasks simply print a message, while the second task waits 100 milliseconds before printing its message.

`Parallel.Invoke` limits what you can do because it doesn't expose any information about the individual tasks, nor does it provide any feedback about whether the tasks succeeded or failed. You can catch and handle exceptions raised by the tasks and cancel them by providing a cancellation token (similar to the approach used in "Cancelling Parallel Loops" on page 233), but that's about it. When you want to do anything more advanced with tasks, you'll need to create them manually.

There are two ways to create tasks manually: directly via a constructor, or through a `TaskFactory`. For our purposes, the primary difference between the two approaches is that when creating tasks with the constructor you must manually start them. Microsoft recommends favoring the `TaskFactory` when task creation and scheduling don't need to be separated.

To create a new task with the `Task` constructor, you need only provide a function that serves as the task's body, like this:

```
open System.Threading.Tasks

let t = new Task(fun () -> printfn "Manual Task")
```

This creates a new task that prints a string. To start the task, call its Start method.

```
t.Start()
```

Alternatively, you can combine the two steps into one with a `TaskFactory`. Conveniently, the `Task` class has a static `Factory` property that is preset to a default `TaskFactory`, so you don't need to create one on your own. Here, we create and start a task using the default factory's `StartNew` method:

```
open System.Threading.Tasks

let t = Task.Factory.StartNew(fun () -> printfn "Factory Task")
```

Returning Values from Tasks

The tasks we've looked at so far simply invoke an action, but you also need to know how to return a value—a commonly needed but cumbersome process under traditional asynchronous models. The TPL makes returning values trivial through a generic `Task<'T>` class, where `'T` represents the task's return type.

WARNING *The random-number generation used in the following examples is sufficient for demonstration purposes, but be aware that the `System.Random` class is not thread-safe and even creating a new instance per task may not be sufficient. Should your solution require a more robust approach to concurrently generating random numbers, I recommend reading Stephen Toub's article on the subject at* http://blogs.msdn.com/b/pfxteam/archive/2009/02/19/9434171.aspx.

Creating tasks that return values is almost identical to the basic tasks we've already looked at. The Task<'T> class provides a set of constructor overloads that are comparable to that of the non-generic Task class, and the TaskFactory includes a generic overload of StartNew. To demonstrate, let's use StartNew<'T> to create and run a task that returns a random number.

```
let t = Task.Factory.StartNew(fun () -> System.Random().Next())
```

The only truly notable thing about this example is that the function passed to StartNew returns an integer and the generic overload is inferred. Of course, returning a value doesn't do much good without a way to access that value, and that's why Task<'T> provides the Result property, which will contain the return value when the task completes. Here, we see how to access the return value:

```
t.Result |> printfn "Result: %i"
```

Because this is an asynchronous operation, there's no guarantee that the task has completed executing before the Result property is accessed. For this reason, Result's get accessor checks whether the task has completed and waits for it to complete if necessary before returning its result. It's more typical to access the result as part of a continuation (as shown a bit later in this chapter) than immediately after the task starts.

Waiting for Task Completion

When your program depends on one or more tasks completing before it can continue processing, you can wait for those tasks using one of the wait mechanisms. For convenience, the examples in this section will use the following function, which returns a new function that sleeps for a random amount of time (simulating a long-running operation lasting up to delayMs) before printing a message:

```
let randomWait (delayMs : int) (msg : string) =
    fun () -> (System.Random().Next delayMs |> Task.Delay).Wait()
              Console.WriteLine msg
```

We can use the TaskFactory to create a task and wait for it to complete with the task's Wait method like this:

```
let waitTask = Task.Factory.StartNew(randomWait 1000 "Task Finished")
waitTask.Wait()
printfn "Done Waiting"
```

In this code, a new task is created and started, but the message "Done Waiting" won't be written to the console until it completes due to the explicit wait. This can be helpful when subsequent code is dependent upon the task's completion.

You'll often want to run a number of tasks in parallel and block until one completes. To do so, you can use the static `WaitAny` method from the `Task` class. The most basic `WaitAny` overload accepts a `params` array of tasks and will stop blocking as soon as one of the tasks in the array completes. Here, we pass three started tasks to `WaitAny`:

```
Task.WaitAny(
    Task.Factory.StartNew(randomWait 2000 "Task 0 Finished"),
    Task.Factory.StartNew(randomWait 2000 "Task 1 Finished"),
    Task.Factory.StartNew(randomWait 2000 "Task 2 Finished"))
Console.WriteLine "Done Waiting"
```

When any of the three tasks complete, `WaitAny` will stop blocking, thus allowing execution to continue to the `Console.WriteLine` call. Note that `WaitAny` doesn't kill the remaining tasks when it unblocks, so they'll continue executing in parallel with the source thread.

Similar to `WaitAny`, the `Task` class provides a static `WaitAll` method. `WaitAll` also accepts a `params` array of tasks, but instead of allowing execution to continue when one task completes, `WaitAll` unblocks only when *all* of the tasks have completed. Because the code differs only by which method is called, I haven't included a sample, but I encourage you to experiment with each. As you do so, run each form several times and observe the differences.

Continuations

Traditionally, whenever you wanted to execute some code as soon as some parallel or asynchronous code completed, you needed to pass a function, called a *callback*, to the asynchronous code. In .NET, callbacks have typically been implemented through the built-in `AsyncCallback` delegate type.

Using callbacks is effective, but they can complicate the code and be tricky to maintain. The TPL greatly simplifies this process with *continuations*, which are tasks configured to start when one or more tasks, called *antecedents*, complete.

The simplest continuations are created from individual tasks. Let's start by creating a task that will serve as an antecedent:

```
let antecedent =
  new Task<string>(
    fun () ->
      Console.WriteLine("Started antecedent")
      System.Threading.Thread.Sleep(1000)
      Console.WriteLine("Completed antecedent")
      "Job's done")
```

Now that we have a task, we can set up a continuation by passing a function to the task's `ContinueWith` method, like so:

```
let continuation =
  antecedent.ContinueWith(
    fun ❶(a : Task<string>) ->
```

```
Console.WriteLine("Started continuation")
Console.WriteLine("Antecedent status: {0}", a.Status)
Console.WriteLine("Antecedent result: {0}", a.Result)
Console.WriteLine("Completed continuation"))
```

As you can see, creating a continuation is very similar to creating a regular task, but notice at ❶ how the function passed to the ContinueWith method accepts a parameter of type Task<string>. This parameter represents the antecedent so that the continuation can branch according to the antecedent's status (for example, RanToCompletion, Faulted, Canceled, and so on) or its result if it has one.

At this point, neither task has been started, so we'll start antecedent. When it completes, the TPL will automatically start continuation. We can observe this behavior as follows:

```
antecedent.Start()
Console.WriteLine("Waiting for continuation")
continuation.Wait()
Console.WriteLine("Done")
```

which should print the following messages:

```
Waiting for continuation
Started antecedent
Completed antecedent
Started continuation
Antecedent status: RanToCompletion
Completed continuation
Done
```

The ContinueWith method is useful when you're dealing with only a single task. When you have multiple tasks, you can turn to the TaskFactory's ContinueWhenAny or ContinueWhenAll methods. Like their WaitAny and WaitAll counterparts, the ContinueWhenAny and ContinueWhenAll methods will start the continuation task when any or all of the tasks in an array complete, respectively. For brevity we'll focus on the ContinueWhenAll method.

```
let antecedents =
  [|
    new Task(
        fun () ->
          Console.WriteLine("Started first antecedent")
          System.Threading.Thread.Sleep(1000)
          Console.WriteLine("Completed first antecedent"))
    new Task(
        fun () ->
          Console.WriteLine("Started second antecedent")
          System.Threading.Thread.Sleep(1250)
          Console.WriteLine("Completed second antecedent"))
    new Task(
        fun () ->
```

```
          Console.WriteLine("Started third antecedent")
          System.Threading.Thread.Sleep(1000)
          Console.WriteLine("Completed third antecedent"))
  |]

let continuation =
  ❶Task.Factory.ContinueWhenAll(
    antecedents,
    fun ❷(a : Task array) ->
      Console.WriteLine("Started continuation")
      for x in a do Console.WriteLine("Antecedent status: {0}", x.Status)
      Console.WriteLine("Completed continuation"))

for a in antecedents do a.Start()

Console.WriteLine("Waiting for continuation")
continuation.Wait()
Console.WriteLine("Done")
```

ContinueWhenAny follows the same pattern as WaitAny. Here we've defined three tasks, which we manually start after creating the continuation at ❶. Notice the continuation task's parameter at ❷. Instead of receiving a single antecedent task as you would with ContinueWith or ContinueWhenAny, continuations created with ContinueWhenAll accept an array of tasks. This array contains all of the tasks supplied to ContinueWhenAll instead of the individual task that caused the continuation to start. This allows you to inspect each antecedent and handle success and failure scenarios as granularly as you need.

Cancelling Tasks

Cancelling a task is fundamentally the same as cancelling a parallel for loop, but it requires a bit more work because the parallel for loops handle the cancellation details for you. The following function demonstrates cancelling a task and follows the typical pattern for handling the cancellation:

```
let taskWithCancellation (cancelDelay : int) (taskDelay : int) =
❶use tokenSource = new System.Threading.CancellationTokenSource(cancelDelay)
❷let token = tokenSource.Token

  try
    let t =
      Task.Factory.StartNew(
        (fun () ->
        ❸token.ThrowIfCancellationRequested()
          printfn "passed cancellation check; waiting"
          System.Threading.Thread.Sleep taskDelay
        ❹token.ThrowIfCancellationRequested()),
          token)
    ❺t.Wait()
  with
  | ex -> printfn "%O" ex
  printfn "Done"
```

As with cancelling parallel for loops, we start by creating a CancellationTokenSource at ❶. For convenience, we then bind the token to a name at ❷ so we can reference it within the function the task is based upon. Within the task body, the first thing we do at ❸ is call the token's ThrowIfCancellationRequested method, which interrogates the token's IsCancellationRequested property and throws an OperationCanceledException if that property returns true. We do this to ensure that no unnecessary work is performed if cancellation was requested when the task was started. When no exception is thrown, execution continues. At ❹ we again check for cancellation to avoid a successful task completion. Finally, at ❺ we wait for the task to complete so we can handle any exceptions thrown by the task.

Exception Handling

Exceptions can be raised by any number of executing tasks at any time. When this happens, we need a way to capture and handle them. In the previous section, we handled the exception in a general manner—by matching any exception and writing it to the console. If you executed the taskWithCancellation function, you may have noticed that the exception we caught wasn't an OperationCanceledException but rather an AggregateException that included an OperationCanceledException. The base exception classes aren't well suited for parallel scenarios because they represent only a single failure. To compensate, a new exception type, AggregateException, was introduced to allow us to report one or more failures within a single construct.

Although you certainly could handle an AggregateException directly, you'll typically want to find a specific exception within it. For this, the AggregateException class provides the Handle method, which iterates over the exceptions contained within its InnerExceptions collection so you can find the exception you really care about and handle it accordingly.

```
try
  raise (AggregateException(
         NotSupportedException(),
         ArgumentException(),
         AggregateException(
           ArgumentNullException(),
           NotImplementedException())))
with
| :? AggregateException as ex ->
     ex.Handle(
       ❶Func<_, _>(
         function
         ❷| :? AggregateException as ex1 ->
             ❸ex1.Handle(
               Func<_, _>(
                 function
                 | :? NotImplementedException as ex2 -> printfn "%O" ex2; true
                 | _ -> true))
             true
         | _ -> true))
```

Handling an `AggregateException` follows the familiar exception-handling pattern: We match against the `AggregateException` and bind it to the name ex as you might expect. Inside the handler, we invoke the `Handle` method ❶, which accepts a `Func<exn, bool>` indicating that the supplied function accepts an exception, and return a Boolean value. (To use pattern-matching functions as we've done here, we explicitly construct `Func<_, _>` instances and allow the compiler to infer the proper type arguments.) Inside the pattern-matching function ❷, we detect whether we have a nested `AggregateException` and handle it at ❸. At each level, we need to return a Boolean value indicating whether the particular exception was handled. If we return `false` for any exception, a new `AggregateException` which contains the unhandled exception will be raised.

Handling `AggregateExceptions` like this can get quite cumbersome, complex, and tedious. Fortunately, `AggregateException` provides another method, `Flatten`, which simplifies error handling by iterating over the `InnerExceptions` collection and recursing over each nested `AggregateException` to construct a new `AggregateException` instance that directly contains all of the exceptions within the source exception's hierarchy. For example, we can revise the previous example to use `Flatten` to simplify the handler, like this:

```
try
  raise (AggregateException(
          NotSupportedException(),
          ArgumentException(),
          AggregateException(
            ArgumentNullException(),
            NotImplementedException()))))
with
| :? AggregateException as ex ->
      ex.Flatten().Handle(
        Func<_, _>(
          function
          | :? NotImplementedException as ex2 -> printfn "%O" ex2; true
          | _ -> true))
```

In this revised example, we call `Handle` against the flattened `AggregateException`. With only one level to process, we can omit the checks for nested `AggregateExceptions` and handle the `NotImplementedException` directly.

Asynchronous Workflows

Despite the many improvements that the TPL brings to asynchronous and parallel programming, F# offers its own model, which better matches the functional paradigm emphasized by the language. While it's sometimes desirable to use the TPL in F# (particularly when working across language boundaries) you'll often turn to F#'s asynchronous workflows, which are best suited for I/O-based operations.

Asynchronous workflows provide a uniform and idiomatic way to compose and execute asynchronous code against the thread pool. Furthermore, their very nature often makes it difficult (if not impossible) to fall into some of the asynchronous traps present even in the TPL.

NOTE   *Like our TPL discussion, this section is intended to give you a basic working knowledge of asynchronous workflows rather than serving as a comprehensive guide.*

Creating and Starting Asynchronous Workflows

Asynchronous workflows are based on the `Async<'T>` class that resides in the `Microsoft.FSharp.Control` namespace. This type represents a bit of code you want to run asynchronously, ultimately returning some value. Instead of creating `Async<'T>` instances directly, though, we compose them through async expressions much like we compose sequences or queries.

Async expressions take the following form:

```
async { async-expressions }
```

Here, *async-expressions* represents one or more expressions that will participate in the asynchronous operation. In addition to the standard expressions we've seen throughout this book, asynchronous workflows allow you to easily invoke additional workflows and wait for results without blocking through specialized variants of some familiar keywords such as `let` and `use`. For instance, the `let!` keyword invokes an asynchronous workflow and binds the result to a name. Similarly, the `use!` keyword invokes an asynchronous workflow that returns a disposable object, binds the result to a name, and disposes of the object when it goes out of scope. It's also possible to invoke an asynchronous workflow and immediately return the result with the `return!` keyword.

To demonstrate, we'll turn to the "hello world" example of asynchronous workflows: requesting multiple web pages. To begin, let's define some functions that encapsulate the logic needed to create an asynchronous page request (note that a similar function, `Http.AsyncRequestString`, is available in the `FSharp.Data` framework):

```
open System
open System.IO
open System.Net

type StreamReader with
  member x.AsyncReadToEnd () =
    async { do! Async.SwitchToNewThread()
            let content = x.ReadToEnd()
            do! Async.SwitchToThreadPool()
            return content }

let getPage (uri : Uri) =
  async {
```

```
    let req = WebRequest.Create uri
    use! response = req.AsyncGetResponse()
    use stream = response.GetResponseStream()
    use reader = new StreamReader(stream)
    return! reader.AsyncReadToEnd()
}
```

After opening the relevant namespaces, we extend the StreamReader class with a single AsyncReadToEnd method. This method, adapted from the F# PowerPack, is similar to the existing ReadToEndAsync method except that instead of using the TPL, it returns an asynchronous workflow that we can evaluate as the final step of the larger workflow in the getPage function where we describe how to make the page request. The overall flow of the expression is pretty standard: Create a WebRequest, wait for the response, and then explicitly return the response stream's contents.

NOTE *The AsyncGetResponseMethod is an extension method defined in the F# core library. It conveniently wraps the standard .NET code within another asynchronous workflow, which makes it possible to employ use! and greatly simplifies the code.*

It's important to recognize that getPage doesn't actually execute the request; it merely creates an instance of Async<string> that represents the request. This allows us to define multiple requests or pass them around to other functions. We can even execute the request multiple times. To execute the request we need to turn to the static Async class, which you can think of as a controller for asynchronous workflows.

There are a number of methods for starting an asynchronous workflow. Some common methods are listed in Table 11-1.

Table 11-1: Common Async Start Methods

Method	Description
RunSynchronously	Starts an asynchronous workflow and waits for its result.
Start	Starts an asynchronous workflow but does not wait for a result.
StartImmediate	Starts an asynchronous workflow immediately using the current thread. Useful for UI updates.
StartWithContinuations	Immediately starts an asynchronous workflow using the current thread, invoking a success, exception, or cancellation continuation depending on how the operation completed.

The method you choose is largely dependent upon what the workflow does, but you'll typically use Start unless your application requires one of the others. The workflow created by the getPage function returns the result of a web request. Since we're making the request, we probably don't want to ignore the result, so we'll need to wire up a continuation to do something with it. The easiest way to do that is to wrap the call to getPage inside another asynchronous expression, passing the result to another function when it completes, and starting the entire workflow with Start. Here, we call getPage and print the result:

```
async {
  let! content = Uri "http://nostarch.com" |> getPage
  content.Substring(0, 50) |> printfn "%s" }
|> Async.Start
```

> **USING ASYNC**
>
> The fact that Async is a static class rather than a module has ramifications for how you interact with it. Rather than providing let-bound functions as a module would, Async provides methods, many of which are overloaded primarily to aid in cancellation. Furthermore, Async's methods are typically designed with a more object-oriented approach than is typical in the core F# libraries. Accordingly, their parameters are often tupled, making it difficult to use them with pipelining.

Alternatively, we can use the StartWithContinuations method, which accepts an asynchronous workflow and three functions to invoke when the workflow finishes successfully, raises an exception, or is cancelled, respectively. The following code shows such an approach:

```
Async.StartWithContinuations(
  ❶getPage(Uri "http://nostarch.com"),
  ❷(fun c -> c.Substring(0, 50) |> printfn "%s..."),
  ❸(printfn "Exception: %O"),
  ❹(fun _ -> printfn "Cancelled")
)
```

When the asynchronous operation ❶ completes successfully, the success continuation ❷ is invoked and the first 50 characters from the page source will be printed. Should the operation throw an exception, the exception continuation ❸ will execute and print the exception. Finally, if the operation is cancelled, as described in "Cancelling Asynchronous Workflows" on page 245, the cancellation continuation ❹ will execute and display a note informing the user of the cancellation.

Instead of relying on continuations, we can use the RunSynchronously method and get the result directly, like this:

```
let html =
  Uri "http://nostarch.com"
  |> getPage
  |> Async.RunSynchronously
```

Of course, running a single asynchronous workflow like this defeats the purpose of running it asynchronously because RunSynchronously waits for the result. Instead, RunSynchronously is often used in conjunction with Async.Parallel to run multiple workflows in parallel and wait for all of them to complete. For instance, we can make multiple requests, starting with an array of asynchronous workflows, as follows:

```
open System.Text.RegularExpressions

[| getPage(Uri "http://nostarch.com")
   getPage(Uri "http://microsoft.com")
   getPage(Uri "http://fsharp.org") |]
|> Async.Parallel
|> Async.RunSynchronously
|> Seq.iter (fun c -> let sample = c.Substring(0, 50)
                      Regex.Replace(sample, @"[\r\n]| {2,}", "")
                      |> printfn "%s...")
```

Here, we employ the Parallel method to combine each of the asynchronous workflows into a single workflow that is then piped to the RunSynchronously method. When each of the requests has completed, we iterate over the resulting array, stripping a few characters from the content for readability and printing the result.

Cancelling Asynchronous Workflows

In the previous section I indicated that asynchronous workflows can be cancelled. Just as in the TPL, asynchronous workflows use cancellation tokens to control cancellation. It's possible, and sometimes even necessary, to manage tokens on your own, but in many cases you can rely on the Async class's default token.

For simple scenarios, such as when you're starting a single workflow via the Start or StartWithContinuations methods, you can use the CancelDefaultToken method to cancel the workflow, like this:

```
❶ Async.StartWithContinuations(
     getPage(Uri "http://nostarch.com"),
     (fun c -> c.Substring(0, 50) |> printfn "%s..."),
     (printfn "Exception: %O"),
     (fun _ -> printfn "Cancelled")
  )

❷ Async.CancelDefaultToken()
```

The StartWithContinuations method ❶ monitors the default token and cancels the workflow when the token is marked as cancelled via the CancelDefaultToken method ❷. In this example, because the workflow is cancelled before it completes, the cancellation callback is invoked instead of the success callback, resulting in the cancellation message being displayed.

The `TryCancelled` method, which accepts a workflow and a function that will be invoked when cancellation is requested, is a nice alternative for workflows that don't return a value. Here, the `displayPartialPage` function wraps a call to getPage within another asynchronous workflow. The outer workflow waits for the response and writes out the first 50 characters when the message is received. Because `TryCancelled` returns yet another workflow and doesn't automatically start it, we need to explicitly do so with a call to Start.

```
let displayPartialPage uri =
  Async.TryCancelled(
    async {
      let! c = getPage uri
      Regex.Replace(c.Substring(0, 50), @"[\r\n]| {2,}", "")
      |> sprintf "[%O] %s..." uri
      |> Console.WriteLine },
    (sprintf "[%O] Cancelled: %O" uri >> Console.WriteLine))

Async.Start(displayPartialPage (Uri "http://nostarch.com"))

Async.CancelDefaultToken()
```

The default token is often sufficient for cancelling workflows. When you're executing multiple workflows and want to coordinate cancellation or if you want more control over cancellation, you can supply your own. Consider what happens when you request three pages but request cancellation with the default token.

```
[| Uri "http://nostarch.com"
   Uri "http://microsoft.com"
   Uri "http://fsharp.org" |]
|> Array.iter (fun u -> Async.Start(displayPartialPage u))

Async.CancelDefaultToken()
```

Executing the preceding code usually results in all three workflows being cancelled. (Usually, but not always, because there's a chance that one or more workflows complete before the cancellation is handled.) To isolate each workflow's cancellation, we can use an overload of the Start method that accepts a user-specified token, like this:

```
open System.Threading

let tokens =
  [| Uri "http://nostarch.com"
     Uri "http://didacticcode.com"
     Uri "http://fsharp.org" |]
  |> Array.map (fun u -> ❶let ts = new CancellationTokenSource()
                         Async.Start(displayPartialPage u, ❷ts.Token)
                         ts)
❸ tokens.[0].Cancel()
❹ tokens.[1].Cancel()
```

In this revised version, we use `Array.map` to map each `Uri` to a workflow with its own `CancellationTokenSource` created at ❶. We then pass the associated token to `Async.Start` as the second argument ❷ before returning the `CancellationTokenSource`. Finally, at ❸ and ❹, respectively, we request cancellation of the first and second requests, allowing the third to proceed as normal.

What's especially nice about cancelling asynchronous workflows is that, unlike the TPL, cancellation tokens are propagated through the entire workflow automatically. This means that you don't have to manually ensure that each new workflow is given a token, leaving you with cleaner code.

Exception Handling

Because exceptions can and do occur within asynchronous workflows, it's important to know how to handle them properly. There are a few exception-handling options available, but their utility may vary depending on what you're doing.

The most uniform way to handle exceptions in an asynchronous workflow is to wrap the potentially offending code inside a `try...with` block within the async expression. For instance, we can provide a version of our `getPage` function that handles exceptions raised during the page request and read, like this:

```
let getPageSafe uri =
  async {
    try
      let! content = getPage uri
      return Some content
    with
    | :? NotSupportedException as ex ->
      Console.WriteLine "Caught NotSupportedException"
      return None
    | :? OutOfMemoryException as ex ->
      Console.WriteLine "Caught OutOfMemoryException"
      return None
    | ex ->
      ex |> sprintf "Caught general exception: %O" |> Console.WriteLine
      return None }
```

There's nothing unusual about the `try...with` block in the preceding code—we simply wrap the asynchronous call to `getPage` in the `try...with` block and return a successful read as an option. Should the operation raise an exception, we match the exception type, print a message, and return `None`.

Another way to handle exceptions from asynchronous workflows is the `Async.Catch` method. `Async.Catch` takes a more functional approach than `StartWithContinuations` in that rather than accepting an exception-handling function, it returns `Choice<'T, exn>`, where `'T` is the asynchronous workflow's return type and exn is the exception thrown by the workflow.

The Choice type is a discriminated union with two union cases: Choice1Of2 and Choice2Of2. For Async.Catch, Choice1Of2 represents successful completion of the workflow and contains the result, whereas Choice2Of2 represents failure and contains the first raised exception.

Handling exceptions with Async.Catch lets you structure your asynchronous code to create an idiomatic, pipelined data flow. For example, the following code shows how we can model an asynchronous operation as a series of function applications, beginning with a Uri.

```
Uri "http://nostarch.com"
|> getPage
|> Async.Catch
|> Async.RunSynchronously
|> function
   | Choice1Of2 result -> Some result
   | Choice2Of2 ex ->
     match ex with
     | :? NotSupportedException ->
       Console.WriteLine "Caught NotSupportedException"
     | :? OutOfMemoryException ->
       Console.WriteLine "Caught OutOfMemoryException"
     | ex ->
       ex.Message |> sprintf "Exception: %s" |> Console.WriteLine
     None
```

Here, a Uri is piped into the getPage function to create an asynchronous workflow. The resulting workflow is piped into Async.Catch to set up another workflow, which we then pipe to Async.RunSynchronously so we can wait for the result. Finally, we pipe the Choice into a pattern-matching function where we either return Some result or handle the exception before returning None.

Asynchronous Workflows and the Task Parallel Library

In addition to the ThreadPool-based asynchronous operations we've seen so far, the Async class provides a few methods for working with TPL tasks. Most notable among them are StartAsTask and AwaitTask.

The StartAsTask method invokes an asynchronous workflow as a TPL task. You would typically use this for CPU-bound operations or to expose an asynchronous workflow to code using the TPL in C# or Visual Basic. For instance, we can treat the result of our getPage function as a TPL task like this:

```
Uri "http://nostarch.com"
|> getPage
|> Async.StartAsTask
|> (fun t -> ❶t.Result.Substring(0, 50))
|> printfn "%s"
```

The presence of the Result property at ❶ indicates that the result of StartAsTask is indeed a Task. In a more real-world scenario, you likely wouldn't fire off a task and immediately block by waiting for the result, but this example is intended only to show how to start an asynchronous workflow as a TPL Task.

The StartAsTask method is handy when you need to create a new task, but what about when you need to handle an existing task? Consider the DownloadStringTaskAsync method added to the System.Net.WebClient class in .NET 4.5. This method serves the same purpose as our getPage function except that it encapsulates downloading a resource within a TPL task.

In C#, you can easily handle such methods with the async modifier and await operator, as shown here:

```
// C#
// using System.Threading.Tasks

private static ❶async Task<string> GetPageAsync(string uri)
{
    using (var client = new System.Net.WebClient())
    {
      return ❷await client.DownloadStringTaskAsync(uri);
    }
}

static void Main()
{
    var result = GetPageAsync("http://nostarch.com").Result;
    Console.WriteLine("{0}", result.Substring(0, 50));
    Console.ReadLine();
}
```

From a greatly simplified perspective, what happens in the preceding C# code is this: The async modifier ❶ is applied to the GetPageAsync method to signify that part of the method will run asynchronously. The await operator ❷ then signifies that execution should return to the caller and the remainder of the method should be treated as a continuation to be executed when the task completes.

Asynchronous workflows allow us to follow a similar pattern in F# using the AwaitTask method in combination with a TPL task and let!, use!, or return!. Here is the corresponding code in F#:

```
// F#
open System.Threading.Tasks

let getPageAsync (uri : string) =
  async {
    use client = new System.Net.WebClient()
    ❶return! Async.AwaitTask (client.DownloadStringTaskAsync uri)
  }

async {
❷let! result = getPageAsync "http://nostarch.com"
  result.Substring(0, 50) |> printfn "%s"
} |> Async.Start
```

Although they're not quite functionally equivalent (the C# version waits for the result in Main while the F# version passes the result to a continuation), the F# approach is similar to that of C#. In the F# version, the asynchronous workflow created by the getPageAsync function uses return! and Async.AwaitTask ❶ to wait for the task to complete before returning the result. Then, in the second asynchronous workflow, let! ❷ is used to evaluate getPageAsync, while printing the result is treated as a continuation.

Agent-Based Programming

As if the TPL and asynchronous workflows didn't make parallel and asynchronous programming accessible enough, F# has borrowed a message-processing mechanism from Erlang. The MailboxProcessor<'T> class implements a queue-based system for asynchronously routing messages (data items) to handlers using shared memory. This is especially useful in scenarios where multiple sources (clients) need to request something from a single target (server), the canonical example being a web server. Furthermore, because MailboxProcessor instances are extremely lightweight, an application can manage thousands of them without breaking a sweat. This fact enables mailbox processors to work independently or together by passing messages between instances.

MailboxProcessor instances are usually referred to as *agents*, and I'll follow this convention throughout this section. In that regard, a common practice in agent-based programming is to alias MailboxProcessor<'T> as Agent<'T> as follows:

```
type Agent<'T> = MailboxProcessor<'T>
```

With the type aliased, we can create agents using the more convenient name.

Getting Started

I think the best way to understand agent-based programming is with an example. We'll start with a simple agent that simply prints whatever is sent into it.

```
type Message = | Message of obj

let echoAgent =
❶ Agent<Message>.Start(
    fun inbox ->
  ❷let rec loop () =
      async {
        let! (Message(content)) = ❸inbox.Receive()
        printfn "%O" content
      ❹return! loop()}
  ❺loop())
```

In the preceding code, we create an agent called echoAgent by passing a function to the Start method as shown at ❶. By convention, the function's parameter is called *inbox* because it's the *mailbox* from which we'll receive new messages. At ❷ we define the recursive loop function, which we'll call continually to receive new messages.

It's certainly possible to loop imperatively using a while loop, but the recursive function is the more typical approach. Functional loops provide the additional benefit of easily allowing you to provide different looping logic when you need to manage multiple states. For instance, if your agent needs to behave differently in a paused state than a running state, you could define a pair of mutually recursive functions that both return a workflow that handles the corresponding state accordingly.

Inside the loop, we create an asynchronous workflow that first asynchronously receives a message from inbox using the Receive method as shown at ❸. Next, the received message is printed before making an asynchronous recursive call to loop at ❹. Finally, at ❺ we initiate recursion by making a standard, synchronous call to loop.

With echoAgent actively listening, we can send it some messages via the Post method, like this:

```
> Message "nuqneH" |> echoAgent.Post;;
nuqneH
> Message 123 |> echoAgent.Post;;
123
> Message [ 1; 2; 3 ] |> echoAgent.Post;;
[1; 2; 3]
```

As you can see, when echoAgent receives a message, it is written to the console and then echoAgent waits for another message, and the process repeats ad infinitum.

Scanning for Messages

In the echoAgent example, we used the Receive method to get messages from the underlying queue. In many cases, Receive is appropriate, but it makes it difficult to filter messages because it removes them from the queue. To selectively process messages, you might consider using the Scan method instead.

Scanning for messages follows a different pattern than receiving them directly. Rather than processing the messages inline and always returning an asynchronous workflow, the Scan method accepts a filtering function that accepts a message and returns an Async<'T> option. In other words, when the message is something you want to process, you return Some<Async<'T>; otherwise, you return None. To demonstrate, let's revise the echoAgent to process only strings and integers.

```
let echoAgent2 =
  Agent<Message>.Start(fun inbox ->
    let rec loop () =
      inbox.Scan(fun (Message(x)) ->
        match x with
        | ❶:? string
        | ❷:? int ->
          Some (async { printfn "%O" x
                        return! loop() })
        | _ -> printfn "<not handled>"; None)
    loop())
```

At ❶ and ❷ you can see standard dynamic type-test patterns used to
filter incoming messages to strings and integers, respectively. When the
message is one of those two types, we associate an asynchronous workflow
with Some and return it. For all other messages, we return None. Scan then
examines the returned value, and when it is Some, the message is consumed
(removed from the queue) and the workflow is invoked. When the returned
value is None, Scan immediately waits for another message.

Passing messages to echoAgent2 is the same as before—just pass the messages via the Post method:

```
> Message "nuqneH" |> echoAgent2.Post;;
nuqneH
> Message 123 |> echoAgent2.Post;;
123
> Message [ 1; 2; 3 ] |> echoAgent2.Post;;
<not handled>
```

Scanning for messages does offer some flexibility with how you process messages, but you need to be mindful of what you're posting to the
agent because messages not processed by Scan remain in the queue. As the
queue size increases, scans will take longer to complete, so you can quickly
run into performance issues using this approach if you're not careful. You
can see how many messages are in the queue at any time by inspecting
the CurrentQueueLength property. If you need to remove messages from the
queue, you can do so by invoking Receive for each message in the queue,
but needing to do so is probably indicative of a larger design problem that
should be addressed.

Replying to Messages

The agents we've created so far have been self-contained: They receive a
message, do something with it, and wait for another message. Agents don't
have to work in isolation, though. One way you can make agents more interactive is by having them reply via an AsyncReplyChannel. To demonstrate, let's
revise echoAgent again, but this time, instead of printing a message within
the agent, we'll have it reply.

```
❶ type ReplyMessage = | ReplyMessage of obj * AsyncReplyChannel<obj>

let echoAgent3 =
  Agent.Start(fun inbox ->
    let rec loop () =
      async {
        let! ❷(ReplyMessage(m, c)) = inbox.Receive()
        ❸c.Reply m
        return! loop()
      }
    loop())
```

The overall structure of echoAgent3 doesn't differ much from the previous versions. For convenience, we're using a discriminated union ❶ for our message type as is typical in agent-based programming. In this case, the ReplyMessage union type has a single case with two associated values, an object and the reply channel.

Inside the loop body, we use pattern matching ❷ to identify the union case and extract the message and channel. We then pass the message to the channel's Reply method ❸ before repeating. Now all that's left is to send a message to the agent.

ReplyMessage's second value is an AsyncReplyChannel<obj>, as you've already seen. In theory we could manually construct a reply channel and send the ReplyMessage to the agent with the Post method, but then we'd have to handle waiting for the result manually. There are much better ways to get the reply channel—namely, the PostAndReply method and its variants.

The PostAndReply methods differ a bit from Post in that, instead of accepting the message directly, they are higher-order functions that accept a function that takes in a preconstructed reply channel and returns the fully constructed method. For our purposes, we'll simply create a ReplyMessage like this:

```
echoAgent3.PostAndReply(fun c -> ReplyMessage("hello", c))
|> printfn "Response: %O"
```

Internally, PostAndReply (and its variants) construct reply channels that they pass on to the supplied function, which then creates the message that is ultimately posted to the agent.

Example: Agent-Based Calculator

Now that you've seen a variety of ways to create and interact with agents, let's look at a more interesting example that ties together several of the concepts for something a bit more useful than simply regurgitating its input: an agent-based calculator. We'll begin by defining a discriminated union that represents the messages the calculator will support.

```
type Operation =
| Add of float
| Subtract of float
| Multiply of float
| Divide of float
| Clear
| Current of AsyncReplyChannel<float>
```

The `Operation` union type defines six cases. Of those, four represent basic mathematical operations and have an associated `float` that is used in the calculation. The `Clear` case allows us to clear the stored value. Finally, the `Current` case lets us interrogate the agent for its current value using its associated reply channel. From this definition, we can create a new agent that handles each case as follows:

```
let calcAgent =
  Agent.Start(fun inbox ->
    let rec loop total =
      async {
        let! msg = inbox.Receive()
        let newValue =
          match msg with
          | Add x -> total + x
          | Subtract x -> total - x
          | Multiply x -> total * x
          | Divide x -> total / x
          | Clear -> 0.0
          | Current channel ->
            channel.Reply total
            total
        return! loop newValue }
    loop 0.0)
```

Even though `calcAgent` appears to keep a running total, it is a bit of an illusion in that we keep state only by passing a value (`total`) to the recursive `loop` function. When `calcAgent` receives a message, it uses pattern matching to determine the appropriate action, binding the result to `newValue`. For instance, when it receives an `Add`, `Subtract`, `Multiply`, or `Divide` operation, it applies the corresponding mathematical operation to `total`. Similarly, when it receives a `Clear` operation, it simply returns `0.0` and `Current` returns `total` after replying.

To see `calcAgent` in action, we just need to send it some messages:

```
[ Add 10.0
  Subtract 5.0
  Multiply 10.0
  Divide 2.0 ]
|> List.iter (calcAgent.Post)

calcAgent.PostAndReply(Current) |> printfn "Result: %f"
calcAgent.Post(Clear)
calcAgent.PostAndReply(Current) |> printfn "Result: %f"
```

In the preceding snippet, we simply pass a list of `Operations` to `List.iter`, posting each message to `calcAgent`. When those have been processed, we query for the current value, clear, and then query again to ensure that the total has been zeroed out. Invoking the preceding snippet results in the following:

```
Result: 25.000000
Result: 0.000000
```

Summary

Asynchronous and parallel programming have long been viewed as tools for specialized software and reserved for experienced developers. With processor manufacturers improving processor performance by adding cores instead of increasing clock speed, software developers can no longer solve performance issues solely by upgrading hardware, nor can they continue expecting users to wait for long-running operations to complete before returning control.

Languages such as F# make asynchronous and parallel programming more accessible by providing multiple, robust mechanisms. The TPL makes it easy for developers to efficiently handle CPU-bound operations such as processing large data sets while effectively using available system resources. Language features such as asynchronous workflows excel at keeping applications responsive during IO-based operations such as web requests or file accesses. Finally, agent-based programming lets you easily coordinate complex systems by firing off individual asynchronous processes without having to directly manage the complexity of traditional thread-based models. Together, these approaches help you build scalable, responsive applications that meet the demands of modern computing while keeping you focused on the actual problems your software is trying to solve.

12

COMPUTATION EXPRESSIONS

In Chapter 6, we looked at how sequence expressions simplify creating sequences. In Chapter 10, we saw how query expressions provide a unified approach to querying data from disparate data sources. Similarly, in Chapter 11, we explored how asynchronous workflows can be employed to simplify creating and executing asynchronous operations. Each of these constructs serves a very different purpose, but what they all have in common is that they're examples of another F# language feature: the computation expression.

Computation expressions, sometimes referred to as *workflows*, provide a convenient construct for expressing a series of operations where data flow and side effects are controlled. In that regard, computation expressions are similar to what other functional languages refer to as *monads*. Where computation expressions differ, though, is that they're designed in such a way that individual expressions look like a natural part of the language.

Within the context of a computation expression, you can repurpose several familiar language elements—such as the let and use keywords, and for loops—to unify the syntax with the language. Computation expressions also provide an alternative "bang" syntax for some of these elements, allowing you to nest computation expressions for inline evaluation.

This feature's generalized nature means that computation expressions can simplify working with complex types and are applicable to a variety of situations. For instance, we already know that the built-in computation expressions streamline sequence creation, querying, and asynchronous processing, but they also have applications in logging and in projects such as the {m}brace framework that aim to simplify offloading computations to the cloud.

In this chapter, we'll explore the inner workings of computation expressions. We'll forego discussing monadic theory because it doesn't really help you understand how computation expressions can fit into your solutions. Instead, we'll begin with a look at builder classes and how they enable computation expressions. With that foundation established, we'll then walk through two examples of custom computation expressions.

Anatomy of a Computation Expression

You're already familiar with the basic pattern for writing computation expressions, but until now, you haven't seen how they work beyond a brief glimpse behind the scenes when we created some additional query operators in "Extending Query Expressions" on page 214. To reiterate for the more general case, computation expressions take the following form:

```
builder-name { computation-expression-body }
```

Computation expressions are designed around an underlying *computation type* (sometimes called a *monadic type*) that we compute by transparently invoking methods exposed by a *builder class*. In the preceding syntax, `builder-name` represents a concrete instance of a builder class, and `computation-expression-body` represents the series of nested expressions that map to the method calls necessary to produce an instance of the computation type. For example, asynchronous workflows are based on Async<'T> and built via AsyncBuilder. Similarly, query expressions are based on QuerySource<'T, 'Q> and built via QueryBuilder.

NOTE *Sequence expressions are an anomaly in the realm of computation expressions in that they don't follow the normal implementation pattern. Although sequence expressions use the computation expression syntax and are based on IEnumerable<'T>, they don't have a corresponding builder class. Instead, the details that would normally be handled by the builder class are handled directly by the F# compiler.*

Builder classes define the operations supported by a computation expression. Defining a builder class is largely a matter of convention, as there are no specific interfaces to implement or base classes to inherit. There aren't any steadfast rules for naming builder classes, but you typically do so by appending `Builder` to the underlying type name (for example, `AsyncBuilder` and `QueryBuilder`).

Although computation expressions are part of the language, they are really just syntactic sugar—a more convenient way to call into the builder class's methods. When the compiler encounters what appears to be a computation expression, it attempts to convert the code to a series of method calls through a process called *desugaring*. This process involves replacing each operation in the computation expression with a call to a corresponding instance method on the builder type (similar to how LINQ query expressions are translated to extension method calls and delegates in C# and Visual Basic). I like to think of the builder class methods as belonging to either of two groups. The first group, listed in Table 12-1, controls various syntactic elements such as bindings, `for` and `while` loops, and return values.

Table 12-1: Control Methods for Syntactic Elements

Method	Description	Signature
Bind	Enables `let!` and `do!` bindings	`M<'T> * ('T -> M<'U>) -> M<'U>`
For	Enables `for` loops	`seq<'T> * ('T -> M<'U>) -> M<'U>` or `seq<'T> * ('T -> M<'U>) -> seq<M<'U>>`
Return	Enables `return`	`'T -> M<'T>`
ReturnFrom	Enables `return!`	`M<'T> -> M<'T>`
TryFinally	Allows exception handling through `try...finally`	`M<'T> * (unit -> unit) -> M<'T>`
TryWith	Allows exception handling through `try...with`	`M<'T> * (exn -> M<'T>) -> M<'T>`
Using	Enables creating `IDisposable` objects with `use` and `use!`	`'T * ('T -> M<'U>) -> M<'U>` when `'U :> IDisposable`
While	Allows you to use `while...do` loops within a computation expression	`(unit -> bool) * M<'T> -> M<'T>`
Yield	Returns items from a nested computation expression using a sequence-like approach with the `yield` keyword	`'T -> M<'T>`
YieldFrom	Returns items from a nested computation expression using a sequence-like approach with the `yield!` keyword	`M<'T> -> M<'T>`

The second group of methods, those that control how computation expressions are evaluated, is listed in Table 12-2.

Table 12-2: Methods Affecting Computation Expression Evaluation

Method	Description	Signature
Combine	Merges two parts of a computation expression into one	M<'T> * M<'T> -> M<'T> or M<unit> * M<'T> -> M<'T>
Delay	Wraps a computation expression in a function for deferred execution, thereby helping prevent unintended side effects	(unit -> M<'T>) -> M<'T>
Run	Executed as the last step in evaluating a computation expression; can "undo" a delay by invoking the function returned by Delay and can also transform the result into a more consumable format	M<'T> -> M<'T> or M<'T> -> 'T
Zero	Returns a default value for the expression's monadic type; used when a computation expression doesn't explicitly return a value	unit -> M<'T> ('T can be unit)

Because computation expressions are intended to be designed in such a way that they apply to a variety of situations, it's important to keep them as generic as possible. This is reflected in the highly generalized structure of the signatures. For instance, the notation M<_> is used to indicate that the underlying type wraps another value.

It is not necessary to implement each method listed in Table 12-1 in your builder classes. Should you omit any of those methods, though, the corresponding mapped syntax will not be available within the computation expression and the compiler will produce an error. For example, if you try to include a use binding within a custom computation expression but omit the Using method from the builder class, compilation will fail with the message:

```
error FS0708: This control construct may only be used if the computation
expression builder defines a 'Using' method
```

Likewise, it is not always necessary to implement each method from Table 12-2, but failure to do so in some situations can lead to undesirable results. For instance, not implementing the Delay method will prevent you from composing expressions that yield multiple results. Furthermore, when your computation expression involves side effects, not implementing the Delay method can invoke the side effects prematurely—regardless of where they appear within the expression—because they are evaluated immediately when they're encountered instead of wrapped up in a function for deferred execution.

Computation expressions can be difficult to understand when discussed in abstract terms focused on the builder classes and method calls. I think it's far more helpful to walk through some simple implementations to see how the pieces work together. We'll spend the remainder of the chapter discussing two examples. In particular, we'll look at the builder implementations, their corresponding expression syntax, and the desugaring process.

Example: FizzBuzz

In Chapter 7, we looked at a few ways to solve the FizzBuzz problem by iterating over a sequence using Seq.map and using pattern-matching functions with active patterns and partial active patterns to identify which value should be printed. At its core, however, the FizzBuzz problem is essentially just an exercise in sequence transformation. As such, the problem can easily be solved with a computation expression.

When implemented as a computation expression, our FizzBuzz sequence can be constructed in a manner such that it looks and behaves like a standard sequence expression. With the computation expression, though, mapping a number to the corresponding string will be completely abstracted away within the builder class.

Because FizzBuzz transforms integers to strings and carries no intrinsic state, we'll forego creating an intermediary wrapper type and jump right into creating the builder class incrementally, beginning with the Yield method.

```
type FizzBuzzSequenceBuilder() =
  member x.Yield(v) =
    match (v % 3, v % 5) with
    | 0, 0 -> "FizzBuzz"
    | 0, _ -> "Fizz"
    | _, 0 -> "Buzz"
    | _ -> v.ToString()
```

Now that we have a rudimentary builder class, we can create the instance that we'll use for every FizzBuzz computation expression, like this:

```
let fizzbuzz = FizzBuzzSequenceBuilder()
```

That's it! There's nothing fancy here; we just create an instance of the class via its primary constructor. To use the instance as a computation expression, we can write something such as the following:

```
> fizzbuzz { yield 1 };;
val it : string = "1"
```

As you can see, evaluating the preceding expression doesn't give us quite the result we're looking for. Instead of returning a sequence of strings, it gives us only a single string, because so far the builder class doesn't know how to create a sequence; it simply yields a string based on an integer value. You can see this a bit more clearly in the desugared form, which resembles this:

```
fizzbuzz.Yield 1
```

To get a sequence of strings, we could make Yield return a singleton sequence (a sequence containing only a single item), but doing so would complicate implementing other methods, such as For and While. Instead, we'll extend the builder class to include the Delay method as follows (be sure to re-create the builder instance after updating the builder class to ensure that the fizzbuzz expressions are evaluated using the latest definitions):

```
type FizzBuzzSequenceBuilder() =
  -- snip --
  member x.Delay(f) = f() |> Seq.singleton
```

Evaluating the previous fizzbuzz expression with the Delay method in place gives us a slightly more desirable result:

```
> fizzbuzz { yield 1 };;
val it : seq<string> = seq ["1"]
```

Again, the desugared expression can help clarify what's happening. With the inclusion of the Delay method, the desugared form now looks like this:

```
fizzbuzz.Delay(fun () -> fizzbuzz.Yield 1)
```

As it stands now, though, all we'll ever get from a fizzbuzz expression is a singleton sequence because we can't yield multiple values. In fact, trying to do so as follows will result in a compiler error indicating that the builder class must define a Combine method:

```
fizzbuzz {
  yield 1
  yield 2
  yield 3 }
```

To make the preceding snippet work, we'll provide two overloaded implementations of the Combine method. The reason for overloading the methods is that, depending on their position within the expression, we'll either be combining individual strings into a sequence or appending a new string to an existing sequence. We want to be careful that we don't create a sequence containing a sequence, so we'll also need to overload the existing Delay method to simply return a supplied sequence. We can implement each of these methods as follows:

```
type FizzBuzzSequenceBuilder() =
  -- snip --
  member x.Delay(f : unit -> string seq) = f()
  member x.Combine(l, r) =
    Seq.append (Seq.singleton l) (Seq.singleton r)
  member x.Combine(l, r) =
    Seq.append (Seq.singleton l) r
```

Now evaluating the preceding `fizzbuzz` expression will result in a sequence containing three strings:

```
> fizzbuzz {
  yield 1
  yield 2
  yield 3 };;
val it : seq<string> = seq ["1"; "2"; "Fizz"]
```

When yielding multiple results like this, the desugaring process produces a much more complicated chain of method calls. For instance, desugaring the preceding expression that yields three items results in code that resembles this:

```
fizzbuzz.Delay (fun () ->
  fizzbuzz.Combine (
    fizzbuzz.Yield 1,
    fizzbuzz.Delay (fun () ->
      fizzbuzz.Combine(
        fizzbuzz.Yield 2,
        fizzbuzz.Delay (fun () -> fizzbuzz.Yield 3)))))
```

Yielding instances one at a time as we've been doing isn't a very effective way to build a sequence of any length. It would be much nicer if we could compose a `fizzbuzz` expression using a for loop. For this we need to implement the `For` method. The approach we'll take is to simply wrap a call to `Seq.map`, as shown here:

```
type FizzBuzzSequenceBuilder() =
  -- snip --
  member x.For(g, f) = Seq.map f g
```

Now it's trivial to generate FizzBuzz sequences because instead of using multiple yield expressions, we can nest a single yield expression within a for loop, like this:

```
fizzbuzz { for x = 1 to 99 do yield x }
```

Part of the beauty of implementing the `Yield`, `Delay`, `Combine`, and `For` methods in the builder class is that we can combine the styles for more flexible expressions. For instance, we can yield values directly before yielding them from a loop:

```
fizzbuzz { yield 1
           yield 2
           for x = 3 to 50 do yield x }
```

As it's currently written, the builder class doesn't support every way you could combine the various expressions, but you shouldn't have trouble adding the appropriate overloads to support many more scenarios.

For your convenience, here's the builder class in its entirety:

```
type FizzBuzzSequenceBuilder() =
  member x.Yield(v) =
    match (v % 3, v % 5) with
    | 0, 0 -> "FizzBuzz"
    | 0, _ -> "Fizz"
    | _, 0 -> "Buzz"
    | _ -> v.ToString()
  member x.Delay(f) = f() |> Seq.singleton
  member x.Delay(f : unit -> string seq) = f()
  member x.Combine(l, r) =
    Seq.append (Seq.singleton l) (Seq.singleton r)
  member x.Combine(l, r) =
    Seq.append (Seq.singleton l) r
  member x.For(g, f) = Seq.map f g
```

Example: Building Strings

FizzBuzz does a nice job showing how you can use computation expressions to create your own sequence-like constructs with the For and Yield methods, but it's not particularly practical for everyday computing. For a more useful example, we turn to a common programming task: combining strings.

It has long been established that constructing strings using a StringBuilder is usually more efficient than concatenation. StringBuilder's fluent interface keeps the code fairly clean, as shown in the following snippet:

```
open System.Text

StringBuilder("The quick ")
  .Append("brown fox ")
  .Append("jumps over ")
  .Append("the lazy dog")
  .ToString()
```

Creating a StringBuider instance and chaining calls to the various Append methods doesn't really fit into the functional-first paradigm, however. The Printf module tries to address this disconnect through the bprintf function, which formats a string and appends it to a StringBuilder instance as shown here:

```
let sb = System.Text.StringBuilder()
Printf.bprintf sb "The quick "
Printf.bprintf sb "brown fox "
Printf.bprintf sb "jumps over "
Printf.bprintf sb "the lazy dog"
sb.ToString() |> printfn "%s"
```

All `bprintf` really accomplishes, though, is replacing an instance method call with a call to a function that accepts a `StringBuilder` as an argument. What's more, you still have to manage the `StringBuilder` instance and pass it to each `bprintf` call. With a computation expression, not only can you make string construction look like a natural part of the F# language, you can also abstract away the `StringBuilder`! The computation expression we'll define shortly will allow us to compose strings using the following syntax:

```
buildstring {
  yield "The quick "
  yield "brown fox "
  yield "jumps over "
  yield "the lazy dog" }
```

Here, we chain together a number of strings by yielding them within a buildstring expression. To make this magic happen, we first need to define the underlying type for the expression. For convenience we'll use a discriminated union called `StringFragment` to track all of the strings as we yield them. The `StringFragment` type is defined as follows:

```
open System.Text

type StringFragment =
| ❶Empty
| ❷Fragment of string
| ❸Concat of StringFragment * StringFragment
  override x.ToString() =
    let rec flatten frag (sb : StringBuilder) =
      match frag with
      | Empty -> sb
      | Fragment(s) -> sb.Append(s)
      | Concat(s1, s2) -> sb |> flatten s1 |> flatten s2
    (StringBuilder() |> flatten x).ToString()
```

The `StringFragment` union has three cases, Empty ❶, Fragment ❷, and Concat ❸. The Empty case represents empty strings, while the String case contains a single string. The final case, Concat, forms a hierarchy of `StringFragment` instances that will eventually be joined together through the ToString method. The beauty of this type is that once the builder is in place, you never have to manually manage these instances or the `StringBuilder`.

The builder class, which we'll call `StringFragmentBuilder`, is similar to the `FizzBuzzBuilder`, but instead of creating sequences it creates `StringFragments`. We already know based on the earlier syntax that we'll be using the yield keyword, so we'll need to provide a Yield method. To yield multiple items, we'll need to implement the Combine and Delay methods as well. It would be nice to allow nested expressions, too, so we'll implement a YieldFrom method. Here is the StringFragmentBuilder class in its entirety along with the instance used with buildString expressions:

```
type StringFragmentBuilder() =
  member x.Zero() = Empty
  member x.Yield(v) = Fragment(v)
  member x.YieldFrom(v) = v
  member x.Combine(l, r) = Concat(l, r)
  member x.Delay(f) = f()
  member x.For(s, f) =
    Seq.map f s
    |> Seq.reduce (fun l r -> x.Combine(l, r))

let buildstring = StringFragmentBuilder()
```

The StringFragmentBuilder class is considerably simpler than FizzBuzzSequenceBuilder because it's concerned only with mapping strings to StringFragments and controlling execution. Let's look at each method individually to understand how it's used within the context of the computation expression.

The first method, Zero, returns a default value for the expression. In this case, we return Empty to indicate an empty string. During the desugaring process, a call to Zero will be inserted automatically in scenarios such as the expression returning unit, or a nested if expression not including an else branch.

The Yield method enables the yield keyword within the buildstring expression. In this implementation, Yield accepts a string, which it wraps in a new Fragment instance.

The YieldFrom method allows you to evaluate a nested buildstring expression through the yield! keyword. This method is similar to Yield, but instead of returning a new StringFragment, it returns the one created by the nested expression.

Each yield or yield! in the computation expression represents the end of a portion of the expression, so we need a way to merge them all together. For that we turn to the Combine method, which essentially treats the remainder of the expression as a continuation. Combine takes two StringFragments and wraps them each within a Concat instance.

COMBINE, EXPOSED

I think it's easier to understand the Combine method's role by looking at the desugared form. Say you're writing a buildstring expression that combines "A" and "B" into a single string like this:

```
buildstring {
  yield "A"
  yield "B" }
```

The corresponding desugared form of this expression would look very much like this:

```
buildstring.Combine(
  buildstring.Yield("A"),
  buildstring.Yield("B"))
```

For clarity, I simplified the desugared form to just the parts essential for understanding the process. Here, the first call to Yield returns Fragment("A") and the second returns Fragment("B"). The Combine method takes both of these and produces the following:

```
Concat (Fragment "A", Fragment "B")
```

Combine is called for every yield after the first. If our hypothetical example were extended to also yield "C", then the desugared form would then resemble this simplified code:

```
buildstring.Combine(
  buildstring.Yield("A"),
  buildstring.Combine(
    buildstring.Yield("B"),
    buildstring.Yield("C")))
```

The resulting StringFragment should then be:

```
Concat (Fragment "A", Concat (Fragment "B", Fragment "C"))
```

The next method in the StringFragmentBuilder class, Delay, controls when the computation expression is evaluated. When a computation expression has multiple parts, the compiler requires you to define Delay to avoid prematurely evaluating expressions that contain side effects and control execution as expressions are combined. Many of the method calls are wrapped in a function that's passed to Delay, so that those portions of the expression won't be evaluated until Delay is invoked. More specifically, the entire expression is wrapped in one Delay call, as are the calls that compute the second argument to each Combine call. The desugared form looks a bit like this (simplified for clarity):

```
buildstring.Delay(
  fun () ->
    buildstring.Combine(
      buildstring.Yield("A"),
      buildstring.Delay(
        fun () ->
          buildstring.Combine(
            buildstring.Yield("B"),
```

```
buildstring.Delay(
    fun () ->
      buildstring.Yield("C"))))))
```

Finally, the For method allows us to use for loops within a buildstring expression. Unlike the FizzBuzz implementation, however, this version employs the Map/Reduce pattern to map the supplied sequence values to individual StringFragment instances and then reduce them into a single StringFragment instance through the Combine method. This flattened instance can then be used in conjunction with other instances.

Now that you've seen the builder class and understand how the methods work together through the desugaring process, let's look at an example that exercises the entire chain. For this, we can use buildstring expressions to build the lyrics to a popular children's song about a farmer and his dog, Bingo. The song's simple lyrics and its repetitive nature make it easy to represent programmatically, like this:

```
let bingo() =
  let buildNamePhrase fullName =
    buildstring {
      yield "And "
      yield fullName
      yield " was his name-o\n"
    }
  let buildClapAndSpellPhrases maxChars chars =
    let clapCount = maxChars - (List.length chars)
    let spellPart =
      List.init clapCount (fun _ -> "*clap*") @ chars
      |> Seq.ofList
      |> String.concat "-"
    buildstring {
      for i in 1..3 do yield spellPart
                       yield "\n" }
  let rec buildVerse fullName (chars : string list) =
    buildstring {
      yield "There was a farmer who had a dog,\n"
      yield! buildNamePhrase fullName
      yield! buildClapAndSpellPhrases fullName.Length chars
      yield! buildNamePhrase fullName
      match chars with
      | [] -> ()
      | _::nextChars -> yield "\n"
                        yield! buildVerse fullName nextChars
    }
  let name = "Bingo"
  let letters = [ for c in name.ToUpper() -> c.ToString() ]
  buildVerse name letters
```

Nested within the bingo function are three functions: buildNamePhrase, buildClapAndSpellPhrases, and buildVerse. Each of these functions constructs a StringFragment through a buildstring expression. At the end of each verse, the buildstring expression includes a match expression to determine whether it should end with the Zero value (implied by returning unit) or recursively include another fully constructed verse via the yield! keyword.

Evaluating the preceding snippet should print the following string (remember, the %0 token formats the corresponding argument by calling its ToString method):

```
> bingo() |> printfn "%0";;
There was a farmer who had a dog,
And Bingo was his name-o!
B-I-N-G-O
B-I-N-G-O
B-I-N-G-O
And Bingo was his name-o!

There was a farmer who had a dog,
And Bingo was his name-o!
*clap*-I-N-G-O
*clap*-I-N-G-O
*clap*-I-N-G-O
And Bingo was his name-o!

There was a farmer who had a dog,
And Bingo was his name-o!
*clap*-*clap*-N-G-O
*clap*-*clap*-N-G-O
*clap*-*clap*-N-G-O
And Bingo was his name-o!
-- snip --
```

Summary

Computation expressions play an important role within F#. Out of the box, they make creating sequences, querying data from disparate data sources, and managing asynchronous operations appear to be a native part of the language by reusing familiar language elements. They're also fully extensible, so you can define your own computation expressions by creating a builder class that constructs an instance of an underlying type. Creating custom computation expressions can be a tricky endeavor, but once you understand the purpose of each builder class method and the desugaring process, the result can be cleaner, more descriptive code.

It can be difficult to find good information about computation expressions, but there are a few resources you can use for further study. First, the computation expressions series at *F# for Fun and Profit* (*http://fsharpforfunandprofit.com/series/computation-expressions.htm*) has plenty of examples covering the range of builder methods. For some more real-world examples, check out the ExtCore project on GitHub (*https://github.com/jack-pappas/ExtCore/*), which contains several practical applications for computation expressions, such as a lazy list implementation.

INDEX

exn type abbreviation, 53
explicit properties, 69–70
exponent operator (**), 35
expressions, 8–9
expression trees, 187, 188–190
Expr<'T> type, 190
Expr type, 190, 191, 192, 194
ExtCore project, 269
ExtensionAttribute, 100, 105
extension methods (C# and Visual Basic), 99

F

F# for Fun and Profit, 269
F# Interactive
 defined, 13
 directives
  #help, 16
  #I, 17, 21
  #load, 16–17, 21
  #quit, 16
  #r, 17, 21
  #time, 17–18
 expression terminator (;;), 14
 fsi.exe, 13
 it identifier, 15
 options
  --, 22
  --define, 21
  --exec, 22
  -I, 21
  --lib, 21
  --load, 20–21
  --optimize, 23
  --quiet, 22–23
  -r, 21
  --reference, 21
  --tailcalls, 23
  --use, 21
  in Visual Studio, 20
 reset interactive session, 16
 timing, 17
 val (output), 15
 Visual Studio window, 13–14
F# Software Foundation, 2
Factory pattern, 90
FailureException, 56
failwithf function, 56
failwith function, 56
fields, 68–69
 explicit, 68–69
 let bindings, 68

file extensions
 .fs, 18
 .fsx, 18
FileNotFoundException, 54
filter function (Event module), 78
find operator (query expressions), 208
FizzBuzz example
 active patterns, 173-174
 computation expressions, 261–264
 partial active patterns, 174–175
FlagAttribute enumerations, 43–45
flexible types, 52
float32 data type, 35
float data type, 34
flow control, 45–48
 for loops, 46–47
 if...then expressions, 47–48
 while loops, 46
foreach loop (C#), 46
for loops, 46–47
For method (computation expressions), 259, 263
forward function composition operator (>>), 108, 109
forward pipelining, 107–108
forward pipelining operator (|>), 42, 79, 107, 108
FSharpFunc (delegate), 105, 112
FSharpFuncUtil class, 105
FSharpList<'T> class, 149
.fs files, 18
FSI. *See* F# Interactive
fsi.exe, 13
fst function, 114
.fsx files, 18
Func (delegate), 105
function
 composition, 108–109
 expressions, 78, 112
 keyword, 161
 values, 105
functional purity, 27–28
functions, higher-order, 105

G

generic measures, 184
generics
 constraints, 50–52
  comparison, 52
  default constructor, 51
  defined, 50
  delegate, 51

The Book of F# is set in New Baskerville, Futura, and Dogma. The book was printed on demand at Lightning Source Incorporated in La Vergne, Tennessee.

UPDATES

Visit *http://nostarch.com/fsharp/* for updates, errata, and other information.

More no-nonsense books from **NO STARCH PRESS**

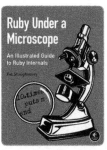

RUBY UNDER A MICROSCOPE
An Illustrated Guide to Ruby Internals
by PAT SHAUGHNESSY
NOVEMBER 2013, 360 PP., $39.95
ISBN 978-1-59327-527-3

PERL ONE-LINERS
130 Programs That Get Things Done
by PETERIS KRUMINS
NOVEMBER 2013, 168 PP., $24.95
ISBN 978-1-59327-520-4

REALM OF RACKET
Learn to Program, One Game at a Time!
by MATTHIAS FELLEISEN, ET AL.
JUNE 2013, 312 PP., $39.95
ISBN 978-1-59327-491-7

LEARN YOU A HASKELL FOR GREAT GOOD!
A Beginner's Guide
by MIRAN LIPOVAČA
APRIL 2011, 400 PP., $44.95
ISBN 978-1-59327-283-8

LEARN YOU SOME ERLANG FOR GREAT GOOD!
A Beginner's Guide
by FRED HÉBERT
JANUARY 2013, 624 PP., $49.95
ISBN 978-1-59327-435-1

LAND OF LISP
Learn to Program in Lisp, One Game at a Time!
by CONRAD BARSKI, M.D.
OCTOBER 2010, 504 PP., $49.95
ISBN 978-1-59327-281-4

PHONE:
800.420.7240 OR
415.863.9900

EMAIL:
SALES@NOSTARCH.COM

WEB:
WWW.NOSTARCH.COM

CPSIA information can be obtained
at www.ICGtesting.com
Printed in the USA
LVOW04s1617131217
559594LV00017B/378/P